WRITINGS AND MUSINGS

Being a collection of articles published in

The Ceylankan,

the Journal of the Ceylon Society of Australia

by

Thiru Arumugam

First published in 2016 by Ohm Books, UK

© 2016 Thirumugam Arumugam

All rights reserved. This book is sold subject to the condition that it shall not, by way of trade or otherwise, be lent, re-sold, hired out, or otherwise circulated without the publishers prior consent in any form of binding or cover other than that in which it is published and without a similar condition including this condition being imposed on the subsequent purchaser.

ISBN-13: 978-1532702730

A CIP catalogue record for this book is available from the British Library.

Cover design and original sketch by Dharshan Rajarayan of the bridge built at Kitulgala, Ceylon for the set of the film "The Bridge on the River Kwai"

To: Malini; Sudhu, Bala and Siva, their wives and children,
around whom my life revolves

CONTENTS

		Page
	Introduction	6
1.	Medieval Hindu Temples and Bronze Sculptures of Polonnaruva	9
2.	The American Ceylon Mission, Midwifery and childbirth customs in Jaffna 150 years ago	15
3.	The medical science of childbirth in Jaffna	19
4.	Robert Knox – a Postscript	24
5.	D J Wimalasurendra – Pioneer Ceylonese Engineer	26
6.	A River for Jaffna	32
7.	High praise for Thiru Arumugam's book	40
8.	Dr Mary Rutnam (1873-1962): Pioneer for Women's Rights (Part 1)	42
9.	Dr Mary Rutnam (1873-1962): Pioneer for Women's Rights (Part 2)	49
10.	Dr Mary Rutnam (1873-1962): Pioneer for Women's Rights (Part 3)	54
11.	Ceylonese Teenager granted a Royal Patent – 100 years ago (Part 1)	61
12.	Ceylonese Teenager granted a Royal Patent – 100 years ago (Part 2)	68
13.	Basil Wright and the film *Song of Ceylon*	76
14.	Don Martino de Zilva Wickremasinghe (1865-1937) – Savant, Linguist and Epigraphist: and Notes about H C P Bell, Archaeologist (1851-1937)	82
15.	Cocos Islands – and the Ceylon Garrison Artillery Mutiny (1942)	90
16.	Am I My Brother's Keeper? – the life and outline of four selected books by Ananda K Coomaraswamy (1877-1947)	98
17.	Devinuwara – the City of Gods	106
18.	The first Ceylonese family in Australia – revisited	115
19.	Ceylon Cricket Team nearly had Australians, led by Don Bradman, on the ropes in 1948!	126
20.	A Tale of Two Bridges: over the River Kwai in Thailand and over the River Kelani in Ceylon	129
21.	A Fighter Plane called "The Jaffna" fought against the Germans in World War One!	141
22.	Was there a Ceylonese in the First Fleet?	149

INTRODUCTION

This book is a collection of articles written by the author. Eighteen of the articles have been published in *The Ceylankan*, the quarterly Journal of the Ceylon Society of Australia. The last four articles have been submitted to the Editor of *The Ceylankan* for consideration for publication. The Society and Journal (originally a Newsletter) were founded in 1997 and its main objectives are to study, foster and promote interest in the cultural heritage of Sri Lanka, especially the post-medieval period when the country was first exposed to globalisation. David Goodrich, the first Editor of *The Ceylankan* wrote in an editorial about the Society's philosophy as follows *"It is important that we maintain the standard of non-confrontational, non-political, non-racial and sectarian outlook. Those principles must be maintained."* These principles have been faithfully followed since then and will no doubt continue to be upheld. The Society also has active Chapters in Melbourne and Colombo who hold regular Lecture Meetings.

The first article in this collection is about the Medieval Hindu Temples and Bronze Sculptures of Polonnaruva and was published in *The Ceylankan* in its November 2007 issue. The Editor of that issue was Sumane Iyer. All subsequent articles were published under the continuing editorship of Doug Jones. I am very grateful to the two of them for encouraging me to write and for publishing my articles without any hesitation.

Thanks are due to Darshan Rajarayan for the cover design, including his original sketch of the wooden bridge built in 1957 over the Kelani Ganga at Kitulgala for the set of the multiple Academy Award winning film *The Bridge on the River Kwai*. The Bridge is the subject of an article in this collection.

Many thanks are due to my wife, Malini, for her unfailing support and encouragement throughout this endeavour. A special thanks to Valentine Perera for suggesting this book.

Thanks also to the Publishers, Ohm Books, UK. Seggy T Segaran of Ohm Books has spent many hours formatting the text and putting this publication together. If not for his enthusiasm and encouragement this book would not have been possible.

A brief summary of the contents of each article follows.

The Chola dynasty reached its zenith from the 9th to the 13th centuries when they ruled over the whole of South India as well as some overseas territories. They occupied Northern and Central Ceylon for about 70 years during the 11th century. They moved the capital from Anuradhapura to Polonnaruva where they built numerous small Hindu temples. The first article titled *Medieval Hindu Temples and Bronze Sculptures of Polannaruva* describes a Siva Devale built by them which is still standing after a thousand years. Numerous bronze statues were found at these temples and the article describes how these were made, the process remains basically unchanged after a thousand years.

The second article, *The American Ceylon Mission, Midwifery and childbirth customs in Jaffna 150 years ago* describes the work of this Mission which arrived in Jaffna in 1816. Apart from their missionary work they also started schools and hospitals. Dr Samuel Fisk Green, an American missionary, started the first Medical School in Ceylon in Jaffna in 1848. After a few years he decided to change the medium of instruction to Tamil, and to do this he translated about 4500 pages of key medical textbooks, including Gray's *Anatomy*, into Tamil. The third article *The medical science of childbirth in Jaffna* continues on this theme and is an overview of a treatise on childbirth practices in Jaffna over 150 years ago. It was written in 1856 by Dr Charles McIntyre, a Ceylonese who was trained as a Doctor by Dr Green.

In 1681 Robert Knox published his book *An Historical Relation of the Island Ceylon in the East Indies*. The fourth article titled *Robert Knox – a Postscript* reproduces a manuscript page in Knox's own handwriting from a copy of the book and also includes a translation of a Latin inscription which is on the same page.

The fifth article *D J Wimalasurendra – Pioneer Ceylonese Engineer* describes how Wimalasurendra, a Chartered Civil and Electrical Engineer, proposed the Laxapana Hydro-electric Scheme in 1919, but the first stage of this scheme was completed only in 1950. The final stage is presently under construction. His proposal made in 1918 to electrify the railways is still to be implemented.

In the 1950s, Sanmugam Arumugam proposed that Elephant Pass Lagoon be converted into a fresh water lagoon and a channel constructed to convey this water to the Vadamarachchi and Upparu Lagoons in the Jaffna Peninsula. Work started on the project but it was not completed as funds ran out. The sixth article *A River for Jaffna* outlines the current status and work still needed to complete this project which will transform agricultural productivity in the Jaffna Peninsula.

The seventh article is a reproduction of a short article from *The Ceylankan* titled *High praise for Thiru Arumugam's book*. It is a brief note about the renowned writer Sir Christopher Ondaatje and reproduces an email from him to this author about his comments on the book *Nineteenth century American Medical Missionaries in Jaffna, Ceylon*. Sir Christopher and the author were schoolmates for a brief period at St Thomas College, Gurutalawa.

Articles 8, 9 and 10 are a three part set of articles about the life and times of Dr Mary Rutnam (1873-1962). She was a Canadian Medical Doctor who was recruited by the American Ceylon Mission to work in their Jaffna Hospitals, A few months after she commenced work the Mission came to know that she was secretly married to a Ceylonese, S C K Rutnam, who had a Master's degree from Princeton University and was training to become a missionary. The Mission immediately insisted that she resign from her post. The articles record the intense opposition from the Mission and their supporters to their marriage. She moved to Colombo where she practised as the first woman Obstetrician and Gynaecologist. She was also deeply involved in founding many organisations promoting women's and children's rights, some of these organisations are still in existence. In the evening of her life she was awarded the inaugural Ramon Magsaysay Award for Public Service. This award is considered to be the Asian equivalent of the Nobel Peace Prize.

Articles 11 and 12 are a two part set of articles about the life of Bertram Dawapurarathna (1895-1918). When he was a 14 year old schoolboy at Royal College he applied to the UK Patent Office for a patent for *Improvements in Reversing Gear for Steam Engines* and was duly awarded a Royal Patent. He proceeded to UK to study engineering at the University of Glasgow where he obtained a second Royal Patent for *Improved Valve Mechanism for Internal Combustion Engines*. World War I then intervened and the family lost all track of him. Research conducted for this article has established that he was returning to Ceylon in the P & O ship *Nyanza* which was torpedoed by the Germans resulting in Dawapurarathna being injured. He subsequently died of his injuries and was buried in Leeds. This new information was passed on to his relations, enabling them to know definitely of his fate for the first time.

In 1933 the Ceylon Tea Propaganda Board commissioned the Empire Marketing Board in London to produce a documentary film to promote the export of tea. The British Director, Basil Wright, was entrusted with the task of making the film and Article 13 describes how the film was made. The film *Song of Ceylon* went on to become a world famous documentary film and was awarded Best Documentary Film and Best Film in all classes at the International Film Festival in Brussels in 1935. At that time there was no Academy Award for Documentary films.

The fourteenth article is about the Epigraphist, D M de Zilva Wickremasinghe (1865-1937). Reproduced below is an excerpt from the editorial of the issue of *The Ceylankan* which carried the article.

"He had no university degree to his name, but a young Don Martino de Zilva Wickremasinghe was appointed, firstly in 1887, as Assistant Librarian in the Colombo Museum Library and thereafter, received appointments to research and study his chosen subject in Oxford University and at the Universities of London, Erlangen, Munich and Germany as well as the British Museum. He was fluent in nine languages and spent a good part of his lifetime doing his research. He bequeathed copious books and papers on Ceylon epigraphy to the world at his death in 1937.

This is the subject of Thiru Arumugam's erudite article on the pioneer linguist and epigraphist of Ceylon (along with notes on Wickremasinghe's contemporary, archaeologist HCP Bell) appearing in this issue. Thiru is one of our writers who needs little or no introduction to our readers. His well-researched contributions have appeared in the journal for some time now.

'I came across Wickremasinghe's work when trying to find information about the inscriptions in the 1000 year old Siva Devale No. 2 in Polannaruva' Thiru says. The information for this article was collected while Thiru was visiting in May at the British Library, London (formerly known as the British Museum Library) where Wickremasinghe collected material for his two books about Sinhalese

Manuscripts and Books; in the School of Oriental and African Studies Library, London where Wickremasinghe was on the teaching staff; and also in the University of Chicago Library which has one of the largest collections of South Asian books in the USA.

'I felt (and still feel) that he has not been given the due recognition that his work deserves' Thiru laments. Even small efforts like this article will help fill the lacuna of giving proper value and acknowledgement to the immense contribution Wickremasinghe has made to the study of epigraphy in Ceylon/Sri Lanka."

The fifteenth article is titled *Cocos Islands – and the Ceylon Garrison Artillery Mutiny (1942).* The article outlines the history of these coral islands which lie almost exactly half-way between Ceylon and Australia. During World War II the defence of these islands was entrusted to Ceylonese troops. In 1942 there was a mutiny by some of the Ceylonese troops which was quelled. The three ring leaders were sentenced to death and hanged in Welikade Jail. They were the only Commonwealth soldiers executed for mutiny in World War II.

The next article is about the life and work of Ananda K Coomaraswamy. He was born in Colombo and was the first Director of Mineralogical Surveys. He later moved to USA where he was for thirty years the Curator of Indian and Oriental Art at the Boston Museum of Fine Arts and a Visiting Lecturer at Harvard University. He was a prolific writer and was the author of 95 books and 909 contributions to journals and periodicals. The article includes overviews of four important books written by him and the illustration on the back cover of this book is from his book *Medieval Sinhalese Art* published in 1908.

The seventeenth article is about the history from ancient times of Devinuwara, the southernmost point in Ceylon. It is marked on the map of Ceylon prepared by the Greek Cartographer, Ptolemy, as far back as 110 AD. It has been the site of Buddhist and Hindu temples, and the seventh century stone temple still standing here is probably the oldest existing stone temple in Ceylon.

The first Ceylonese family in Australia – revisited is the subject of the eighteenth article which is about the O'Dean family who arrived in Sydney in 1816, two hundred years ago. O'Dean, who was of Malay origin, was a Drum-Major in the British Army in Kandy and was sentenced to banishment for life to Australia for desertion from the army. He and his Kandyan wife had six children and he lived in Australia for 44 years. His descendants in Australia have been traced.

The nineteenth article is a short article titled *Ceylon cricket team nearly had Australia, led by Don Bradman, on the ropes in 1948.* The Australian cricket team on their way to England by ship stopped over for a one-day match in Colombo. When word got around that Bradman was definitely playing, a crowd of about 20,000 descended on the Wanathamulla Oval. Australia batted first and declared at 184 for 8, with Bradman out for 20 runs. Ceylon were motoring at 46 for 2 wickets when a tropical thundershower ruled out further play for the day.

The twentieth article is the story of Two Bridges. The first bridge is the one built over the River Kwai in Thailand by the Japanese in World War II using as forced labour Allied Prisoners-of-War and Asian 'slaves' who were treated atrociously. The bridge was part of a railway line built by the Japanese to link Thailand with Burma. The railway line was through mountainous tropical jungle and it is estimated that 100,000 men died in the construction of the line, one for every sleeper on the line. The second bridge is the wooden bridge built in 1957 over the River Kelani at Kitulgala for the set of the award winning film *The Bridge on the River Kwai*. The climax of the film was when a steam engine and carriages (from the Kelani Valley narrow gauge railway) steamed over the bridge which was then blown up.

The next article describes how the Ceylon Tamils resident in Malaya during World War One collected funds to meet the cost of a fighter plane named 'The Jaffna' to battle against the Germans. The final article describes the First Fleet which was sent to colonise Australia in 1788 and considers whether there was a Ceylonese on board.

Thiru Arumugam
Sydney, Australia
February 2016

1

Medieval Hindu Temples and Bronze Sculptures of Polonnaruva

by Thiru Arumugam

The Chola dynasty held sway continuously in South India from the 9th to the 13th centuries reaching its zenith in the reigns of Rajaraja I (985AD to 1016AD) and his son Rajendra I (1012AD to 1044AD), who expanded their empire to stretch from Kanyakumari, the southern-most tip of India, up to the Deccan Plateau.

The Cholas were great temple builders and built Hindu temples to exhibit their domination, as well as serve their religious needs. The Cholas built the 66 metre high, majestic *Brihadeeswarar* (Great Lord Sivan) temple in Thanjavur and the *Gangaikonda Choleswarar* (Chola Ganges Conqueror's Sivan) temple, were built by them in the 11th century. These temples were the tallest buildings in India for several centuries.

During the Chola occupation of Polonnaruva in the 11th century AD, they constructed several small Hindu temples. In the 19th century, British archaeologists re-discovered and excavated the ruins of 16 Hindu temples in Polonnaruva, which include Siva, Vishnu, Ganesha and Kali temples, either in isolation or in groups of two or three. The Temples, built of stone or brick or a mixture of the two materials were in the Chola style of temple architecture of the 11th and 12th centuries, but some are in 13th century Pandyan style. This would indicate that some of these Hindu temples were built under the patronage of Sinhalese royalty after the departure of the Cholas.

In most of the temples the brickwork has collapsed, leaving only the stone structures such as pillars, pavements and doorways. The seven temples of Siva are the largest temples. Siva Devale No. 2 (Fig. 1) is in a remarkable state of preservation. Describing this temple, the first Sri Lankan Archaeological Commissioner, S. Paranavitana, has stated that: "It is still preserved, and is the best example of Dravidian architecture to be seen anywhere in the Island." (*Sinhalayo,* Colombo, 1970, p.47).

Fig. 1: 11th century Siva Devale No. 2, Polonnaruva
(Photo: Thiru Arumugam)

Siva Devale No. 2 is constructed of granite and limestone. The sanctum and the antechamber have survived intact, while the rest has collapsed and their remains have totally disappeared. The outer walls of the *garbagraha* (main sanctum) are about 6 metres square. The *vimanam* (sanctum turret) rises to a *sthoopi* (octagonal dome) over 9 metres high. The *lingam* (symbol of Siva) and its pedestal were assembled in the sanctum. The *avudaiyar* (base) of the *lingam* is 70 cm square and the *rudra pakam* (vertical shaft) rises about 45 cm. (Full details are in Archaeological Survey of Ceylon, Annual Report, (ASCAR), 1906, pp 18-20).

There are five inscriptions on the walls of the temple. One of these is partially legible and confirms that the temple was established during the reign of Rajendra I (1012-1044) and was named after his mother as *Vanavan Madevi Isvaram* (Great Queen Vanavan's Sivan temple). Another inscription in Grantha Tamil characters is almost totally legible. It describes how the temple officials and those that perform the sacred worship after them in this place "having agreed to burn a perpetual lamp (*tirunanta vilakku*) till the sun and the moon endure, received five kasu and one lamp stand".

In the year 1950, a group of local Hindu residents sought an interview with the Hon. Minister D. S. Senanayake and the Archaeological Commissioner and obtained permission to re-use this temple as a place of worship. The temple was re-consecrated and pujas were performed regularly for a few years (Fig. 2), and this must surely make this nearly 1000 year old temple the oldest existing Hindu temple in Sri Lanka where pujas have been held in the recent past. The Archaeological Survey of Ceylon, Annual Report of 1910-11 (page 40) states that "….this Saivite shrine, thus saved from further dilapidation, is the sole example existing in the Island of a medieval temple of the Hindu cult, virtually complete." The existing temples in much older sites such as Muneeswaram, Thiruketheeswaram, Koneswaram etc. are of more recent construction, the original temples there having been destroyed by the Portuguese in the 16th and 17th centuries. In the Jaffna District alone the Portuguese destroyed over 500 temples, but the temples of Polonnaruva were not affected because the Portuguese were mainly in the maritime areas.

Fig. 2: Religious ceremonies in Siva Devale No. 2 in 1950 after 650 years of disuse
(Photo: Sanmugam Arumugam)

The art of bronze sculpture in South India reached its zenith during medieval Chola rule. Several bronze images were excavated at the Hindu temples of Polonnaruva. These bronzes are up to the standards of Chola bronzes found in India. These include finds by Archaeological Commissioner H. C. P. Bell of more than twenty bronzes, mainly in 1907, at the Siva Devale Nos. 1, 4 and 5, Archaeological Commissioner C. E. Godakumbare's finds at the Siva Devale No. 5 in 1960 and the finds in 1975 at Vishnu Devale No. 4 (Figs. 3 and 4). Six bronzes were also unearthed at a Kali Kovil during the Cultural Triangle excavations. The bronzes include the Hindu gods Siva in his various manifestations but mainly as Nataraja; Parvati, Uma, Ganesa, and the *Nayanmar* or canonized saints of Siva.

Fig 3: Nataraja 12th century bronze, 90 cm high, excavated in 1907 at Siva Devale No. 1, now in the Colombo Museum.
(Photo: Thiru Arumugam)

Fig. 4: Parvati 12th century bronze, 51 cm high, excavated at
Siva Devale No. 5 in 1907, now in the Colombo Museum.
(Photo: Thiru Arumugam)

The technique of bronze casting used was as follows. The amalgam used consisted mainly of copper, with small quantities of brass and white lead. The process employed in casting the images is the 'lost wax' method (O C Gangoly, *South Indian Bronzes,* Calcutta 1915, pp 29-32). The image to be cast was first modelled in beeswax. It could be a solid model, or modelled over a heatproof former if a hollow image is to be made. If the proposed bronze is that of a deity, the dimensions, proportions, pose, ornaments, *mudras* (hand gestures) and *bhavas* (states of being) are defined in the *Shilpa Sastras* (ancient texts on architecture and arts). The *Dhyana Slokas* (contemplative verses) as mentioned in the *Shilpa* texts are meditated upon by the sculptor, so that the image of the deity fills the artist's mind. It is because of this need to comply with the *Sastras* when sculpting a deity that, for example, all Nataraja sculptures are similar in pose and general proportions and differ only in details.

The wax image is then coated in layers of fine clay, using earth from termite hills. The image is then baked in an oven using cow dung cakes as fuel. This causes the wax to melt and run out. The molten bronze alloy is then poured into the mould. After it has set, the mould is broken and the finishing touches made to the bronze image. This includes removing blemishes, adding finer details like ornaments and polishing the image. The whole process can take several months for a large image. In this process the wax mould is destroyed. Therefore, every image cast is an original, unique image.

This process of bronze casting has continued virtually unchanged over a thousand years, and *sthapathis* (bronze casters) using this process can be seen at work in their workshops in Swamimalai, near Thanjavur in Tamil Nadu, making bronze images for use in temples. Swamimalai was the ancient home of Chola *sthapathis* and many of today's artisans claim to be descended from several generations of *sthapathis*. There is a Government regulation that they are not allowed to make exact replicas of antique bronzes, this follows the theft of bronzes from temples, in particular the case of the Sivapuram Temple Nataraja bronze sculpture.

In 1965 Douglas Barett, Keeper of Oriental Antiquities in the British Museum visited India to collect material for his forthcoming book on Early Chola Bronzes. He went to Sivapuram, near Thanjavur, to see the 10th century Chola era Nataraja bronze in the temple. He was not satisfied with what he saw and suspected that it was a replica. The following month he saw a Nataraja in the private home of an art dealer in Chennai and suspected that this was the original Sivapuram Nataraja. He mentioned this in his book, and the Indian Government started investigating the matter.

This bronze had been excavated in the temple premises in 1951 and as it had been buried for several hundred years it was tarnished. It was sent to a *sthapathi* for restoration. He is supposed to have surreptitiously made a replica and given it to the temple and sold the original to an art dealer. The original had passed through several intermediaries and was finally purchased by Norton Simon in USA for a million dollars in 1973 for the Norton Simon Museum in Pasadena, California which has a fine collection of South Asian art. The Indian Government threatened legal action and after long negotiations it was agreed that it could be exhibited in US Museums for ten years and then returned to India in 1986. This bronze was recently valued at 100 million dollars, while this valuation may be optimistic, it does indicate the order of value of the beautiful Polonnaruva bronzes now in the Colombo and Polonnaruva Museums.

The most unusual of the bronzes in the Polonnaruva Museum is the bronze of *Karaikkal Ammaiyar* (revered Mother from Karaikkal) excavated at Siva Devale No. 5 in 1960 (Fig 5). She was a beautiful lady who lived in the 6th century AD in the east coast of India. After her marriage she was abandoned by her husband who feared that she had supernatural powers. She prayed to Siva to divest her of her physical beauty and she was turned into an emaciated hag and became a life-long devotee of Siva. She was later canonised as one of the 63 *Nayanmars* or Saints of Siva. Because she was a mortal, a *sthapathi* making a bronze image of her was not tied down by the rules of the *Sastras* but can allow his imagination free reign; therefore, all images of her in her emaciated form are totally different. The stunning Polonnaruva bronze of her can hold its own in any museum of modern art. Archaeological Commissioner C.E. Godakumbura has described this bronze as the best example of this subject in the world.

Fig. 5: Karaikkal Ammaiyar 12th century bronze, 28 cm high, found at Siva Devale No. 5, now in the Polonnaruva Museum.
(Courtesy: Dept. of National Museums)

The medieval Hindu temples and bronze sculptures of Polonnaruva are a significant and important chapter in the history of art and architecture of Sri Lanka. To quote Prof. Anuradha Seneviratna (*Polonnaruva: Medieval Capital of Sri Lanka,* Colombo, 1998, p.13): "With Buddhist and Hindu shrines on the same grounds embracing a common architectural tradition, and royal palaces once occupied by both Sinhala-Buddhist and Tamil-Hindu kings surrounded by large reservoirs shaded by primeval forests, Polonnaruva was a city that symbolised the unity and integrity of the island as well as the religious and ethnic harmony which prevailed in medieval Sri Lanka".

Article originally published in "The Ceylankan", Journal No. 40, November 2007.

2

The American Ceylon Mission, Midwifery and childbirth customs in Jaffna 150 years ago

by Thiru Arumugam and Dr Malini Arumugam

The American Board of Commissioners for Foreign Missions (ABCFM) was formed in Massachusetts, USA in 1810 with the object of spreading Christianity in the developing world. In 1812 the first batch of five missionaries, three of whom were accompanied by their wives, set sail for India. By the time the missionaries reached Calcutta, the Anglo-American War of 1812 had broken out and the East India Company ordered the missionaries to return to America or face deportation to England. One of the missionaries, Samuel Newell decided to go to Mauritius with his teenage wife Harriet Newell, who gave birth to a daughter during the voyage. Sadly, mother and daughter passed away soon after reaching Mauritius. It is recorded that Harriet died of consumption i.e. tuberculosis. The emotional diary of her last days were later publicized in the USA and led to the increased involvement of women in missionary activity.

By 1813 the War was beginning to peter out and Newell decided to return to India from Mauritius, stopping on his way in Ceylon for about a year. He wrote to the ABCFM in USA that the British Governor in Ceylon, Sir Robert Brownrigg, was receptive to the suggestion that American missionaries work in Ceylon and that a group of missionaries could be sent out. He visited Jaffna and was very much taken up by the place and wrote "What a field is here for missionary exertions!" In 1815, after the War was over, a group of four missionaries was sent out to Ceylon. They reached Jaffna in 1816 and thus began a continuous presence of American missionaries in Jaffna until about World War II under the auspices of American Ceylon Mission (ACM). The impact of their missionary activity was not just in the religious field. Apart from their missionary work, they also engaged in educational and medical activities and in social welfare activities. Their medical activities included establishing Ceylon's first medical school and the next article is a study of a treatise on midwifery by Dr Charles McIntyre, a product of that medical school. One of Dr McIntyre's great-grandsons is the Sydneysider playwright and CSA member, Ernest Macintyre.

In 1823 ACM established the Vaddukoddai Central High School, later to be called the Batticota (i.e. Vaddukoddai) Seminary in 1846, the forerunner of present day Jaffna College. These institutions were ahead of their time. The British Colonial Secretary, Sir James Emerson Tennant, visited the Seminary in 1848 and wrote in his Book *Christianity in Ceylon* (John Murray, London, 1850) "The knowledge exhibited by the pupils was astonishing; and it is no exaggerated encomium to say that, in the course of instruction and in the success of the systems of communicating it, the Collegiate Institution of Batticotta is entitled to rank with many European Universities....." Nevertheless the British Government turned down the application for a Charter for the Seminary and said that the title of University was reserved for a Government Institution to be established shortly in Colombo. The 'shortly' turned out to be several decades as the University College, Colombo which prepared students for external degrees of the University of London was founded only in 1921, and became the fully fledged University of Ceylon only in 1942.

In 1824 ACM established the Oodooville (i.e. Uduvil) Girls School. This was the first girls' boarding school outside the western world, and is still functioning. The first Principal was Harriet Winslow, the great-grandmother of John Foster Dulles, the former US Secretary of State. He visited her grave in 1956 and thanked the people of Tellipallai for keeping the gravesite in such good order over the years.

The ACM also started the *Morning Star* newspaper in 1841. This was the second English language newspaper in the country. There was also a Tamil edition. These papers had a wide readership in Jaffna as well as in Colombo and were printed in the ACM's own printing press in Manipay.

The first fully qualified medical missionary to come to Jaffna under the auspices of the ACM was Dr John Scudder MD who arrived in 1819. He was in fact the first Medical Missionary in the world, a singular honour for Jaffna. He set up dispensaries in Pandatheruppu and Chavakachcheri and practised there until 1836 when he was transferred to South India. The Scudder family and 42 direct descendants over four generations provided about 1100 person-years of combined missionary service to India. Dr John Scudder's grand-daughter, Dr Ida Scudder MD, started one of Asia's foremost clinical medical schools in 1918, the Christian Medical College and Hospital in Vellore, South India.

In 1805, Sinnathamby Asirvatham was born in Maviddapuram. He later moved to Vaddukoddai and got married there and cultivated a small farm. He also obtained employment under an American missionary attached to the Batticotta Seminary. In 1830 his second child Nallathambi was born. Nallathambi was educated at the Batticotta Seminary and on conversion to Christianity chose the baptismal name of Charles Nallathambi McIntyre (Fig. 1). This is recorded in the book *Through Memory Lane* written by his grandson Tan Sri S Chelvasingam-MacIntyre (University Education Press, Singapore, 1973, pp 5-13). The family name McIntyre (now spelt MacIntyre or Macintyre) still lives on in Sri Lanka, Singapore and Australia. After completing his education in the Batticotta Seminary, Charles McIntyre applied to Rev. Pargiter the Principal of the Nallur Boys Seminary (now called St Johns College) for a teacher's post but was unsuccessful. On his return home, Charles met Dr Samuel Fisk Green, an event that was to change the course of the rest of his life.

Fig. 1: Dr C N McIntyre

In 1848, 25 year old medical missionary Dr Samuel Fisk Green MD (Fig. 2), a recent graduate of the College of Physicians and Surgeons, New York, arrived in Jaffna. (*Life and Letters of Samuel Fisk Green MD,* Ebenezer Cutler, USA 1891). This College was the first medical school in USA to award the degree of MD and is now the post-graduate medical school of Columbia University.

Fig. 2: Samuel Fisk Green MD

Dr Green served the ACM in Jaffna from 1847 to 1873 with a five year gap in between. He went beyond the terms of his reference by establishing a hospital in Manipay (Fig. 3), presently called the Green Memorial Hospital, and also established the first medical school in Ceylon in 1848. The British Government recognized the medical school and its graduates and gave it an annual grant. Over the years he trained 62 Doctors, one of whom, Dr E Waitilingam, joined Government service and rose to become Assistant Colonial Surgeon. Another ex-student Dr J Danforth was awarded the degree of Doctor of Medicine by the College of Physicians and Surgeons, New York for his work in Jaffna on cholera. Cholera and small-pox were the major epidemics in Jaffna at that time and decimated the population with high morbidity rates particularly among children.

Fig. 3: Dr Green's Hospital in Manipay, circa 1850

The medical historian, Dr C G Uragoda in his address in 1996 to the College of Surgeons, Sri Lanka, said "The real advances in Surgery took place in the British period. At first it was a private hospital namely Green Memorial Hospital, Manipay that took the lead in Surgery. General Hospital

Colombo was established only subsequently. Samuel F Green was a medical missionary.......He established the first medical school in Sri Lanka." (C G Uragoda, *Surgery in Sri Lanka – the past,* Ceylon Medical Journal, 1996, V. 41, pp 111-114).

Dr Green also became very proficient in Tamil and translated or supervised the translation during his lifetime of over 4500 pages of key medical textbooks into Tamil. The books translated include such classics as Gray's *Anatomy,* Maunsell's *Obstetrics,* Druitt's *Surgery* etc for which he purchased the original woodcuts used by the authors for illustrations. This was a tremendous achievement considering that western science was totally new to the Tamil language. Dr Green had to coin hundreds of new Tamil words for the medical and scientific terms, which he set about in a very systematic way. There was a substantial demand for his books from South India.

Dr Green's medical school closed down after the Colombo Medical School was established in 1870 and the grant to Dr Green's school was withdrawn. When Dr Green finally left Ceylon in 1873, Dr James Loos, the Colonial Surgeon in Colombo wrote to him "....I am grieved that sickness has prevented me from seeing you. I should have been happy to take you round our hospital and show you the work we are carrying on – a work in which we are humbly imitating you. Medical education in Ceylon is deeply indebted to you and your predecessors" (Cutler p. 312).

Dr Green suggested to Charles McIntyre that he study medicine and Charles was enrolled as a student in Dr Green's medical school in the batch of 1853. The curriculum was based on the American University system at that time and consisted of a three year course followed by a year of Internship. McIntyre completed the course in 1856. He initially worked as a Lecturer in Dr Green's school and in other Jaffna hospitals. In 1866 he joined the Government medical service. During his lifetime he was posted to several outstation hospitals and in 1891 he was serving in Kurunegala. On 17 January 1891 he attempted to separate two of his bulls which were fighting with each other and he was severely gored. He was taken to the General Hospital Colombo for treatment by the eminent surgeon Dr Rockwood but suppuration was setting in. He became delirious due to septic absorption from the wound, diabetic coma set in and he passed away on 11 February 1891 (Chelvasingam-MacIntyre pp. 8-11). A life that could have been saved if only antibiotics had been invented.

In 1856, Dr Charles McIntyre wrote a 50 page handwritten manuscript treatise in English titled *Yatpana Piravasa Vyththiyam.* This can be loosely translated as *The medical science of childbirth in Jaffna.* When the treatise was received in the ABCFM headquarters in Boston in 1863 they re-named the title as *Hindu Midwifery.* Communication between Jaffna and Boston was very slow and was by handwritten reports which took several months to reach the destination by sailing ships. The preface states that it is "A view of Midwifery as held and practiced by the Hindus of Jaffna – compiled from various sources (including) a Midwife of note...by Dr Charles McIntyre alias Asirvatham Nallathambi, educated in medicine by the American Ceylon Mission". [*Papers of the American Board of Commissioners for Foreign Missions,* Ceylon Mission (ABC 16.1.5), Microfilm Reel No. 451, Vol. 7, 1857-1871, Documents, Reports, Letters, Section 158, pp. 1-50, Houghton Library, Harvard University, Massachusetts, USA].

(To be continued in the next article)

Article originally published in "The Ceylankan", Journal No. 46, May 2009 and is continued in the next article.

3

The Medical Science of Childbirth in Jaffna

by Thiru Arumugam and Dr Malini Arumugam

This article is continued from Article No. 2. In 1856, Dr Charles McIntyre wrote a 50 page handwritten manuscript treatise in English titled *Yatpana Piravasa Vyththiyam*. This can be loosely translated as *The medical science of childbirth in Jaffna*. Dr McIntyre was trained by the American Missionary, Dr Samuel Fisk Green. Dr Green studied Medicine at the New York College of Physicians and Surgeons and would have studied Midwifery under Professor Gilman who would have used as a text book Dr Maunsell's book *The Dublin Practice of Midwifery, with notes and additions by Prof. Gilman*. Later Dr Green translated this book into Tamil, see Fig. 1 for page 1 of the translated book. The Midwives of Jaffna at that time were illiterate and would not have access to this book.

THE

THEORY AND PRACTICE

OF

MIDWIFERY

ADAPTED TO INDIA

AND

TRANSLATED INTO TAMIL

BY

SAMUEL F. GREEN, M.D.

FOR THE

AMERICAN CEYLON MISSION.

JAFFNA:
RIPLEY & STRONG, PRINTERS.
1857.

Fig. 1: The first page of Dr Green's translation of a Midwifery book into Tamil

The contents of Dr McIntyre's treatise relate to Midwifery as practiced in Jaffna over 150 years ago and must therefore be read in the light of circumstances of that time. Western medical science was new to Jaffna and indeed to the whole of Ceylon. The vast majority of the population went to the Native Physicians when they fell sick. It is significant to note that in the entire treatise there is no mention of Native Physicians in Midwifery. It is entirely left to the Midwife. The Sastri (priest) is called in if there is a problem. It is significant also that Dr McIntyre does not interject at any time with comments arising from his knowledge of western medicine. He lets the Midwife's commentary flow smoothly along.

When Dr McIntyre's treatise was received in the American Board of Commissioners for Foreign Missions headquarters in Boston in 1863 they re-named the title as *Hindu Midwifery*. Communication between Jaffna and Boston was very slow and was by handwritten reports which took several months to reach the destination by sailing ships. The preface states that it is "A view of Midwifery as held and practised by the Hindus of Jaffna – compiled from various sources (including) a Midwife of note…by Dr Charles McIntyre alias Asirvatham Nallathambi, educated in medicine by the American Ceylon Mission". [*Papers of the American Board of Commissioners for Foreign Missions,* Ceylon Mission (ABC 16.1.5), Microfilm Reel No. 451, Vol. 7, 1857-1871, Documents, Reports, Letters, Section 158, pp. 1-50, Houghton Library, Harvard University, Massachusetts, USA].

The treatise is dated 1856 which is the year that Dr McIntyre completed his medical course and started his internship. At the time of writing the treatise his clinical experience would have been limited, or the treatise may even have been written as a course requirement. The rest of this article is a review of the treatise.

The treatise is divided into two parts, the first part deals with the pregnant woman and the second part deals with the child. It is interesting to note that some of the customs and beliefs have persisted to the present day, particularly in rural areas.

The Mother

The first part is further sub-divided into three sections (ibid p.1):

"(a) Events and practices previous to confinement

(b) Events connected with labour itself

(c) What happens after the completion of labour"

If the soot at the bottom of the rice pot catches fire it is a sure sign that someone in the house has menstruated. When a girl first menstruates, an auspicious day is selected and she is bathed and a feast given to all friends and relations with much pomp and ceremony. It is a custom that is followed to the present day. It is a way of informing the village that the girl will in due course be available for marriage. Biological changes in the girl soon appear, usually between the ages of 12 and 15 years.

After marriage when the monthly discharge ceases, she "must not see either a child, or a stranger or any poverty stricken person, or any white people, but must first look upon the sun….. If a mud-wasp comes and builds its nest in the house, it is taken as a sure sign that someone in the house is starting with child" (ibid p.4). The latter belief is still prevalent in rural areas to this day. In the fifth month "a white disc the size of the palm of the hand will form on the lower abdomen. This disc will be found on the right side, if the child is a male, and on the left side if the child is a female" (ibid p. 6). This is not looked for or recognized these days. In certain cases if there is a flow of menses during pregnancy it is believed that the woman has incurred the displeasure of a *Devathy* (i.e. evil spirit). A votive offering must be made to placate this evil spirit.

Diet during pregnancy should consist of easily digestible food items like rice *kanji* (i.e. porridge), *odiyal* (i.e. dried palmyrah sprout bulb) soup, etc. She must not eat *kiranthi* (i.e. eruptive) foods because they will cause eruptions upon the child (ibid p.7). Delivery occurs ten lunar months (40 weeks) after stoppage of menses, and about a month before the due date items necessary for the mother and child must be purchased. The items include garlic, ginger, tumeric, rice flour, dry fish, sesame oil, margosa oil and jaggery. "If among the garlic bought and brought home, either one or several of the single stem garlic be found, it is a sure sign that the conceived is a male child" (ibid p. 9). In a typical village home where elders are present, these rituals are still followed.

The pregnant woman must not be allowed to fry cakes or knead dough because if any unnatural shapes occur the child may assume that shape. Nor should she braid mats or baskets since if crowding of the strips occurs, the opening of the womb may be similarly narrowed (ibid p. 10). The actual delivery occurs in an out-house temporarily built for the purpose. As the Midwives at that time were women of the scheduled caste of Nalavar (i.e. mainly toddy tappers), one suspects that the out-house may have been used because of the reluctance to admit them into the main house. Margosa leaves must be hung from the thatch to keep out devils, a practice current to this day and margosa has been found to be an effective antiseptic. "Also a lamp is lit and oil kept ready by it to keep it burning continuously till labour is completed. If the lamp burns brightly the child will be boy, if dimly it will be a girl. Should the lamp go out, it would be a very ill omen" (ibid p.13).

When labour commences, the woman is encouraged to walk about as this help the child in its descent. When delivery actually starts "the midwife sits down upon the ground placing both her own legs upon a bag of sand. Then she makes the woman sit down, in front of her, face to face, the patient placing her thighs upon the midwives feet. Another woman sits behind the patient to brace up her back" (ibid p.15). If the child's head is well descended but there is great difficulty in the birth it means that a *Devathy* has been offended and is holding on to the child's legs. A *Sastri* (i.e. priest) must be immediately consulted. The *Sastri* may direct the sacrifice of a sheep or fowl or other offerings to be made to the *Devathy* to appease her (ibid p. 17).

If after this the woman's distress does not abate, a little water should be charmed by mantras and rubbed over her abdomen, or a coconut split in two and stroked over body. The head normally emerges first, but if an arm emerges first the midwife will push it in, and if the head still does not emerge, nothing can be done. If the leg emerges first, the midwife should pull the child down as far as the shoulders and then try to pull the child out completely. If it will not come out then nothing can be done (ibid pp.19-20). The solemn 'nothing can be done' repeated twice above probably implies maternal and/or infant mortality.

The after-birth must be removed as soon as the delivery has been completed. If there are any lesions in the placenta or cord it is bad for the child. If the cord is full of lumps then it is a sign that the next child will be a boy. It is the duty of the midwife to bury the after-birth and bathe the mother using water in which the leaves of margosa, cotton and castor-oil plants have been boiled. After this a paste of tumeric and margosa oil is smeared all over the body (ibid p. 22). No doubt this acts as an antiseptic. This is repeated for the next five days, and twice daily the woman must eat with *kanji* a ladle full of a paste of garlic, ginger, pepper, tumeric and cumin seed. For the next fifteen days she should not drink cold water as this would hinder the healing process (ibid p. 23). On the thirty-second day a Brahmin is called in to purify the house by sprinkling holy water using a mango leaf. Until this is done, none of the inmates should go to a temple (ibid p.25).

The Child

"When a child is born, if it appears with its face downwards, it will be possessed of plenty of worldly good. If it be born feet foremost, even though unlearned in physic, the touch of its foot, or stroking a part therewith, will heal all fractures, bruises, pains and sicknesses. Maladies that would not yield to any medicine are cured by this" (ibid p. 27). It is interesting to note that this belief persisted until relatively recent times. If the head of a child appears to be very large, then a coconut must be split into two and one half pressed on the child's head like a cap to make it small. The time of birth must also be carefully noted so that the horoscope can be cast.

Soon after birth the cord is cut and knotted, and after a while the child is given a dose of *codi calli* juice. This is from a slender cactus like plant which has a milky juice. After this the midwife spreads a paste of tumeric on the child and carefully washes the child (ibid p. 30). "If the child exits with the cord round its neck, it is a bad sign for the father and his relatives, but a very good sign for the mother and her relatives" (ibid p. 31). The child is initially fed on jaggery or sugar dissolved in water and after the third day the child can be nursed. If the child has one crown in its hair it will obtain authority, if it has two it will be a beggar, but if it has three it will be wealthy. On the morning of the seventh or ninth day a very elaborate ceremony is carried out to ward off the influence of devils and also to thank *Cothy*, a *Devathy* specially honoured by midwives for a successful childbirth. The child must sleep with its head pointing to the east as only corpses are laid with the head pointing west (ibid pp. 33-34).

Each time the child is bathed, a mixture of lamp-black and oil is smeared around the eyes. This is to ensure that the child does not get cats-eyes i.e. like white people (ibid p.37). On the thirty-second day the child is taken to the temple and the hair is shaved off and also any vows made during delivery must be honoured. The Brahmin priest is asked to name the child, usually one of the names of that temple's deity (ibid p. 38).

Moles on children are supposed to be placed according to the influence of stars. A mole on the right side is lucky for the male and unlucky for the female. A mole on the left side has the opposite effect. If the mole cannot be seen by the child it is considered lucky. A squint eye is also considered lucky. If a near relative dies at about the time the woman conceives, it is believed that the same person is conceived by the mother. "If the child born be a male, the thought is that he was in a former birth a debtor to the parents and has come in this birth to earn something to give them. If a female, then it is thought that she was a creditor in a former birth and has come to take her dowry" (ibid p. 40).

"Generally when it is ascertained that the child born is a girl, there is sorrow. When a boy, there is great joy. This is because the girl must receive a portion from her parents, whereas the boy will bring a portion with his wife" (ibid p. 41). Not much has changed nowadays, particularly in India where many abortions are induced when it is realised that the expected child is a girl.

If the mother has been away from the house for a while, she must not give the child milk immediately on her return, as an evil spirit may come and seize the child. If this happens an image of the child must be made of mud and placed on a braided coconut leaf with flowers and the *Devathy* driven off (ibid p.42).

For a woman to die with a child in her womb is considered a great calamity. If this happens, it is better to separate them before burial (ibid p. 43). "Twin children, if of different sexes will not live long. If both are males or both are females there is more prospect of surviving. If of different sexes it is thought that they were in a former birth husband and wife" (ibid p.44). The birth of twins is generally considered to be a bad sign for the household.

Children must be hidden from the sight of visitors with an evil eye or tongue. If such a calamity happens then the child must be stroked with chillie and margosa leaves and the leaves burnt at a cross-road. If the sighting cannot be avoided, then the child must be blackened with charcoal to ward off the evil eye (ibid p.45).

When the child is just under a year old, the first feeding of solid food takes place. On an auspicious day, a mixture of rice, jaggery, milk and banana is fed to the child. This feeding must not be in the view of others (ibid p.45). Nowadays solid foods are introduced a little earlier in life. When teething commences, in order that they may grow nicely, a small ceremony is performed. Some small rice cakes called *kolukattai* are steamed and the child placed in a big basket and fed (ibid p.46). Nowadays small pieces of coconut kernel the size of teeth are cut and embedded along the outer edge of the *kolukattai*.

If for some reason the mother's milk supply fails before the child is weaned "the practice is to beg breast milk round the village, letting the child suck a little from this and that woman. (This giving of milk is counted as among the thirty two acts of charity or merit). Cows milk is on no account to be given to the child, being considered indigestible" (ibid p. 48). Clearly lactose intolerance has been recognized. When the mother becomes pregnant again, or if she falls seriously ill, the child may be weaned. This is done by smearing margosa oil on the mother's nipples to make them bitter, or the child sent away for a few days (ibid p. 48). Children start their schooling at the age of five years. The course of study must start on an auspicious day and begins with the offering of a coconut to the God Ganesha.

Fig. 2 is a picture of Nurses and their charges taken in the 1890s at the McLeod Hospital, Inuvil, Jaffna, which was an American Mission Hospital for Women and Children.

Fig. 2: Nurses and their charges Inuvil Mission Hospital, 1890s.

This article was first published in the "The Ceylankan", Journal No. 47, August 2009

4

Robert Knox - a Postscript

By Thiru Arumugam

The November 2007, 10th Anniversary Collectors Edition of The Ceylankan included an interesting and comprehensive article by Dr Brendon Gooneratne about Robert Knox and his 1681 book *An Historical Relation of the Island Ceylon in the East Indies*. The book describes life in the 17th century Kandyan Kingdom where Robert Knox was incarcerated for 19 years. Daniel Defoe is believed to have been influenced by the book when he wrote *Robinson Crusoe*. A Postscript to that article is a reproduction of the first text page of the copy of Knox's book in the Bodleian Library, Oxford (Fig. 1).

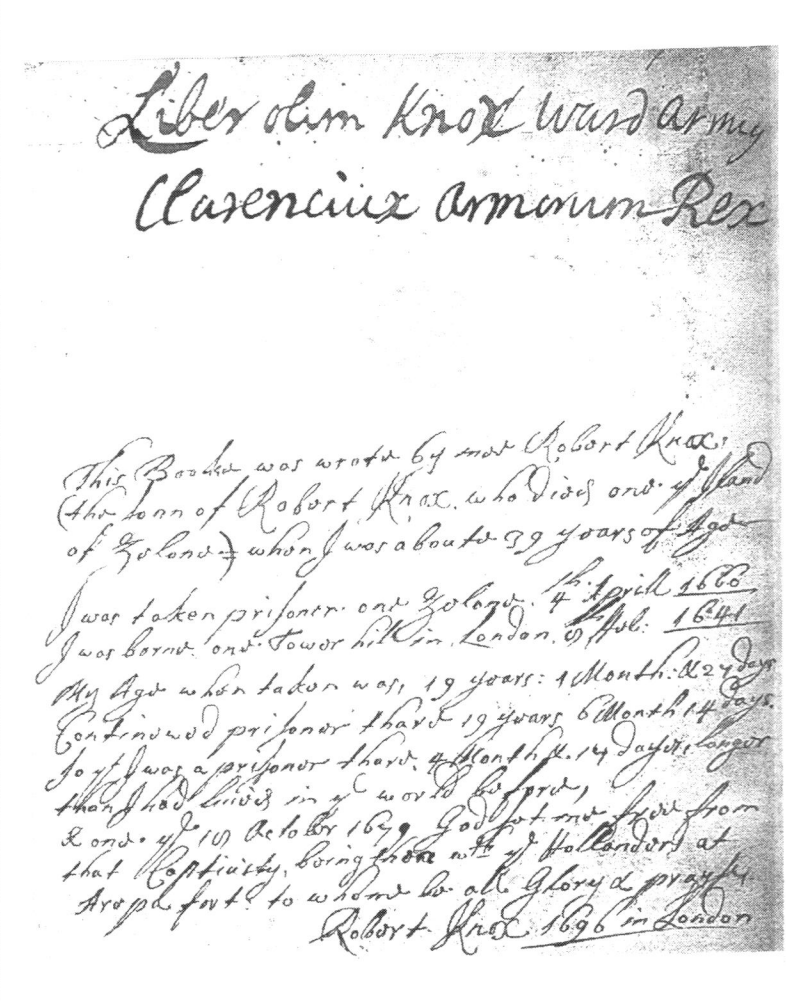

Fig. 1: Inscription in Robert Knox's own handwriting (except for the Latin tag) in a 1681 first edition of his book *An Historical Relation of the Island Ceylon in the East Indies*.

The Latin inscription at the top of the page:
Liber olim Knox Ward armiger(?) Clarenceux Armorum Rex
has been translated by CSA Members and Classicists, Valentine Perera and Nalini MacIntyre as :
A book formerly (of) Knox Ward, arms bearer (of) Clarenceux King of Arms

The only doubtful word is the fifth word which is probably *armiger*. Perhaps an erudite *Ceylankan* reader may be able to resolve this issue.

Robert Knox is believed to have been a misogynist and that could explain why he did not join most of his captive shipmates who formed liaisons with local women during their long captivity. He remained a life-long bachelor and having no progeny, he bequeathed "The Manuscript of my own life" to his nephew, Knox Ward (Richard Garnett, *The Age of Dryden,* 1895, p. 273). Knox Ward was the son of Sir John Ward, Lord Mayor of London in 1718, which shows that Robert Knox was well connected. The manuscript subsequently went missing for many years.

Knox Ward was Clarenceux King of Arms from 1726 to 1741. The College of Arms in London was founded in 1420 and still exists. It is the official repository of the Coats of Arms and is the office regulating heraldry and the grant of new armorial bearings. Clarenceux is the senior of the two provincial Kings of Arms and has jurisdiction over England, south of the River Trent.

The manuscript page, except for the inscription, is in Robert Knox's own handwriting. The date given in the last line is 1696, which is fifteen years after *Historical Relation* was published in 1681. It therefore probably forms part of the proposed revised edition which was to include his autobiography also, but was never published.

The text of the manuscript reads as follows (note his use of the word "one" instead of "on" and "in", and that his father was also Robert Knox):

This Booke was wrote by mee Robert Knox (the sonn of Robert Knox who died one the Iland of Zelone) when I was aboute 39 years of Age.

I was taken prisoner one Zelone, 4th Aprill, 1660. I was borne one Tower hill in London, 8th Feb. 1641. My Age when taken was, 19 years: 1 month : & 27 dayes. Continewed prisoner thare 19 years 6 month 14 dayes So I was a prisoner thare 4 Month & 17 dayes, longer then I had lived in the world before, & one the 18 October 1679 God set mee free from that Captivity, being then with the Hollanders at Arepa fort to whome be all Glory & prayse.

Robert Knox, 1696 in London

Authors Note: For those who are interested a genuine 1681 first edition of Robert Knox's book is available for reference in the National Library of Australia, Canberra. The reader has to wear soft kid gloves before being allowed to handle the book and photocopying is not allowed because of the weak binding of the book.

This article was originally published in "The Ceylankan", Journal 52, November 2010.

5

D J Wimalasurendra - Pioneer Ceylonese Engineer

By Thiru Arumugam

D J Wimalasurendra (1874 - 1953) (Fig. 1) was a pioneer Ceylonese engineer and was almost certainly the first Ceylonese to qualify as a Chartered Civil Engineer as well as a Chartered Electrical Engineer, a rare dual qualification which very few Ceylonese have achieved since then. His father was a jewellery craftsman from Galle who had mastered the art of engraving on diamonds. When Governor Gordon heard of his skills, he got him to engrave his seal on a diamond which he wore as a pendant. Later when he met Queen Victoria in London she noticed this pendant and asked him where it was carved because the art of engraving diamonds was unknown to British jewellers. The upshot was that Queen Victoria sent for Wimalasurendra Senior, gave him a room in Windsor Castle for a few months and asked him to train British craftsmen. In return she awarded him the rank of *Mudaliyar*.

Fig. 1: Statue of D J Wimalasurendra at Norton Bridge (Courtesy Ceylon Electricity Board)

D J Wimalasurendra studied at Ananda College where he was the first student to pass the London Matriculation examination. Had there been a University in Ceylon at that time he would have automatically gained entry to it. He joined the Public Works Department (PWD) Government Factory in Kolonnawa as an Apprentice. In 1893 when the Government Technical School (later to become the Ceylon Technical College) in Maradana started a Diploma in Civil Engineering course, he enrolled in the first batch of students. After completing the course, he was appointed Head Overseer in the PWD in 1898. He later sat for and passed the Graduate Membership examination of the Institution of Civil Engineers, London and was promoted as a District Engineer in the PWD in 1904 and was posted to Diyatalawa.

The upcountry railway line had reached Bandarawela by 1894 but progress on the last leg from there to Badulla was very slow. One of the reasons for the delay was the problem of crossing the Demodera gap. Soon after the proposed site of the Demodera railway station there was a wide and deep gorge below which had to be crossed. The only way of crossing this was thought to be a ten mile detour, until Wimalasurendra suggested the ingenious idea of the railway line looping around itself like a snake and passing under the station through a tunnel and crossing the gorge over a nine arch masonry viaduct. The result is the well-known tourist attraction of the 'Demodara loop' with a substantial saving in track length, cost and travel time.

Another of his assignments when he was at Diyatalawa was to prospect for gold in the Maskeli Oya in the foothills of Adams Peak. Ian Van Geyzel, a Boer prisoner-of-war from Transvaal, who was also an engineer was assigned to assist him. When they came to the Kiriwan Eliya waterfall downstream of Maskeliya, Van Geyzel remarked that there may not be solid gold here but there is liquid gold in the energy of the waterfall. This started Wimalasurendra thinking about how this energy could be tapped and it became a life-long quest for him. He promptly re-named the waterfall Laxapana Falls (Fig. 2) because he calculated that it had the potential to light up 100,000 light bulbs (i.e. Laksa-pahana). We now know that his assessment was approximately correct, amazing because of the very limited hydrological data that would have been available to him.

Fig. 2: Laxapana Falls (Courtesy Ceylon Electricity Board)

In 1915, although he was already a Chartered Civil Engineer, he decided to qualify as an Electrical Engineer. He took long leave and proceeded to London where he enrolled in a sandwich course at Faraday House. He passed the qualifying examinations and returned to Ceylon in 1917. His first assignment after his return was to design and build a small hydro-electric scheme in Nuwara Eliya using excess water from Lake Gregory. The Provincial Engineer said that Wimalasurendra's scheme was not practical, but Wimalasurendra nevertheless went ahead and built the scheme which subsequently provided electricity to Nuwara Eliya for many decades to come.

In 1918 Wimalasurendra read his path breaking paper titled *Economics of Power Utilisation in Ceylon* before the Engineering Association of Ceylon, now known as The Institution of Engineers, Sri Lanka. This paper was the launching pad for hydro-electric power development in Sri Lanka. He assessed the hydro-electric potential of the Mahaweli Ganga and the upper reaches of the Kelani Ganga and said that if the potential was exploited, then Ceylon can start large scale industrialisation, electrification of tea and rubber factories and electricity supply can spread beyond the larger towns. Furthermore he said that the availability of cheap power can be used for the electrification of the railways, but this has yet to be implemented to this day. The majority of the audience was overwhelmingly British engineers and Rylands, his superior officer in the PWD said in the discussion that followed that Wimalasurendra's estimates of the hydro-power potential were seven times too high. We now know that Wimalasurendra's estimates were of the correct order.

In 1919 the Director of Public Works (DPW), his Deputy and Wimalasurendra outlined a proposal to the Government to supply hydro-electric power to Colombo. The Kehelgamu Oya flows from near Dickoya at an elevation of about 4000 feet. In the next valley to the south the Maskeli Oya flows from the foothills of Adams Peak also at an elevation of about 4000 feet. Both rivers flow westwards and parallel for about the next 25 miles dropping in elevation to about 300 feet until their confluence just upstream of Kitulgala to form the Kelani Ganga. The proposed Laxapana hydro-electric scheme utilises the fall in elevation of these two Oyas by a cascade of power stations, including a trans-basin diversion. The generated power is transmitted to Colombo by high voltage overhead lines, a distance of about 60 miles.

In 1921, the DPW submitted a revised proposal called Scheme A which proposed the utilisation of the Kehelgamu and Maskeli Oyas in three stages, with a final installed power of 71 megawatts (MW). It must be remembered that the total power load in Colombo at that time was about two megawatts and the Government could not foresee how such a vast amount of power could be utilised. In 1923 Wimalasurendra proposed an alternative cheaper proposal which he called Scheme B. In this Scheme the final output would be 54 MW, but in the first stage only 17 MW of generating plant would be installed and this would be sufficient to meet the demand of the Western Province for the first three years from commissioning. The first stage consisted of a 90 foot high dam across the Kehelgamu Oya at Norton Bridge, a 8100 foot long tunnel to convey the water under a mountain range to the next valley, a 60 inch diameter pipeline to drop this water to the Laxapana power house 1500 feet below on the banks of the Maskeli Oya where there would be three generators rated at 5.6 MW each.

The Government consulted Evan Parry, one of the world's leading authorities on hydro-electric power at that time. He visited the site and highly commended Wimalasurendra's Scheme B on its engineering merits and said that it was the most economical development of the two rivers. Scheme B was adopted and forms the basis of the subsequent development of the utilisation of the hydro-power potential of the two rivers. The original 1923 design drawing of Scheme B is reproduced (Fig. 3) and it shows Norton Dam, the tunnel trace, the pipeline route, Laxapana Power House, Glencairn (Castlereagh) Dam, Kintyre (Mousakelle) Dam and the trace of the take-off of the power line to Colombo. In 1924 the Secretary of State for the Colonies in London approved Scheme B for construction and in his letter expressed his appreciation "in particular of the ability with which the detailed plans and estimates had been drawn up by Mr Wimalasurendra". High praise indeed.

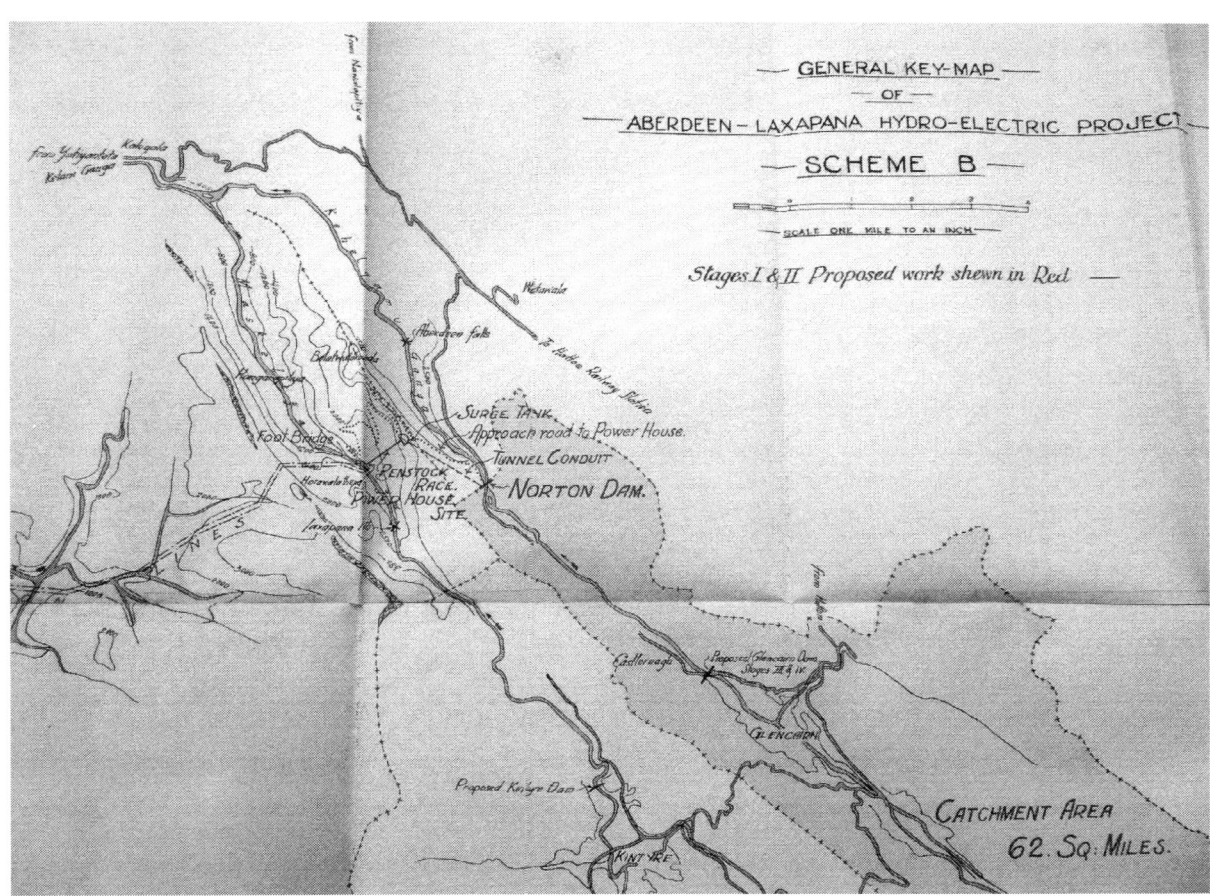

Fig 3: Wimalasurendra's submission of Scheme B in 1923 forms the basis of the present day Scheme. It includes Norton Dam, Laxapana Power House, Glencairn Dam (Castlereagh Dam) and Kintyre Dam (Mousakelle Dam).

Construction work on Scheme B started in 1924 and Wimalasurendra was surprised to find that although the Scheme had been designed by him and he was the Chief Electrical Engineer in the PWD, he was to play no role in the project. He was asked to hand over all designs and drawings to Hughes, a relatively junior British engineer who had no hydro-electric experience. Hughes was appointed Construction Engineer and asked to report directly to the DPW. Disappointed at the turn of events, Wimalasurendra applied for commuted half-pay leave and left for England on a long holiday. When he returned in 1925 he found that the work on the Scheme was in a complete mess. Three million rupees had been spent and there had been severe over-expenditure on several items without approval and some structures had been incorrectly built. The new DPW who had just been appointed decided to stop all work on the project.

In 1927 the Legislative Council decided to appoint a Select Committee which included D S Senanayake to investigate what had gone wrong with the project. In their Report the Select Committee, referring to Wimalasurendra, said that the DPW had "failed to utilise to advantage the services of the only man available who had any first hand or intimate knowledge of the works".

Due to stoppage of work on the hydro-electric scheme, the Government realised that there would soon be a power crisis as the diesel power station in Pettah would not be able to meet for much longer the rapidly growing Colombo power demand. It was decided to build a steam turbine powered power station in Kolonnawa, initially to consist of two nos. 3 MW generators. Wimalasurendra was appointed to be directly in charge of building this power station. The opening ceremony was in March 1929 and the

Governor named it after himself as the Stanley Power Station. Wimalasurendra was the only Ceylonese present at the opening ceremony.

In September 1929, Wimalasurendra reached the age of 55 years and decided to retire without asking for an extension of service. In June 1931 he contested the Ratnapura seat in the first State Council elections and was duly elected. While he was a State Councillor he campaigned for the resumption of work on the hydro-electric scheme but because of the great depression and the collapse of export prices for tea, rubber and coconut, the Government had to cut down capital expenditure to the absolute minimum. In 1937 he re-contested the Ratnapura seat, but he was not re-elected.

In 1937, John Kotalawala was the Minister for Communication and Works and he was able to get the State Council to pass a resolution to resume work on the hydro-electric scheme. Only four Councillors voted against the proposal, two Englishmen and Dr N M Perera and Philip Gunawardhana. Tenders were invited for the work and in 1939 the contract for the civil work was awarded to Hindustan Construction Company and the mechanical and electrical contracts were awarded to three British firms. However, with the outbreak of World War II later that year, all work stopped again. The contracts were re-awarded after the war ended and the 25 MW Laxapana Power House was finally opened in October 1950 (Fig. 4).

Fig. 4: Old Laxapana Hydro Power Station with the
3 nos. Stage 1 machines in the background.
(Courtesy Ceylon Electricity Board)

Before the 8100 foot long trans-basin tunnel was filled with water, 74 year old Wimalasurendra rode through the tunnel on a trolley. When he emerged at the other end he said "Although it was not my good fortune to execute the Scheme I had originated, I am happy that I have lived to see it brought to fruition by my countrymen, and that I should have in the evening of my life, been able to see the light, the dawn of which I beheld fifty years ago....".

Subsequent stages in the cascade of power stations in the two valleys in the hydro-electric scheme were constructed as the demand for electricity increased. An additional 25 MW of generators in the Laxapana power house and the Castlereagh Dam near Dickoya were completed in 1958, financed by the first World Bank loan to Ceylon. Sadly, Wimalasurendra passed away in 1953 and did not live to see these completed. A 50 MW power station was built at Norton Bridge in 1965 and named Wimalasurendra Power Station. A 75 MW power station was built in 1969 at Polpitiya downstream of Laxapana and the Mousakelle Dam near Maskeliya completed in 1972. The 100 MW New Laxapana Power Station, alongside the original Laxapana Power Station, was completed in 1974. The 60 MW Canyon Power station at the head of Laxapana falls was completed in 1989. The final power station in this scheme is the 35 MW Broadlands Power Station which is presently under construction and is due for completion in 2017.

All this arose from the vision and foresight of one man who battled against all the odds. He was ridiculed by his peers who could not comprehend how Ceylon could ever utilise what they considered to be vast amounts of power. In fact at one stage the DPW transferred Wimalasurendra from Colombo to a remote outstation as he said that access to libraries and sources of information in Colombo seemed to be feeding "his flights to the realms of fantasy"!

Article originally published in "The Ceylankan", Journal No. 56, November 2011.

6

A RIVER FOR JAFFNA

by Thiru Arumugam

INTRODUCTION

The Jaffna Peninsula which is the northernmost tip of Sri Lanka, has an area of about 1000 square km and being relatively flat has no rivers and is totally dependent on the annual rainfall of about 1270 mm, of which about 87% falls during the north-east monsoon from October to December, for recharge of the water table in the underground aquifer. In the past, water was drawn from wells for domestic and agricultural use by well sweeps, but from the 1950's onwards pumps have been used to draw water from these wells. There are about 100,000 wells in the Peninsula. This over pumping for agricultural use has drawn down the fresh water stored in the limestone aquifer resulting in sea water percolating into the wells through the fractured limestone, as no part of Jaffna is more than about 15 km from the sea.

Of the 1000 sq km area of the Jaffna Peninsula, about 60% is occupied by residential usage, home gardens, roads, parks, public buildings etc., about 13% (13,700 hectares) is cultivated with food and subsidiary crops and about 13% (13,000 hectares) is cultivable with rain-fed rice paddy. 4% of the land is not arable due to soil salinity and the balance 10% of the Peninsula is occupied by two lagoons. At present about 30% of the wells in the Jaffna Peninsula are saline. Recent reports from agricultural experts state that more than 4500 hectares of fertile agricultural land have turned saline and have become unsuitable for cultivation.

It is anticipated that due to climate change causing rising sea levels and drought the present trend of losing arable land in the Jaffna Peninsula due to soil salinity will progressively increase, causing further losses in food production. It is therefore necessary to consider what urgent measures could be undertaken to combat climate change and maintain (and increase) food production in the Jaffna Peninsula. An appropriate solution is to complete the 'River for Jaffna Project' (Fig. 1). Construction work on this project was carried out in the 1950s, but it was never completed due to lack of funds.

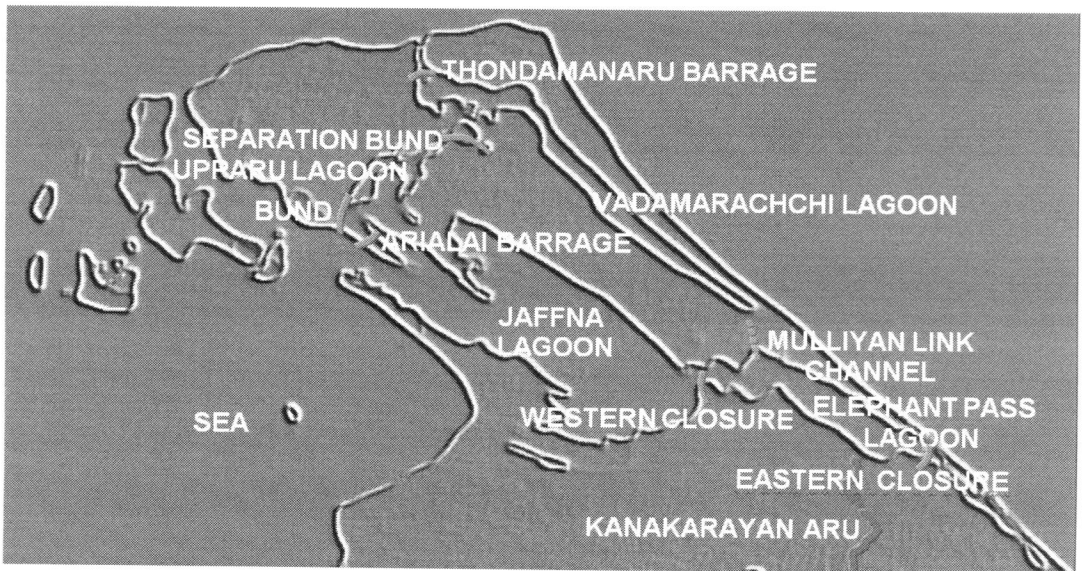

Fig. 1: Sketch of Jaffna Peninsula showing River for Jaffna Project Area

Within the Jaffna peninsula there are two large lagoons, the Vadamarachchi lagoon and the Upparu lagoon with surface areas of about 77 and 26 square km respectively. These are large shallow lagoons and cover a significant proportion (10%) of the peninsula's land area of 1000 square km. These lagoons have openings to the sea and are salt water lagoons but during the north-east monsoon rain water from their catchment areas also collects in them. The total catchment area of these lagoons is about 50% of the area of the Peninsula.

Paddy cultivation in the Jaffna Peninsula is essentially rain-fed cultivation. Cash crops and market garden crops are, however, irrigated using well water. The British Colonial Secretary, Sir James Emerson Tennant in 1859 has described market gardening in Jaffna as follows and his description remains basically unchanged to this day except that pumps have, for the most part, replaced well sweeps:

"In the immediate vicinity of Point Pedro (and the description applies equally well to the vicinity of Jaffna and the western division of the peninsula in general), the perfection of the village cultivation is truly remarkable; it is horticulture rather than agriculture, and reminds one of the market gardens of Fulham and Chelsea more forcibly than anything I have seen out of England. Almost every cottage has a garden attached to it, wherein are grown fruit-trees and flowers, the latter being grown in great quantities for decoration and offering in the temples. Each is situated in a well-secured enclosure, with one or more wells. From these night and day, but chiefly during the night, labourers are employed for raising water by means of vessels (frequently woven of palm leaves) attached to horizontal levers; something like the sakkias used by the peasants on the Nile for a similar purpose, except that in Jaffna two persons at least are required for each well, one of whom walks back and forward along the lever, whilst the other below directs the bucket in its ascent and empties its contents into a reservoir, whence by removing a clod of earth with the foot, it is admitted into conducting channels, and led to the several beds in succession. The value of these wells is extreme in a country where rivers and even the smallest stream are unknown, and where the cultivators are entirely dependent on the rains of the two monsoons. But such has been the indefatigable industry of the people in providing them, that they may be said to have virtually added a third harvest to the year, by the extent to which they have multiplied the means of irrigation around their principal towns and villages."

The earliest known recorded observation about improving the fresh water situation in the Jaffna Peninsula was made nearly 350 years ago in a recently translated report by the Dutch Captain Hendrile van Reede, who had accompanied the Dutch Governor of Ceylon, Rijckloff van Goens, on a visit to Jaffna in 1665 in which he states:

"A dike to contain the sea at Condemanaer and Navacolli, with sluices to claim the rain water and a canal to the salt pans at Nieweli would create more useful arable land."

Van Reede suggests a barrage at Thondamannaru and another at Navatkuli (Ariyalai) to convert Vadamaradchi and Upparu lagoons into freshwater lagoons, and a separate canal for salt water from the sea to the Upparu salterns. He was a remarkably perceptive man to realize this on a casual visit to Jaffna. Only a Dutchman with their long history of land reclamation would have thought of this scheme.

In 1879, the Northern Province Government Agent, Twyneham, proposed that dams be constructed to prevent salt water from entering the lagoons, but before it could be implemented there was a severe cyclone and flooding, possibly a tsunami caused by the eruption of the volcano Krakatoa in Indonesia in 1883 which caused severe flooding in Jaffna and Twyneham withdrew his proposals. He feared that if the dams had been already constructed, the flooding would have been much worse.

In 1916 the Government Agent, Horsberg, suggested that as an experiment the culverts where the Point Pedro – Chavakacheri road crosses the Vadamaradchi lagoon be temporarily blocked by wooden gates, thus making the upper reaches of Vadamaradchi lagoon a freshwater lagoon. The work was done in 1920 and the scheme operated successfully for four years. Although it was decided to make the scheme permanent, this was never done, possibly due to the great depression which followed and placed the Government in serious financial difficulties.

In the 1930s and 1940s the Divisional Irrigation Engineer, Webb, produced detailed plans for barrages at Thondamannaru and Ariyalai. The scheme was supported in the State Council by Balasingham who was a member of the Council, but the war intervened and construction work on the Thondamannaru

Barrage commenced only in 1947 and was completed in 1953, and the Ariyalai Barrage was completed in 1955. After a few years the wooden gates and stop logs perished and sea water passed through them freely.

If we are to increase the availability of fresh water in the Jaffna peninsula we need to look at sources alternative to rain in the peninsula. South of the peninsula is the sea water Elephant Pass Lagoon which is relatively shallow but has a surface area of about 77 square km. It has a catchment area of about 940 square km in the mainland Vanni, mainly consisting of the Kanakarayan Aru and three smaller streams. During the north-east monsoon these streams discharge the surplus rain water from the Vanni into the Elephant Pass lagoon. From this lagoon this fresh water flows into the sea through the eastern end at Chundikulam and formerly also through the western end Elephant Pass bridge, and is at present being wasted.

During the 1960's a scheme was proposed to utilise the monsoon rain water running to waste from the Elephant Pass lagoon, for the benefit of the Jaffna peninsula.

KEY POINTS of the RIVER for JAFFNA Project

Key points of the scheme and details of the work done at that time are as follows:

- Close off the openings in the road and rail bridges in the Elephant Pass causeway at the western end of the Elephant Pass lagoon to prevent fresh water going to the sea from this end. This work was completed.

- Build a bund at the eastern end of the Elephant Pass lagoon at Chundikulam to prevent fresh water going to the sea at that end and also provide a spillway to discharge excess flood water to the sea. This work was completed and Elephant Pass lagoon became a fresh water lagoon for a few years but unfortunately the bund was breached by subsequent heavy floods, thus allowing sea water access since then.

- Excavate a 12 metre wide, 4 km long channel, called the Mulliyan Link Channel, from the northern side of the Elephant Pass lagoon to convey fresh water from the Elephant Pass lagoon to the southern end of the Vadamarachchi lagoon, including regulatory gates to control the flow. Unfortunately this work was never completed. About 80% was completed when funds ran out and work stopped.

- Refurbish the existing Thondamanaru Barrage (where the northern end of Vadamarachchi lagoon joins the sea) to make it watertight, and improve the discharge gates to allow for discharge of flood water. This will make Vadamarachchi lagoon a fresh water lagoon. This work was carried out but a few years later the wooden stop logs perished and allowed sea water to enter the lagoon.

- Provide a spillway and gates at the southern end of Upparu Lagoon where it connects to the sea, near Ariyalai. This will make Upparu lagoon a fresh water lagoon. The spillway and gates were constructed but a few years later the wooden stop logs perished and allowed sea water to enter Upparu lagoon.

It can be seen from the above that the scheme was only partially completed in the 1960's and the main key element of the Mulliyan link channel to convey fresh water from Elephant Pass lagoon to Vadamarachchi lagoon was never completed. In the brief period that Vadamarachchi and Upparu were fresh water lagoons the benefits to the peninsula were noticeable and many saline wells became potable water wells.

PROJECT BENEFITS

The benefits of completing this project include the following:

- About 13,000 hectares of land can be cultivated with paddy in the Jaffna peninsula. The area presently cultivated is about 8000 hectares due to soil salinity and other reasons. This cultivation is entirely rain fed unlike paddy cultivation on the mainland which is watered by irrigation channels. As it is rain fed, the yield per acre in Jaffna is very poor and is only about one-third of the average yield per acre on the mainland. If the Vadamarachchi and Upparu lagoons become fresh water lakes, the water table and water quality in the wells will improve, and using lift irrigation it will be possible to irrigate these paddy fields without depending purely on the rain and the paddy land now lying fallow can also be cultivated. The potential for improvement in yield and rice production is staggering.

- About 4400 hectares of land bordering the Vadamarachchi and Upparu lagoons are uncultivable at present as they are saline. When these become fresh water lagoons, after the salt is leached out of the soil, it will be possible to cultivate this land with cash crops and paddy.

- There will be a dramatic improvement in the water quality of the 30% of the Jaffna wells which are now saline. In many cases the water will become suitable for domestic use and agricultural use, increasing the acreage under agricultural cultivation.

- In the existing wells it will be possible to increase the amount of daily pumping without the water going saline, thus increasing agricultural cultivation and livestock production.

- Fresh water prawn farming can commence on the banks of the lagoons, with potential for export earnings.

- Converting Elephant Pass lagoon into a 77 sq km fresh water lagoon will provide fresh agricultural possibilities on both sides of the lagoon i.e. the Jaffna peninsula side on the north, as well as the Vanni side on the south, once the salinity has been leached out of the soil.

WORK NEEDED TO COMPLETE THE SCHEME

K Shanmugarajah who was Chief Engineer of this project in the 1970's has written a comprehensive book on this project in 1993 titled *Water Resources Development Jaffna Peninsula*. The book details the history of the project, contains detailed designs, details of the work carried out and work remaining to be done. Detailed cost estimates have also been included. Implementation of the project involves the following steps:

Step 1: Thondamanaru Barrage

This barrage has now been completely repaired and refurbished about two years ago with steel gates and new lifting gear. The barrage is now watertight and Vadamarachchi lagoon has become a fresh water lagoon fed with rain water from its 300 sq km catchment area (Fig. 2). The benefits are already beginning to appear as this extract from the Island newspaper of 10 March 2012 shows:

Fig 2: Thondamannar Barrage, rebuilt and fitted with new gates
(Photo: Sakthi Arumugam)

Finally the delegation visited the Vallai region to observe the onion cultivation where the lands were found unsuitable for onion cultivation. The Governor (Chandrasiri) was able to make his own personal observation as to how the construction of the water prevention bund at Thondaimannaru by the Irrigation Department was successful in changing the former high salinity lands into fertile agricultural lands.

Step 2: Recondition Ariyalai Barrage

This Barrage has been completely repaired a few months ago and refurbished and new gates fitted (Fig. 3). This makes Upparu lagoon into a fresh water lagoon fed with rain water from its 220 sq km catchment area.

Fig. 3: Ariyalai Barrage, rebuilt and fitted with new gates
(Photo: Thiru Arumugam)

Step 3: Complete Mulliyan Link Channel

Complete excavation of Mulliyan Link Channel, form bund and roadway, causeway and provide control regulator. When this work is completed, water can flow from Elephant Pass to Vadamarchchi and Upparu lagoons as required. No immediate plans for carrying out this work have been indicated.

Step 4: Complete Spill cum Causeway at Chundikulam

At the eastern end of Elephant Pass lagoon at Chundikulam, complete the spill cum Chundikulam causeway, zoned embankment, and flanked embankment with gravel road. The spill plus causeway will be 2100 metres long and the bund 1400 metres long. When this work is completed Elephant Pass lagoon will become a fresh water lagoon (Fig. 4). No immediate plans for carrying out this work have been indicated.

Fig. 4: Elephant Pass Lagoon, must be converted to a fresh water lagoon to complete the River for Jaffna
(Photo: Thiru Arumugam)

ATTEMPTS AT SCHEME APPROVAL

In October 2007 at the Annual Sessions of the Institution of Engineers, Sri Lanka, held in Colombo, a Resolution was passed unanimously. The Resolution urged the Government to complete the River for Jaffna Project. This Resolution was conveyed to the Government.

A presentation on the River for Jaffna Project was also made by the writer in November 2007 in Colombo at the Nobel Peace Prize winning Pugwash Organisation's Workshop on *Learning from Ancient Hydraulic Civilizations to combat Climate Change.* A resolution worded as follows was passed at this Workshop, proposed by Ambassador Jayantha Dhanapala, President, Pugwash Conferences on Science and World Affairs and seconded by D L O Mendis:

This Pugwash Workshop resolves to recommend to the Government of Sri Lanka that the project known as A River for Jaffna that was started some fifty years ago, and almost completed, but is now in a state of disuse and abandonment, should be restored without delay, as a most important step towards including Sri Lankans of the Jaffna peninsula in the development and enjoyment of the natural resources of the country, thereby contributing to early achievement of a durable peace.

It is hoped that the Government will carry out the remaining work on this project without delay, namely the Mulliyan link channel and the Chundikulam bund and spillway. When this project is finally completed there will be a complete transformation in the agricultural productivity of the Jaffna Peninsula and the quality of life will also be greatly improved by solving to a large extent the problem of salinity in wells.

This Article was originally published in "The Ceylankan", Journal No. 58, May 2012.

River for Jaffna

(with apologies to Leigh Hunt's Abou Ben Adhem)

Sanmugam Arumugam (may his clan increase!)
Awoke one night from a deep dream of peace,
And saw, within the moonlight in his room,
Making it rich, and like a lotus in bloom,
An angel writing in a book of gold:—
Exceeding peace made Arumugam bold,
And to the presence in the room he said,
"What writest thou?"—The vision raised its head,
And with a look made of sweet deport,
Answered, "A Water Projects Report"
"And is River for Jaffna among?" "Nay, not so,"
Said the angel. Arumugam spoke more low,
But cheerily still; and said, "I pray thee, then,
Write it as one that serves our fellow men."

The angel wrote, and vanished. The next night
It came again with a great awakening light,
And showed the names which the Report had blest,
And lo! River for Jaffna led all the rest!

NOTE: This parody was written by Thiru Arumugam, in Sydney, Australia, to honour his late father on his 108th birthday anniversary, Aug. 31, 2013. A recent (Aug. 12, 2013) UN Environmental Program Report on thirty Sri Lanka water projects, had placed A River for Jaffna at the top of the list.

7

High praise for Thiru Arumugam's book

Sri Lankan born Sir Christopher Ondaatje was a fellow student at St Thomas College in the 1940s until his parents sent him off at the age of 13 to a boarding school in England. After leaving school he worked in a Bank in London and then migrated to Canada where he became a wealthy Stockbroker and also represented Canada in the 1964 Winter Olympics. In the 1990s when he was on holiday in Africa he decided that there are more things in life than the pursuit of money. He sold his Pagurian Corporation which was valued at over $500 million and moved to London to begin a new life as philanthropist, adventurer and writer.

Among the many institutions that he helped include the National Portrait Gallery, London where the Queen opened the Extension naming it the "Ondaatje Wing", the British Labour Party, the Royal Geographical Society, Somerset County Cricket Club, his old school - Blundell's School etc. His books include *Hemingway in Africa: The last Safari, Woolf in Ceylon 1904 - 1911, Journey to the source of the Nile, The Man-Eater of Punanai* etc. His forthcoming book is *The Last Colonial: Curious Adventures & Stories from a Vanishing World,* which has just been published.

Sir Christopher Ondaatje

His younger brother, Michael Ondaatje, is the author of many books including *Anil's Ghost, Running in the Family, The English Patient* etc. The latter book was awarded the prestigious Booker Prize for fiction in 1992 and the film of the book won nine Academy Awards in 1996 including Best Picture and a nomination for Best Writing and Screenplay from another Medium.

Last month Sir Christopher was in Macquarie University, Sydney as Writer in Residence and gave a series of lectures. I was able to meet him and give him a copy of my book, *Nineteenth century American Medical Missionaries in Jaffna, Ceylon,* and his response after reading the book is appended below.

Thiru Arumugam

Dear Aru,

I have now finished your book. Congratulations. It is extraordinary, and I am placing it in a prize position in my "Literary Museum" where it will get some deserved attention.
What a work of love! Quite an achievement. I feel so humble having done my hacking around the world ... just to get something to write about. "The Last Colonial" comes out in September, and I can't wait to get back to Australia again.
It was wonderful meeting you after all these years. Thank you for all your kindness.
And thank you for the book.

Best wishes,
Christopher
(Sir Christopher Ondaatje)

This article originally published in "The Ceylankan", Journal No. 60, November 2012.

8

Dr Mary Rutnam (1873 - 1962): Pioneer for Women's rights (Part 1)

by Thiru Arumugam

"The most famous foreign woman doctor in Sri Lanka" Prof. Kumari Jayawardena, 1993.

Introduction

On 29 December 1896, Dr Mary Helen Irwin, a young newly qualified Canadian gynaecologist arrived in Colombo to work as a medical missionary in the American Ceylon Mission in Jaffna. Little did she imagine that Ceylon would become her home for the rest of her long life. She passed away in Colombo in 1962 at the age 89 years. She married a handsome Ceylonese and had five children, four boys and a girl. She had her own private practice in Colombo and was particularly popular among the Muslim ladies. She spent a large part of her time on social service and founded many social service organisations many of which function to this day, such as the Lanka Mahila Samiti which is the largest women's organisation in the country today. She started the first family planning clinic in the country in the face of intense opposition and ridicule. Her social service work was finally recognised by her receiving the inaugural Ramon Magsaysay award for Public Service in 1958. The prize money for this award was $10,000, a considerable sum of money at that time. The award is considered to be the Asian equivalent of the Nobel prize.

Sources of information for this article include microfilms in the National Library, Canberra of original handwritten letters by the following: Mary; her husband, S C K Rutnam; the American Missionary sisters, Mary and Margaret Leitch who were in Jaffna for seven years, mainly at Uduvil Girls College and raised funds for Jaffna projects in UK and USA thereafter; the American Ceylon Mission (ACM) based in Jaffna; and the parent body the American Board of Commissioners for Foreign Missions (ABCFM) based in Boston. Other sources of information include *Race Antagonism in Christian Missions*, a book published by Mary's husband S C K Rutnam in 1899 in which two chapters are in Mary's own words, and Prof Kumari Jayawardena's book *Dr Mary Rutnam; a Canadian pioneer for Women's Rights in Sri Lanka* which was published in 1993 and describes Mary's social service work in detail. The other major source of information was Brian Rutnam, a grandson of Mary. He is a Sydneysider and an active member of the CSA and he kindly provided access to the text of Mary's personal diary covering the period 1906 to 1910 and also to his own personal notes on the Rutnam family. Information has also been taken from the extensively detailed Family Tree prepared by CSA member Jayantha Somasundaram of Canberra. He is a great-grandson of Elizabeth Agnew Chellama, a sister of S C K Rutnam. Rutnam was very close to this sister. All direct transcripts from these sources are printed in italics in this article.

Mary's early days

Mary was born in Elora, Ontario, Canada on 02 June 1873, the daughter of Presbyterian parents of Irish-Scottish descent. Her father owned a store and later they moved to Clinton, also in Ontario. In the 1880's Canadian Universities started admitting female students for medical courses for the first time. Mary was an early female admission to the Medical College affiliated to the University of Toronto, graduating in early 1896. Many of these early women Doctors worked abroad as medical missionaries particularly in India and China, in fact the Universities offered reduced fees for those who undertook to do medical missionary work after graduating.

Mary responded to an advertisement by the ABCFM inviting applicants for two posts of Women Medical Officers at the new McLeod Hospital for Women and Children which was fast nearing completion in Inuvil, Jaffna. Out of a total of 17 applicants, Mary and Dr Isabella Curr of Scotland were selected. It is interesting to note that as many as 17 women Doctors were prepared to forego financially glittering careers in the west and work in a remote country and live a frugal lifestyle.

As the McLeod Hospital, Inuvil, would be for women and children only, the ABCFM arranged for Mary to undergo post-graduate training in obstetrics and gynaecology in New York prior to her departure to Ceylon. The training program was arranged by the Leitch sisters, Mary and Margaret, of whom more details are given later. The training was under Prof Thompson in one of the post-graduate medical schools, and under Dr Peel, Resident Surgeon at the Roosevelt Hospital. The ABCFM paid all of Mary's training fees and living costs in New York. She was also paid a tropical outfit allowance of $250. In return she had to sign a Bond for $1500 undertaking to work in Jaffna for five years.

S C K Rutnam

Joseph Seth Christmas was a school teacher in Jaffna who had been educated at the Batticotta Seminary which was run by the ACM. He was converted to Christianity by the ACM and changed his surname to Christmas as he was born on Christmas Day 1823. Coincidentally, he passed away also on Christmas day in 1904, having served the ACM for many decades as a Pastor in the Tellipallai Church. He named his second son Samuel Christmas Kanagarutnam (1869 - 1929) (Fig. 1), but the latter found his surname too long when he went to the West and split his last name and became S C K Rutnam. Rutnam was educated at Jaffna College and then sent for further schooling to Salem, South India where his brother-in-law was a successful lawyer. He entered Madras Christian College where he obtained a Bachelor's degree in Philosophy from the University of Madras. He was appointed Headmaster of a Mission School in Belgaum which is now in Karnataka State. He was a fluent speaker and gave public lectures on the evils of the British Government covertly funded opium trade.

Fig. 1 Pastor J S Christmas and son Rutnam
(Courtesy: J Somasundaram)

Similar to the situation today, there was a huge balance of payments problem with China which was exporting vast amounts but was not interested in importing Western goods. Warren Hastings, the first

Governor General of India, hit upon the idea in 1780 of growing opium in India and exporting it to China. This trade grew and peaked in the early twentieth century when it provided about 20% of the Indian revenues.

Because of his eloquence and strong views on the opium trade, Rutnam was invited to tour UK and lecture on the subject. He was sponsored by anti-opium campaigners, particularly by the very rich Lady Henry Somerset who was President of the British Women's Temperance Association. After lecturing for some time in UK, he proceeded to USA where he was sponsored by Frances Willard, President of the Women's Christian Temperance Union. She was a close friend of Lady Henry Somerset. In USA he joined Princeton Seminary to study Theology, but when he later realised that the Americans would never appoint him as a Missionary, he switched over to the Ivy League Princeton University where he ultimately obtained a Master's degree in Logic and Philosophy. In the summer of 1896 he started on a lecture tour in eastern United States and ended up in New York, where he heard that a young Canadian lady Doctor was planning to go and work in Jaffna.

Rutnam called on Mary at her boarding house in New York and says that he was greeted heartily as he was the first Ceylonese that she had ever met. Mary was anxious to learn more about Ceylon, its people, life, customs and invited Rutnam to call on her frequently. In addition she "*wished to improve her evenings by taking lessons in Tamil from me*". They spent many hours together and discussed literary, religious, philosophical topics and also international marriages. They agreed that in such an event, however precious the counsels of parents and friends may be, "*the actual decision always rests or rather should rest with the individuals concerned*".

Their marriage

It was not long before their friendship turned to mutual affection and thoughts of possible marriage. They "*discussed minutely the advantages and disadvantages of such an alliance, the inevitable mountain-like opposition that we must be prepared to meet in carrying out our plans*". Rutnam took great care "*to describe to Dr Irwin as fully and truthfully as ever possible, differences between oriental and occidental tastes, disposition, manner and life*". Rutnam goes on to say that "*the day we arrived at a decision to marry, or as Dr Irwin put it, the day on which 'possibilities were resolved into certainties' was one of special prayer*".

They then carefully considered their circumstances. Mary was due to proceed to Ceylon in a few months time while Rutnam wished to pursue his studies in USA for three or four more years. A long engagement and a long separation were by no means a desirable state of affairs. They decided to make their engagement more binding if such a thing was possible. They considered a registry marriage, but that would entail going to a public place like the City Hall in New York City and have the ceremony performed in the presence of the Mayor or Justice of the Peace. They decided that "*such public function at this stage of our love story, was by no means desirable*".

It is not difficult to see why they were reluctant to have a public marriage. Although they lived in cosmopolitan New York, a little further south, lynching of coloured people for similar acts was not uncommon although the first wave of Ku Klux Klan organisations had begun to fade away.

The couple considered an alternative. Through an intermediary minister they made contact with two other ministers, one Episcopalian and the other Congregationalist, who "*fully satisfied themselves as to the purity of our motives, before they approved of our judgement to have the marriage ceremony secretly performed*". On 16 July 1896 the two ministers performed the marriage ceremony in a Church (Fig. 2).

Fig. 2: S C K Rutnam and Mary Rutnam
(circa 1898) *Courtesy Rutnam family*

At this stage, Mary and Rutnam considered this to be a "betrothal" rather than a marriage. Mary would continue to go under her maiden surname and leave for Ceylon in three months time and Rutnam would remain in USA for four years and complete his studies. The marriage was not consummated at this time, and they looked forward to repeating the ceremony in Ceylon in about five years time, after which only would they become man and wife.

Mary travels to Ceylon

Mary completed her post-graduate training and sailed for Ceylon on 10 October 1896. During their separation they agreed to write to each other daily and mail the letters twice a week. They never sought to conceal their frequent correspondence. Mary sailed from New York for Scotland where she met Dr Isabella Curr, the other Doctor selected by the ABCFM to work in Jaffna, and they travelled together to Ceylon. They landed in Colombo on 29 December 1896 and after a sojourn of a fortnight in the capital they travelled to Anuradhapura by train and from there they took a coach to Jaffna, arriving there on 17 January 1897.

In her letter dated 17 March to Dr Barton, Secretary of the ABCFM, Mary says that she was disappointed that the completion of construction of McLeod Hospital would take several months and that she is meanwhile working in the Green Memorial Hospital in Manipay. She added that Dr Curr and herself "*are both very much in love with the country, surroundings and people*". One of Mary's early letters to Rutnam from Jaffna implies that her mother is aware of the relationship and quotes her mother's letter as saying "*We three still keep the secret, Mary. But of course you will both be true to the Board for five years at any rate*". Mary's letter to Rutnam continues "*You see by this that mother is beginning to look upon this as a settled thing for the future. She at least does not discourage it..........I today for the first time saw your father and mother and I like them so much*".

By this time Rutnam realised that however equal he may be in qualifications and training to the

Americans who were being sent abroad as missionaries, the ABCFM would never appoint a native as a missionary. He therefore abandoned his study of Theology at the Princeton Seminary and started a fund raising campaign in USA to build and run a school in Anuradhapura. He estimated that he would need $12,000 to build and run the school for three years, after which period the school would become self-supporting from school fees.

Mary and Margaret Leitch

Mary and Margaret Leitch were born in Vermont, USA in 1849 and 1857 respectively. Ian Tyrell, who retired last year as Professor of History, University of New South Wales, has devoted the whole of Chapter 2 of his recent book *Reforming the World: The creation of America's Moral Empire,* Princeton, 2010, to a survey of the work of the Leitch sisters and says that they "*had ordinary beginnings but extra-ordinary lives*". The Leitch sisters, or the Misses Leitch as they preferred to be known, signed almost all their letters with the common signature "Mary and Margaret Leitch". It would appear that the younger sister, Margaret, was the more dominant. Their first jobs were six years spent teaching young ex-slaves in Virginia. In 1879 they joined the ABCFM and were posted to Jaffna where they spent seven years, mostly teaching at Uduvil Girls College. This period of their lives was documented in their book *Seven years in Ceylon: Stories of Missionary Life*, which was published in 1890. The book contains copies of many beautiful wood engravings and photographs and provides a vivid 'snapshot' of Jaffna in the closing years of the nineteenth century.

In 1886 the ABCFM informed the Leitch sisters that they would have to do their own fundraising to continue their work in Jaffna. They spent the next three years travelling around and lecturing and fund raising in UK and USA and collected the colossal sum of $150,000 for mission work in Jaffna. These funds were used for major building construction in Jaffna College, Uduvil Girls College, Udupitty Girls College and Green Memorial Hospital, Manipay. As Helen Root, a contemporary American missionary in Jaffna records, the American missionaries in Jaffna "*were embarrassed by the receipt of larger funds than they saw how to expend wisely at that stage of the work*". The surplus funds were used to fund many scholarships and bursaries for students in the mission schools.

Fig. 3: McLeod Hospital, Inuvil, Jaffna, 1897
(Original sketch by Darshan Rajarayan)

Out of the funds raised, the Leitch sisters specifically allocated $30,000 for the purpose of setting up a Medical School at Jaffna College. However, due to personality clashes between the Leitch sisters and Rev Hastings, the Head of Jaffna College, nothing was done to implement this project. The Leitch sisters therefore withdrew this allocation from Jaffna College and used the money to fund the construction of a purpose built hospital for women and children at a green field site in Inuvil, not far from Manipay. It was to work in this hospital, later named McLeod Hospital (Fig. 3) after the principal donor, that Mary Rutnam was recruited by the ABCFM.

The Misses Leitch swing into action

When the Misses Leitch who were now back in USA heard about Rutnam's fund raising campaign in USA for a proposed school in Anuradhapura, they swung into action. In a long letter to Rutnam dated 27 May 1897 they pointed out that his article in the Christian Herald about his scheme was misleading. They said that while it is true that there is no missionary living in Anuradhapura, it is visited regularly by English missionaries. They pointed out that Ceylon already has 61,986 children in mission schools, which is three times the number in China, and Anuradhapura already has a small mission school. The climate is malarial and it will be difficult to recruit teachers. They told him that he was educated in mission schools and had received much help from mission sources but he had not cared to consult any missionaries about his scheme, and that they did not believe a single missionary would endorse his scheme.

They added that *"we would be untrue to the truth and remiss in our duty to the public, to your Committee, and to yourself if we remained silent at this time. It does not seem to us desirable that every foreigner who comes to this country and is aided in his education should attempt when about to return to collect a large fund, establish an independent mission work in his country entirely controlled at that end by himself .... We do not wish to put anything in the religious or secular papers which would discredit you before the public and will not do so if you will give us as soon as you conveniently can after receipt of this letter, your written assurance that you will not proceed to collect funds for this scheme"*. (Emphasis in original). In other words, keep clear of our patch.

The bursting of the storm in America

On 02 June 1897 Rutnam wrote to Dr Barton the Secretary of the ABCFM formally applying for a job as a Missionary in Jaffna. Barton replied that it was not the policy of the Board to employ natives in foreign missions. Rutnam replied to this on 14 June that his case was special because he was 'engaged to be married' to Mary. He mentioned his betrothal to Mary to Barton because he mistakenly thought that Mary's father had already written to Barton about it. Barton immediately wrote a letter to the Leitch sisters that *"Of course he cannot be appointed even if they are engaged. Unless the engagement is broken I cannot see how Dr Irwin can continue her work in Ceylon as a missionary .... the whole affair is most unfortunate"*.

The Leitch sisters replied to Dr Barton on 19 June that *"With regard to what Rutnam has told you of his engagement we believe it is pure fabrication. Dr Irwin wanted to learn a little Tamil while she was in New York and he gave her a few lessons. He once or twice brought her some flowers and she was much annoyed by that much attention .... You perhaps know that it is very hard for a native of India to discriminate between what is true and what he wishes should come true .... We have studied him pretty carefully and he does not appear to us to be a man of spiritual power or moral earnestness. It would be preposterous to give him the salary of a missionary in Jaffna when a native of his ability and education would be receiving in Jaffna about $20 a month"*. Note: Rutnam had an American Master's degree which would have been extremely rare if not unique for a Ceylonese at that time. American missionaries were paid about $100 per month plus children's allowances and free housing and they very rarely had Master's degrees.

The bursting of the storm in Jaffna

Meanwhile the storm had burst in Jaffna also. The missionaries were suspicious of Mary's frequent letters from America in the same handwriting and one of her letters was stolen from the Manipay Post

Office. The contents of the letter were made public and Mary was asked by the ACM if she was married to Rutnam which she admitted. Her 'trial' was conducted at a Committee Meeting of the ACM held on 19 June 1897 which she was asked to attend. The Committee recorded that *"she had acted under pressure from Mr Rutnam, and with the idea that it was to be an utter secret between them, a sort of special betrothal, the actual union not to be consummated till after a public marriage in Ceylon some years later"*. The main points of a lengthy Minute that was passed were as follows: *"......we do sympathise with Mrs Rutnam in the embarrassing position in which she now finds herself placed ...... Mrs Rutnam should at once join her husband .... but failing this, we believe that Mr Rutnam should come out at once to relieve his wife of her present embarrassment ...... the Prudential Committee to secure as speedily as possible a new colleague for Dr Curr to take the place of Mrs Rutnam"*.

Mary objected to the statement in the record of the meeting that she had acted under pressure from Mr Rutnam and that it was incorrect. She was told that there was no time to make any corrections as it had to be sent off to Boston urgently. In the event the statement was only despatched to Boston, uncorrected, twelve days later on 01 July 1897. On the following day, Rev T S Smith wrote a 19 page letter from Jaffna to the Leitch sisters stating that his letter was written as a Missionary and not as Secretary of the ACM. He said that Mary does not regret the alliance and scarcely seems to see how wrong it is even now. She claims that one of her letters was opened by the Acting Postmaster in the Manipay Post Office. Their persistent correspondence had excited gossip even earlier. He said that Rutnam's *"conduct was simply dastardly, to worry her into a secret marriage .... letting her come alone ten thousand miles ...... and making her bear the brunt of all this gossip"*. He added that Mary says that it is a legal marriage and that Rutnam has the marriage certificate. He went on to say that we should all oppose Rutnam's plan for a school in Anuradhapura.

With the opening of the Suez Canal, sea mail letters between Jaffna and Boston took about five weeks each way. The verdict from Boston regarding Mary's future was therefore not expected in Jaffna until early September.

To be continued in the next Article.

This Article was originally published in "The Ceylankan", Journal No.61, February 2013.

9

Dr Mary Rutnam (1873 - 1962) : Pioneer for Women's rights (Part 2)

by Thiru Arumugam

"The most famous foreign woman doctor in Sri Lanka" Prof. Kumari Jayawardena, 1993.

Part 1 of this article ended with Mary from Canada having worked for over six months in the Green Memorial Hospital, Manipay. However, news of her secret marriage in New York to a Ceylonese, S C K Rutnam, had leaked out and she was now awaiting a ruling from the headquarters of the American Board of Commissioners for Foreign Missions (ABCFM) in Boston as regards her future.

The campaign continues in America

Meanwhile in America the campaign against Mary and Rutnam continued. On 26 June 1897 Mary wrote a twelve page letter to Dr Barton of the ABCFM giving her side of the story. She said that when she was doing post-graduate studies in New York, Rutnam called on her and suggested teaching her Tamil. She agreed and the Misses Leitch also thought it was a good idea. *"It was not very long before a feeling deeper than mere friendship became apparent. It was a matter of earnest prayer with me, from the very first I seemed to feel as if something was impending and I was powerless to act ...... and I began to think that God had some special work for me to do in far away Ceylon"*. She added that there were no restrictions on marriage in her contract of employment and the subject was never even mentioned by the ABCFM or Misses Leitch. So when she consented to be Rutnam's wife she did not feel any disloyalty to the ABCFM and did not realise that she was doing wrong in keeping the matter secret. She said that one of Rutnam's letters to her was stolen from the Manipay Post Office and the contents made public. She said that she had written about it all to her parents.

On 29 June 1897 the Leitch sisters wrote a very long letter to Mary. Some of the points mentioned in their letter include *"We think the greatest unkindness you could do to Mr Rutnam would be to marry him .... Our candid opinion is that he is a consummate beggar but without the push or willingness to work hard towards his own support .... A native man is brought up from his infancy to think about the dowry he will get from his wife .... If however you were to marry Mr Rutnam you would be doing the mission and the cause a very serious injury .... nine-tenths of his relatives, near and remote have never handled a knife and fork. Their usual way is to sit on the floor and eat with their fingers. You would not feel happy to sit down and eat with them on the ground"*.

The Leitchs pile on the pressure

To pile on the pressure the Leitch sisters sent another long letter to Mary dated 01 July 1897. Some of the points they mentioned were *"The natives easily take on a veneer. They dress well and make a good appearance when they go abroad. But immediately they return home, they relapse into their native habits going about the house wearing nothing but a loin cloth .... Almost every Hindu thinks that it is a husband's duty to occasionally beat his wife, in order to keep her in proper subjection .... There is scarcely a native in Jaffna who does not claim to be in debt .... It is true that Mr Rutnam is somewhat light complexioned but many of his relatives are very dark and some of his children might be almost black. And what about the laws of heredity? Would it not be reasonable to expect that the Hindu traits of deceit, falsehood, in short moral crookedness, will appear in the children? .... in mixed marriages the worst traits of both sides are likely to appear in the children .... This whole affair seems to us like a nightmare .... a Hindu expects his wife to be a constant servant while he plays the part of a grand lord"*.

On 05 July 1897, the Leitch sisters piled on the pressure with a long letter to Mary's parents in Canada in which they came out with the real reasons for their objection to the union. They wrote *"Dr Irwin is beautiful and attractive and there is no reason she should throw herself away .... if she were to marry a native we would feel that a blow has been struck at our work. How could we go to fathers and mothers and ask them to send out a daughter. They would say 'the last young lady who went out there married a native ' .... Mary would occasion ten times more harm to the cause of missions than all the good she can do in a lifetime"*. They also said that when the news of this union becomes public their fund raising would be affected. The letter continued *"You perhaps do not know that it is the custom among Hindu men, as soon as a man loses his wife to begin to plan whom he will marry for his next wife .... native men are accustomed to think of women only as a convenience"*. It is strange that the Americans consistently refer to Rutnam as a Hindu when he was born a Christian of Christian parents and he was not a convert.

On 07 July, Dr Barton of the ABCFM wrote to Mary's parents in Canada that *"I cannot believe that your daughter has entered into an engagement with him with a full understanding of what it means, and if she has engaged herself to him I feel she would be thoroughly justified in breaking it. There is no way in which we can make Mr Rutnam a missionary of the Board and I see no way in which she could marry him and remain in her work in Ceylon"*. At least he did not go as far as the Leitch sisters who had written to Mary that she should break the engagement if she was only engaged, but if she was actually married she should take steps to get a divorce.

During the last week of July 1897 the Leitches wrote a total of five letters to Dr Barton of the ABCFM stoking up the fires! Some of the thoughts they expressed about Mary were *"She has deceived us all and lived a lie"*, *"She has ruined herself"*, *"The local papers will get hold of the story and hold her conduct up to ridicule. Her usefulness is at an end"*, *"We planned a nursing school at Inuvil, but by her conduct the best native families would not send their daughters"*, *"Missionary enterprise rests on confidence. She cannot behave like that and retain the standing of a missionary ....she must resign .... There is no point in keeping her out of pity"*. They also asked Barton to investigate whether the marriage between them carried out in New York was legal.

The Leitches followed this up with a thirteen page letter to Mary dated 03 August 1897. Some of their thoughts expressed in this letter include *"Your conduct is inexplicable. Yours was not a sudden impulse, but you never cared to take your parents or the Board into your confidence .... You kept your marriage a secret so that when the Board came to know you could force their hand .... It is best if you severe connections with the Board .... It is in your power to do us much harm .... If you cause trouble between the natives and the missionaries we will expose you"*. The Leitches also said that Rutnam's brother-in-law in India met the cost of his education in the hope that he would marry a relation in accordance with Tamil custom. He should therefore pay back what was spent on his education. He is trying to raise funds for a school in Anuradhapura. He should abandon this project and return whatever funds have been raised and go back to his native country.

Mary' rebuttal

On 1 August 1897 Mary wrote to the Leitch sisters with a point by point rebuttal. Some excerpts from her letter are *"both my father and mother had written to me consenting that the marriage might take place after I had served some years in Inuvil (which was exactly what we hoped for and trusted for). It was your long letters to my parents that completely upset them .... We both fully realised that there would be prejudice by many of both nations and much opposition and the object of the secrecy of the affair was that we might have an opportunity of doing something to lessen these feelings .... You speak of incongruities, our Master never used knife and fork .... should we despair primitive manners? .... I also know of men in our own country who slap or ill-treat their wives"*. Mary also wrote that at the Mission Committee Meeting at which her future was discussed, Mr Hastings, the Head of Jaffna College, said that the fact of her marriage *"was made known by treachery"* and that she thought that he was right.

Rutnam's supporters

Rutnam did have his supporters and sympathisers in America. This included Louis Klopsch the Proprietor of the "Christian Herald" which had the largest circulation of all the Christian weeklies in USA. On 29 June 1897 Klopsch wrote to Rutnam to say *"The attack of the Misses Leitch came to us of course. It is very much like the usual attack of Missionary Boards and their friends. It does not influence us one bit"*. Klopsch followed this up with an insertion in the Christian Herald of 25 August 1897 which included the words *"The marriage is announced of Mr S C K Rutnam MA the talented young Christian Hindu who recently graduated at Princeton University, to Miss Mary H Irwin MD. Mr Rutnam is well known to us through his eloquent and scholarly lectures on Christian education among the high caste races of India .... We trust that the united labours of the young couple for the evangelisation of the Ceylonese will be abundantly blessed by God"*.

Rutnam decides to return to Ceylon

On 11 August 1897 Rutnam (Fig. 1) wrote to Barton of the ABCFM that he had decided to return to Ceylon and that if he could catch the connecting ship in England he should be in Ceylon by the end of September. Rutnam said that he had written to Mary's father apologising and he had received a reply, some parts of which he could not understand. Rutnam quotes from Mr Irwin's letter to him *"She* (i.e. Mary) *is now suffering from devices which however clever they may seem in the eyes of some people are sinful in the eyes of that God who is now punishing you (murder <u>will</u> out) .... You led her to believe that this was only a strong form of engagement to be followed up by a public marriage in five years, best thing now is go no further and at the end of five years we will consider the subject again"*.

Fig. 1: S C K Rutnam (1869-1929)

By a letter dated 26 August 1897 the Leitches ramped up their pressure on Rutnam to leave USA and return to Ceylon. The gist of their letter was *"You have done a most dishonourable thing. If the way you have treated Mary is known to the public, you will be mobbed. Plenty of coloured men have been mobbed for less. Leave the country. Do not try Mr Irwin's patience. He may hunt you and put a bullet through you. If you do not leave the country we will make your actions public. Your influence is dead here. You will be made into a laughing stock".*

Rutnam set sail from New York in the *Lucania* on 04 September 1897, bound for Liverpool, England. This Cunard ship was the largest passenger liner afloat when she was launched. He sent a cable to Mary that he was leaving USA. On his arrival in Liverpool he found a cable from Mary which had been sent to New York and re-directed to Liverpool. Mary's message was that she was leaving Ceylon for several reasons to join him and to please reply immediately. He sent a cable to Mary that he was now in Liverpool and would be leaving for Colombo on the Orient Liner *Ormuz* on 17 September. He sailed as planned as he did not receive any further message from Mary.

Mary's story

Two chapters in Rutnam's book *"Race Antagonism in Christian Missions"* were written by Mary and gave her views of the events that unfolded. Some of her narrative has already been included earlier in this article.

She arrived in Jaffna on 17 January 1897 and was disappointed to find that the McLeod Hospital for Women in Inuvil was still under construction and actually was completed more than a year later. This meant that Mary and Dr Isabella Curr had to work for the time being in the Green Memorial Hospital, Manipay where Dr Thomas Scott and Dr Mary Scott were already working. Apart from her medical work in the Hospital, Mary spent a lot of time learning Tamil and also conducting Bible classes. By early June 1897 rumours about her started spreading and she was asked pointedly by an American missionary whether she was married. When she admitted it he said *"It will be death to your influence and his .... Everyone will despise you. You will lower yourself by such a marriage, for no matter how educated a man may be, the born tendencies of the lower races are in him"*.

Mary says that at this time the storm clouds were also gathering round Rutnam in New York and *"it was as if I was compelled to stand helpless and silent and watch the cruel blow that was about to descend and crush the one I loved"*. The American Ceylon Mission (ACM) in Jaffna held a Committee Meeting to discuss Mary's situation on 19 June 1897 and what happened at the Meeting has been described earlier. The covering letter forwarding the Minutes to Boston said *"We especially feel that every such alliance can but be a new menace to the safety, and a new narrowing of the sphere, of every missionary (young and unmarried) of the Women's Board"*.

Mary added that as the matter became known in America her weekly mail increased in volume *"Every week brought lengthy epistles from the Misses Leitch, first against Rutnam's scheme for independent work in Ceylon, then about the engagement, and latterly covering the marriage ceremony"*. It was only later that Mary discovered that that the Leitch's letters to her had been copied to Barton of the ABCFM, her parents and even to the other American missionaries in Jaffna. As a result *"my dear father and mother were led to believe that their daughter had promised herself to one of the greatest rogues in existence and in their broken heartedness wrote to me imploring me to come home at once .... It did seem strange that the Leitches could write so much about one of whom they knew so little. Surely I had one hundred times more opportunity of knowing Mr Rutnam, his life, plans and spirit, than they or anyone else had"*.

Boston's Verdict

On 03 September 1897, Mary received a bundle of foreign mail. It included an official letter from Barton of the ABCFM that considered her *"connection with the ABCFM to have ceased - the Board henceforth having no control over your movements"*. She was also asked to refund immediately all monies spent on her by the Board including the cost of post-graduate training, outfit allowance, passage and travel expenses to Ceylon. Regarding this claim for a refund, a Minister of the Presbyterian Church in Canada later wrote a letter to Mary in which he said "*Your father told me that your former employers were asking him to recoup them for the expenses incurred by them in connection with your relation to them. I dissuaded him from doing that on the ground that **they** and not **you** broke the contract*". It must be noted that not only was it the Board that broke the contract but also that the contract did not say anything about her marital status or place any restrictions on marriage during the period of the contract. Anyway, we may safely assume that the Board backed down from the claim for a refund because later on 26 November 1897 Mary wrote to the ABCFM forwarding receipts for travel expenses from Canada to Ceylon and asking for reimbursement.

Among the letters that Mary received on 03 September was a letter from her mother who said that although they had previously given consent to the "*engagement they now believed after letters from the Leitchs that 'Mr Rutnam was a rascal of the worst kind; and their minds were centred on the one object of saving their child from the clutches of this scoundrel' and begged for her speedy return to Canada*". Mary believed from her parents' letter that the only hope of reconciliation with her parents was by her presence in Canada.

Mary decides to travel to Canada

There was also a cable from Rutnam saying that he was returning from America by the first available steamer. This at once complicated matters "*for how could I think of returning home when he was on his way to me?*". Mary decided to cable Rutnam to wait in America until her return. She also learned that the ACM missionaries Rev and Mrs Howland were leaving Jaffna the following week for America by the Bibby Liner *Cheshire* leaving Colombo on 17 September. If a reply was received from Rutnam in time she could sail in the *Cheshire* with the Howlands to America.

On 10 September she finally received a cable from Rutnam to say that he had arrived safely in Liverpool and was leaving for Colombo on 17 September by the Orient Liner *Ormuz*. Evidently Mary's cable to Rutnam asking him to stay in America until she arrived there had missed him. Not knowing his address in Liverpool, she drafted a cable to the Orient Lines asking them to inform Rutnam to wait in UK until she arrived there, and sent the message to Colombo asking one of Rutnam's friends, a Mr L to hand it over to the Orient Lines Office in Colombo for transmission to England.

The coastal steamer from Kankesanturai to Colombo was leaving on 14 September and she immediately started packing to leave Jaffna. She said goodbye to Rutnam's family whom she said were "*deeply sorrowed at my departure but trusted God to lead and guide me*". She arrived in Colombo on 16 September and found to her utter surprise that Mr L had not forwarded her draft cable to the Orient Lines Office. When she asked him why he had not done so, he simply said that he did not believe God wanted him to do so.

Mary's immediate decision was to wait in Colombo for three weeks until Rutnam arrived and then proceed homewards to Canada to effect a reconciliation with her parents. She explained her decision to Mr L and was astonished when Mr L urged her to travel immediately by the Bibby Liner *Cheshire*. Mr L promised faithfully to meet Rutnam on arrival and explain the reasons for her departure and Mary finally believed that it was God's wish that she should travel by the *Cheshire*. She sailed from Colombo the next day, 17 September 1897, travelling with the Howlands.

This Article was originally published in "The Ceylankan", Journal No. 62, May 2013.

To be concluded in the next Article.

10

Dr Mary Rutnam (1873 - 1962): Pioneer for Women's rights (Part 3)

by Thiru Arumugam

"The most famous foreign woman doctor in Sri Lanka" Prof Kumari Jayawardena, 1993.

Part 2 of this article ended with Mary leaving Colombo for Canada for a reconciliation with her parents over her secret marriage with S C K Rutnam, a Ceylonese. Meanwhile Rutnam was at the same time sailing from England to Colombo, not knowing that Mary had left Colombo.

Ships that pass in the night

On 29 September 1897 the Bibby Liner *Cheshire* entered the Suez Canal and Mary hoped that she could get a glimpse of the Orient Liner *Ormuz* in which Rutnam her husband was travelling to Colombo. She borrowed Rev Howland's telescope and looked for the Ormuz but did not see that ship. At 6 pm the *Cheshire* reached Port Said and a member of the crew told Mary that the *Ormuz* was not expected until early the next morning. The two ships would therefore be crossing in the middle of the night and Mary recorded that *"My desire then was not to be granted; for it was God's will that we should pass in darkness - so near and yet so far, and each day farther, until at length the whole wide world would separate us as before".*

Mary reached London on 09 October and sailed from there to New York in the Cunard Liner *Lucania*, reaching there on 23 October. She travelled by train from New York and finally reached her parental home in Canada on 29 October. Her parents and family were overjoyed at seeing her as they had assumed she would not come because they were aware that Rutnam had sailed for Colombo. Mary recorded that *"As the days passed and the truth of the affair became better known to my people, and the unchristian spirit, and the untruths of the letters sent to my parents became apparent, they began to see things in a different light .... it was not long before they were fully convinced of Rutnam's strong and tender and true love for me".*

Meanwhile Rutnam landed in Colombo and was deeply distressed to find that Mary had sailed for Canada. Mr L failed to keep his promise to Mary to meet Rutnam on his arrival and explain the reasons for Mary's departure. In fact when Rutnam went and met him, Rutnam was treated very coldly. Mary said that when she heard about this she realised that it was not God's wish but Mr L's wish that she should return to Canada. After a few days in Colombo, Rutnam journeyed to Jaffna where he met his parents and family after four years. After a week in Jaffna, he proceeded to his sister's house in Salem, South India to rest and recuperate.

Rutnam has summed up the opposition to their union as follows, *"As soon as people learned of our intentions, ah, how they raged! What utter untruths they wrote! What total misrepresentations they indulged in! What a fearful combination of power was formed against us! Some people threw off their religious cloak and solemnly declared they would do all in their power to separate us altogether".*

Mary returns to Ceylon

After about three months stay in Canada, Mary was fully reconciled with her parents and family and decided that it was time to return to Ceylon. She sailed on the White Star Liner *Teutonic* on 09 February 1898 from New York to Liverpool and from there she sailed by the Bibby Liner *Cheshire* to Colombo. Coincidentally this was the same ship that she sailed in from Colombo to England. Mary records that *"Mr Rutnam had previous to my arrival secured a small bungalow near the sea in Wellawatte, and after arranging for the transport of luggage, we drove together to our future home. Here then did we spend our first day and weeks of married life, doubtless all the more precious after the long separation, and especially after the trying experiences we had both gone through".*

The last days of the Leitch sisters

Prof Ian Tyrell says that Mary and Margaret Leitch spent their last days in penury and obscurity. They never married. They did not return to Jaffna but lived and worked in the USA and had terminated their direct connection with the American Board of Commissioners for Foreign Missions (ABCFM). They were involved in the anti-opium lobby, YMCA, Student Volunteer Movement and temperance campaigns. The latter was a success with nationwide Prohibition in 1919 but was soon repealed as organised crime muscled in. By the end of World War 1, Mary was 69 years old and Margaret was 61 years old and they retired from active campaigning. They had run through their inheritance which was spent entirely on mission work. Their only joint income left was a monthly pension of $83 from the ABCFM. By 1925, Margaret, the younger and more dominant sister, was bedridden and needed care. A lengthy typewritten appeal was sent to the ABCFM to increase their joint pension to $100 a month, no doubt pointing out their work for the Board in their earlier days when they fund-raised $150,000 for mission work in Jaffna. Their appeal was turned down by the Secretary of the ABCFM who drily observed that *"she must have paid a pretty sum of money to have all that typewriting done and it does not strengthen her appeal for a stipend from the Board".* Margaret died in 1926 and Mary lived on until 1940.

The early days in Colombo of the Rutnams

The Rutnams settled down in their Wellawatte home in March 1898 and started looking for suitable jobs. In October of that year Mary was offered a temporary post acting for the Head of the Lady Havelock Women's Hospital as the permanent Head was going on long leave. Mary enjoyed her period of work here which included teaching the first batch of women medical students from the Colombo Medical College. However when the permanent incumbent of the post returned from long leave, the Government refused to give Mary a permanent appointment on the grounds that they only recognised British medical degrees and not did not recognise Canadian medical degrees. Mary spent the rest of her working life as a private practitioner in Colombo mainly in the fields of obstetrics and gynaecology. Mary recorded in her diary that her income as a private practitioner was about equal to the salary paid to her when she worked for the Mission in Jaffna.

Towards the end of 1898, the couple moved from Wellawatte to a house in Maradana. They also had the use of the Hall of the City College in Norris Road. This College had been founded in 1894 by Samuel Green Lee MA, who had taught Rutnam when he was a student in Jaffna College. Rutnam converted the lower floor of the College Hall into a free reading room and in the upper floor they held Sunday School, Bible classes and religious services. Meanwhile Rutnam started looking for a suitable premises to fulfil his long standing dream of starting his own school, not in Anuradhapura as originally planned, but in Colombo. In 1900 he opened Central College in Smallpass, Kotahena. His younger brother Jacob Christmas Vijayarutnam also taught there. He was a graduate of Calcutta University. By 1906 Central College was fully functional with 180 students. In that year, of the 25 students admitted to the Colombo Medical College, seven students were from Central College, an achievement unlikely to have been matched by the long established major schools in Colombo. Rutnam was also Secretary of the Ceylon University Association which was formed to campaign for a University in Ceylon.

Unfortunately, Rutnam's health began to fail in 1909. It was the beginning of a long illness. Mary arranged for him to live in a quiet house outside Colombo (possibly in Ragama) where he lived out the rest of his days, finally passing away in 1929. His brother continued to run Central College in Kotahena. It no longer exists and was probably closed down during World War II.

Mary's social service work

Meanwhile in 1904 Mary got interested in social service. She formed the Girls Friendly Society, a place where young women could meet and discuss various issues. This organisation still exists and has an 89 year old Hall in Green Path. In the same year, 1904, she formed the Women's Mutual Improvement Association which was ridiculed by the press calling them Cinnamon Gardens ladies who want to improve themselves. The group's name was then changed to The Ceylon Women's Union, the object of which was to improve the lives of women as wives, mothers and citizens. This Union was the forerunner of the Lanka Mahila Samiti founded in 1931 with Mary as the founder President. This organisation was dedicated to the upliftment of the lives of rural women. According to its Constitution, it is involved in promoting social intercourse, agricultural enterprise, cottage industries, home-craft and mothercraft, co-operative enterprises and social hygiene, all at village level. It is now the largest women's organisation in the country with 4500 Samitis in the villages registered under the parent organisation.

In 1909 Mary inspired a group of Tamil ladies to form the Ceylon Tamil Women's Union, the object of which was to promote cultural activities. The Union is still very active and runs "Kalalaya" a pioneer institution for the teaching of oriental dancing and music, and celebrates its diamond jubilee this year.

Mary was involved in the work of the Ceylon Social Service League which was founded in 1915 by Sir Ponnambalam Arunachalam. The League focussed on issues of mass education, medical relief and economic improvement. Working with the League, Mary founded the country's first free Day-Care Centre and Crèche for children of working mothers.

Mary highlighted women's health issues by articles and speeches. She wrote two books, *"A Health Manual for Schools"* which was first published in 1923 and was a Hygiene text-book for schools and was translated into Sinhala and Tamil, and *"Home-craft Manual for Ceylon Schools"* which was first published in 1933. Prof Kumari Jayawardena, whose 1993 book *Dr Mary Rutnam: A Canadian pioneer for Women's Rights in Sri Lanka,* which has a detailed description of Mary's work, says that Mary's book *"contained much social criticism including sections denouncing cruel behaviour to servants, deploring the system of child servants and even reproducing the Declaration of Geneva (1923) on the Rights of the Child".*

Mary also campaigned for greater milk consumption as Ceylon had an extremely low per capita consumption of milk. In 1928 she opened Colombo's first Milk Bar. She also campaigned for a central depot where all dairies should be compelled to take their milk for testing. She took a major role in the temperance movement and was for many years the President of the Women's Christian Temperance Union of Ceylon. This organisation is now defunct. She was also involved in the Girl Guides Association and the Jayasekera Home, a refuge for destitute women.

More social service work by Mary

Mary introduced the then controversial subject of Family Planning in 1932 and has been described as the mother of family planning in Ceylon. Under her guidance the first Family Planning Clinic was opened in Colombo in 1937, in the face of intensive opposition. On 17 August 1949, Mary proposed a resolution in the Ceylon Medical Association, of which she had been a member for fifty years, that conception control should be part of the activities of Public Health and instruction in control methods should be part of the curriculum of the Colombo Medical College. The resolution was resoundingly defeated. The current President of the Association observes that it would be hard to imagine such a resolution being defeated today. As usual, Mary was ahead of the times. In 1953, Mary formed the Family Planning Association which is now a very active organisation in their field.

She was an active founder member of the Women's Franchise Union which started in 1927, and she made speeches campaigning for limited female franchise. At that time there was only limited male franchise. The campaign was a resounding success, beyond their expectations, because in the Donoughmore reforms of 1931, Ceylon became the first British Colony with universal adult suffrage for males and females over the age of 21 years. Their next success was in women being allowed to contest seats in the State Council and Local Authorities. With the achievement of women's suffrage, this Union transformed itself into the All-Ceylon Women's Conference with Mary as the founder President. The

Conference campaigned for women's rights in the fields of politics, legislation, employment, legal aid for the poor, crèche facilities for children of women employees, adult education etc.

In 1937 Mary contested the Bambalapitiya Ward of the Colombo Municipal Council in the Municipal elections. During the election campaign she was attacked for her advocacy of family planning and she was called a foreigner and a Communist. Nevertheless she won the elections by a substantial majority and was elected as the first Woman Councillor of the Colombo Municipal Council. During her period as a Councillor she served on the Committees for Sanitation and Markets and opened crèches for children of working mothers.

The Rutnam family

The Rutnams had five children. The four boys were Alan, Donald, Robin and Walter all of whom studied at Royal College, and a daughter Helen (named after Mary's middle name) who studied at Ladies College (Fig. 1). In view of Rutnam's long final illness during which he lived away from home, Mary brought up the children virtually as a single parent and still involved herself in all her social work. In 1906 we see from Mary's diary that the household staff consisted of a Housekeeper cum Medical Assistant, Cook, Gardener, Rickshaw Puller and Rickshaw, Horse drawn carriage and Driver

Fig. 1: S C K Rutnam, Mary and sons Alan and Donald
Courtesy Rutnam family

Alan Rutnam

Their eldest son was Alan Rutnam (1899 - 1982) who qualified as a Gynaecologist at Middlesex Hospital, London. He married an Irish Nurse, Gertrude Scollan, whom he met as a medical student in London. He returned to Colombo and had a good practice as a gynaecologist with a Surgery adjacent to the Dutch Burgher Union building in Bullers Road. He was, however, totally disinterested in money matters and quite often did not bill his patients. In 1946 horse racing commenced in Colombo after World War II. Alan got interested in horses and had a string of racehorses but never won a major event. He began spending more time in the stables than in the surgery, and lost a lot of money. He died in 1982 at the age of 83 years.

Donald Rutnam

The second son was Donald Rutnam (1901 - 1968). He was the Captain of the Royal College cricket team which won the 1920 Royal - Thomian cricket match by an innings. The match was over in one day. He won a scholarship to Cambridge where he won Half-Blues in Tennis and Boxing. After graduating from Cambridge he sat for the Colonial Civil Service - Eastern Cadetship's examination in which he was first in order of merit. As there was no vacancy in the Ceylon Civil Service that year, he was posted to the Indian Civil Service. He played first class cricket for Central Provinces for the Ranji Trophy and he also played against visiting Australian and MCC teams.

He was almost certainly the first Ceylonese to participate in the Olympics, being chosen to play for India in the Men's Tennis Doubles in the 1924 Paris (Chariots of Fire) Olympics. His partner was S M Hadi, a Cambridge Blue in Tennis. They reached the quarter-finals where they lost to the legendary French pair, Jean Borotra and Rene Lacoste. The latter pair later won the Wimbledon doubles title, so there was no shame in losing to them. Lacoste, who later became World No. 1 in tennis had the nickname of "Crocodile" because of his tenacity on the court. He founded a Company which marketed a line of tennis shirts with the crocodile logo. The company prospers to this day and has diversified. Donald married an English lady and returned to England after he retired from the ICS in 1958. He passed away in 1968.

Robin Rutnam

Fig. 2 Mary with Robin and Helen
Courtesy Rutnam family

The third son was Robin Rutnam (1904 - 1968) (Fig. 2). Robin obtained his Bachelor's degree from the University of Toronto and a Master's degree in Psychology from McGill University. He was a founder member of the Lanka Sama Samaja Party which was founded in 1935. He was involved in the Youth League's Suriya Mal campaign and was one of the Joint Secretaries. On every Armistice Day (11

November) Poppies were sold for the benefit of British ex-Servicemen. In the Suriya Mal counter campaign, Suriya flowers were sold for the benefit of Ceylonese ex-Servicemen. In 1934-35 there was a drought and crop failure followed by a malaria epidemic in which 125,000 people died. Mary and Robin joined Dr N M Perera and others in distributing quinine and Marmite rolled into the form of vedarala's pills and saved many lives. Robin was a Director of the Oil and Fats Corporation and Chairman of the Leather Products Corporation. He was founder President of the Mercantile Table Tennis Association, founded in 1957. He passed away in 1968.

Walter Rutnam

The youngest son was Walter Rutnam (1905 - 1963). Walter obtained his Bachelor's degree from Antioch College, Ohio, USA and his Master's degree from the University of St Louis, USA. In 1932, together with Richard Pieris, Percy Pieris and Evelyn Fonseka they formed Richard Pieris and Co., and Walter was a founder Director. During World War II the Company's business boomed as they were involved in the retreading of tyres and there was a shortage of new tyres due to natural rubber shortages following the fall of Malaya to the Japanese in 1942. The Company is now the largest tyre retreader in South Asia and has also diversified into various other fields. Starting with a share capital of Rs 12,000 the Group turnover is now Rs 39 billion rupees making it one of the top ten Companies in Sri Lanka.

Walter was also actively involved in the Otter Aquatic Club and in 1950 succeeded in negotiating with the Government and obtained the present site of the Club which is off Bullers Road. Walter's wife Doreen Ferdinands was Principal of Lindsay Girls School. They had three children, a son Brian, and two daughters Sonia Doreen and Romaine. Brian Rutnam is a Sydneysider and active CSA Member and kindly provided access to the text of Mary's personal diary covering the period 1906 - 1909 and also to his personal notes on the Rutnam family.

Helen Rutnam

Their youngest child and only daughter was Helen who was born in 1914. She studied at Ladies College and obtained a Bachelor's degree from the University of Toronto. The St Thomas Times Journal of Ontario, Canada records that on 11 August 1941 she married Dallas Gunesekera. Helen became Principal of Clifton Presbyterian Girls School, now known as Clifton Girls School, in Maradana. Like her brother Robin, she too was actively involved in the Lanka Sama Samaja Party. Fig. 3 is a photo of the extended family.

Fig. 3 The extended Rutnam family
Courtesy Rutnam family

Awards and Honours

Although the Government offered her awards and honours several times for her social service work, Mary turned all of them down. She declined all of them still smarting over the Government's original refusal to recognise her University of Toronto medical degree. In 1958 however she accepted the offer of an Asian award, the inaugural Ramon Magsaysay award of $10,000 (a considerable sum of money at that time) for outstanding Public Service. This award is considered to be the Asian equivalent of the Nobel Prize and was funded by the Rockefeller Foundation. It is named after the former President of the Philippines who had died the previous year in a plane crash and whose funeral was attended by a crowd of five million people.

At the age of 85 years she travelled to Manilla, Philippines accompanied by one of her sons, to receive the award (Fig. 4). The citation for her award ended with the words *"In electing Mary H Rutnam to receive the first Ramon Magsaysay award for Public Service, the Board of Trustees recognises her gift of service to the Ceylonese people and the example set by her full life of dedication as a private citizen to the needs of others"*.

Fig. 4: Mary in her eighties

Mary gave a brief response to the citation and concluded by quoting a verse from Henry Wadsworth Longfellow's *A Psalm of Life:*

The lives of great men all remind us,
We can make our lives sublime
And departing leave behind us,
Footprints on the sands of time.

Dr Mary Helen Rutnam certainly left her footprints on the sands of time of Ceylon.

This Article was originally published in "The Ceylankan", Journal No. 63, August 2013.

11

Ceylonese teenager granted a Royal Patent – 100 years ago (Part 1)

by Thiru Arumugam

Bertram Elibank Dawapurarathna (Fig. 1), a fourteen year old Royal College, Colombo, schoolboy, applied to the London Patents Office for a Royal Patent over one hundred years ago on 21 October 1909 for *Improvements in Reversing Gear for Steam Engines*, and Royal Patent No. 24199 was granted to him on 09 June 1910 when he was fifteen years old.

Fig. 1 Bertram Dawapurarathna in 1912
Courtesy Judge Weeramantry

This event is mentioned in the book written when Royal College was almost one hundred years old, *The History of Royal College, formerly called Colombo Academy / written by boys in the school, 1931*. The book records on page 96 that *"Two remarkable performances must not be left out. First, the unique achievement of P L Jansz, who came first in the British Empire in the Junior Cambridge, and later won the University Scholarship; second the invention of B E Dawapurarathna, who improved the reversing gear for steam engines. This invention was patented in London"*.

Bertram was born in 1895 and was the youngest son of David Dawapurarathna. At the time of Bertram's birth, Sir Arthur Elibank Havelock was the Governor of Ceylon and that is why Bertram was given the middle name of Elibank. David was from Galle and won a scholarship to study at Royal College. He qualified as a lawyer and had a good practice in Colombo. Bertram's older sister Lilian, was one of the first girls to pass the Cambridge Senior Examination. She married Gregory Weeramantry. Gregory was a student at St Benedict's College where in 1909 he came first in the British Empire in the Cambridge Junior Examination. He subsequently studied in the University of London, graduating in 1916. Judge Christopher Weeramantry is the youngest son of Gregory and Lilian. Christopher was a Supreme Court Judge in Ceylon, Professor of Law at Monash University, Melbourne, and a Judge in the International Court of Justice in the Hague. In Volume 1 of his autobiography *Towards One World: The Memoirs of Judge C G Weeramantry,* he has in pages 173 - 179, outlined the life of his uncle (mother's brother) Bertram Dawapurarathna. Judge Weeramantry records (p. 173) that Bertram as a schoolboy *"earned such a reputation for his mechanical skills that people from far and wide would seek his help to repair their motor cars, motorcycles, rice mills or any sort of machinery you could name"*.

Royal Patents

A few years later while still a teenager, Dawapurarathna was granted a second Royal Patent, No. 6883 dated 20 March 1914, for an *Improved Valve Mechanism for Internal Combustion Engines.* There are small variations in the spelling of the surname Dawapurarathna. For the purpose of this article, the spelling will be that used in his patent applications.

The texts of the two Patent applications are reproduced in Judge Weeramantry's book, but not the engineering drawings that would have accompanied the applications. To understand the patent applications, one needs to study the drawings in conjunction with the text. The drawings have now been tracked down and are reproduced here for the first time, together with the texts of the patents.

Dawapurarathna's application for a patent for *Improvements in Reversing Gear for Steam Engines* is dated 21 October 1909. He was then a Form V student in Royal College aged about 14 years (Weeramantry p. 173). Railways were then very much in the news with the opening of the Northern Line to Kankesanthurai in 1905, the Royal Patent was granted to this precocious genius on 09 June 1910, i.e. less than eight months after his application. Nowadays it takes on average about four and a half years between applying for a patent and being informed whether it is successful or not. Last year over 150,000 patents were awarded in the UK.

History of Steam Locomotives

To understand the background in which the patent application was made, a brief history of the steam engine would not be inappropriate. It was the steam engine that sparked off the industrial revolution. With the invention of the stationary steam engine it became possible to locate a manufacturing factory anywhere, whereas previously it had to be located adjacent to a stream to obtain motive power from a waterwheel. The first commercially successful stationary steam engines were built by James Watt in the latter part of the eighteenth century. In 1804 Richard Trevithick demonstrated the first steam powered railway locomotive. In 1825, George Stephenson built a steam locomotive for the Stockton and Darlington Railway and this was the first steam powered railway open to the public.

Steam engines in locomotives are double acting engines. In this respect they differ from internal combustion engines which are single acting engines. Steam is introduced at one end of a cylinder and as the steam expands it pushes a piston towards the other end of the cylinder. Steam is then admitted to the other end of the cylinder and the piston is pushed back, meanwhile the originally admitted steam is released from the cylinder. The piston is connected by shafts and connecting rods to the driven wheels of the locomotive. This is the double acting principle. The introduction of steam to the two ends of the cylinder and the exhausting of used steam is done by a slide valve which slides and uncovers and covers ports leading to the cylinder. The motion of the slide valve is derived from linkages to the wheels, connecting rods or axles and this is the valve gear.

Stephenson's Valve Gear

Early stationary steam engines were used in factories and for driving water pumps, and reversal of the direction of rotation was rarely required. In the case of steam locomotives, reversal of direction of rotation is essential, particularly for shunting locomotives which require frequent reversal. From 1841 to the end of the nineteenth century the most popular type of locomotive valve gear was the Stephenson valve gear. This was developed in Robert (son of George) Stephenson's locomotive works in Newcastle upon Tyne.

It consisted of two eccentrics mounted on the driven locomotive wheel axle, out of phase with each other, which were connected to link rods. The other ends of the two link rods were connected by pins to the top and bottom of a vertical slotted expansion link. This link was connected to a reach rod ending in a lever or screw hand wheel in the engine driver's cab. Forward or reverse motion of the engine was attained by raising or lowering the expansion link from the driver's cab. The slide valve which admitted and released steam to and from the engine cylinder was connected by a valve rod and by a pin to a slide which could move up or down in the slot of the expansion link.

Fig. 2 shows a typical example of the drive mechanism for Stephenson's inside valve gear. This photo was taken of a Beyer Peacock 2-6-0 steam locomotive which was built in 1890 and used by the New South Wales Government Railway. The valve gear is internally mounted, i.e. within the frame and directly under the boiler. The bottom and top link rods get their oscillating simple harmonic motion from eccentrics (not in picture) on the left and mounted on the wheel axle. The second pair of top and bottom link rods in the background are for operating the valve on the other side of the locomotive. The link rods are pinned to the top and bottom of a slotted expansion link which is partially obscured by the vertical reach rod in the front of the picture. It is this reach rod which is used to raise or lower the slotted expansion link. The reach rod is connected by links to a lever and a notched quadrant in the engine driver's cab. This lever controls the forward and reverse motion of the locomotive by bodily lifting or lowering the expansion link. The slotted link position also controls the percentage steam cut-off, i.e. the percentage of piston travel at which the admission of steam to the cylinder is cut off. Long cut-off (say 75%) is required for high torque when starting to move, and this percentage is progressively reduced as the locomotive picks up speed. This procedure is known as 'notching up'. The connection from the valve drive gear in the picture to the actual steam slide valve (not shown) is by a valve rod pinned on to a slide which can move up or down in the slot of the expansion rod. The valve rod passes through a hole in the vertical plate on the right of the picture.

Fig. 2: Stephenson's Inside Valve Gear
(Photo: Thiru Arumugam)

Stephenson and Co. was the largest single supplier of steam locomotives to the Ceylon Government Railway. Of the 410 steam locomotives purchased by the CGR, 64 nos. were manufactured by them, including the first five locomotives purchased by the CGR. Many of them would have been fitted with Stephenson's valve gear, as well other steam locomotives purchased by the CGR. It would have been these examples of Stephenson's valve gear that Dawapurarathna would have studied when formulating his ideas for his patent application.

Fig. 3 shows an early example of a steam locomotive built by Stephenson and Co. which was supplied to the New South Wales Government Railway. This was a 0-6-0 built in 1864, the same year that the first train ran in Ceylon. It has internally mounted Stephenson valve gear with an inside steam cylinder. It weighed 50 tons, had a tractive effort of 18,000 lbf and a top speed of 25 mph (40 km/h).

Fig. 3 Stephenson Steam Locomotive built in 1864
(Photo: Malini Arumugam)

Dawapurarathna's steam valve gear

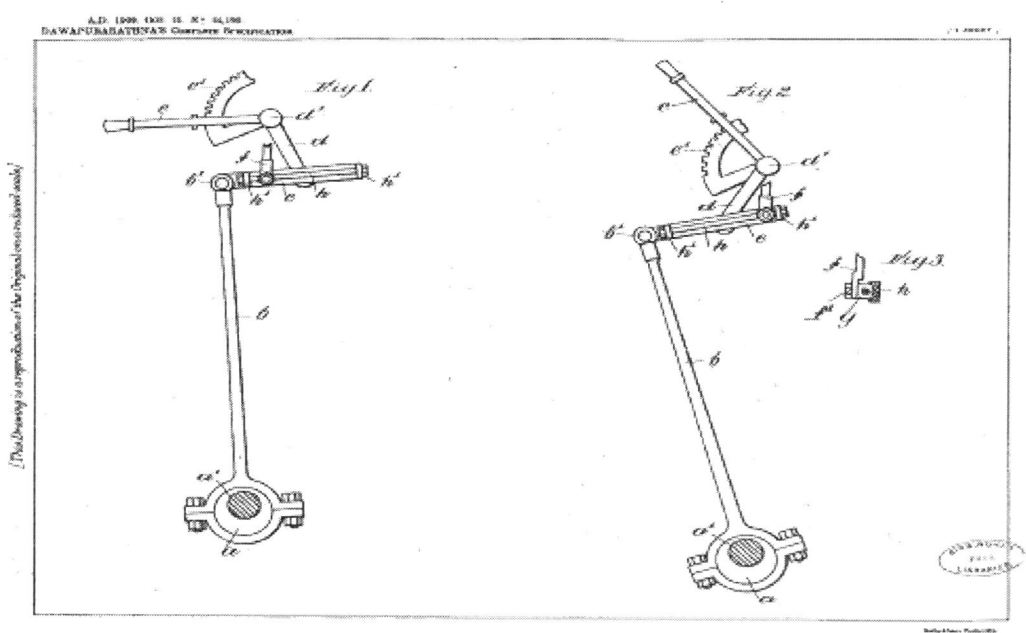

Fig. 4: Diagram attached to Patent Application for Improvements in Reversing Gear in Fig.5

The innovation that Dawapurarathna proposed in his patent was that only one eccentric link be used instead of the two links used in Stephenson's valve gear. This is shown in the drawing (Fig. 4) attached to the patent application in Fig 5. The eccentric 'a' is connected to a link rod 'b' the other end of which is pivoted to a rocking arm 'c' which has a fulcrum to an arm 'd' which leads to the valve control rod 'e' in the driver's cab. The control rod position is adjustable on a toothed quadrant 'e^1'. The rod 'f' which leads to the valve gear is pivoted to a block 'g' which can slide on the guide bar 'h' mounted on the rocking arm. The engine driver by altering the position of the lever 'e' on the toothed quadrant can change the position of the block 'g' and go forward or reverse. It can be seen that the block 'g' will move the valve rod 'f' in the opposite direction when it is on the left hand side of the rocking arm 'c', compared with when it is on the right hand side. The position of the block 'g' will also control the percentage steam cut off. This simplifies the valve gear and also reduces the cost. Also because the valve gear is much lighter, it requires much less physical effort for the engine driver to 'notch up' or change from forward to reverse motion.

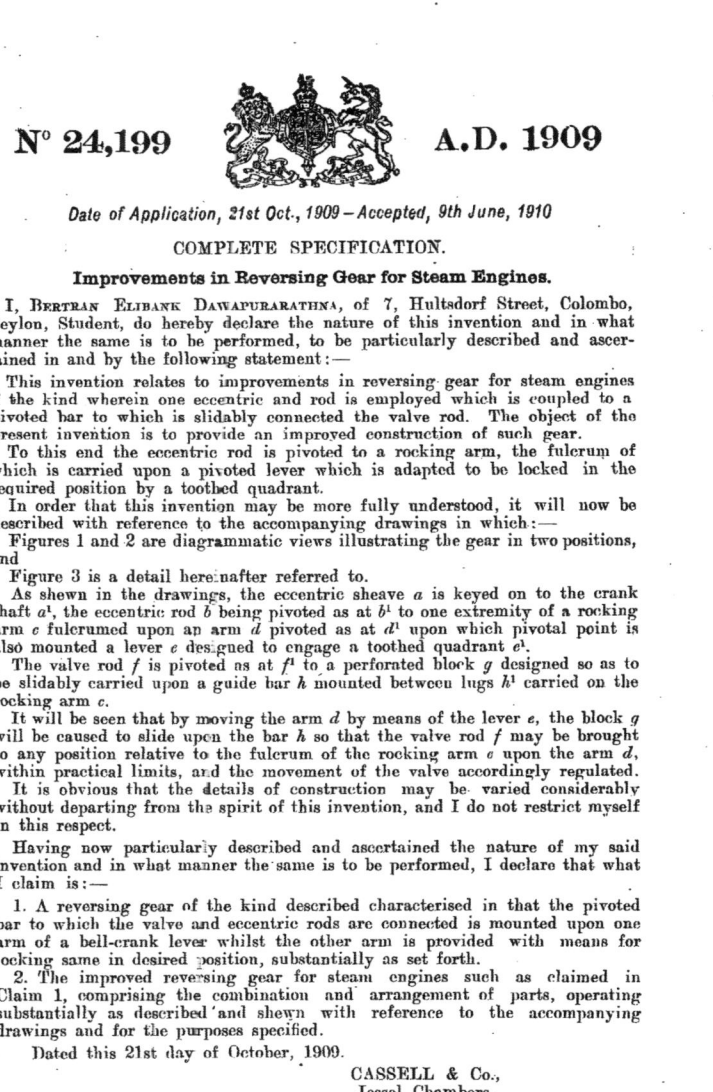

Fig. 5: 14 year old schoolboy's application for a Royal Patent

The only point that remains uncertain is whether the rocking arm 'c' should be a straight link as shown, or whether it should in the form of an arc so that the valve rod is a sort of a radius bar to maintain the required valve lead and lap at different valve cut off settings. Overall, what an ingenious idea to be conceived by a 14 year old schoolboy without any formal engineering training. The boy is nothing short of a genius.

Comparable valve gear

Although a careful search of steam valve gear literature was made, a commercial application of this arrangement could not be found. At that time patents were valid for fourteen years provided the annual renewal fees were paid. If a manufacturer wants to make commercial use of someone else's patent, he must buy the patent outright from the patentee or obtain a licence from the patentee and pay him royalties. An example of a royalty payment was when the locomotive manufacturer Beyer Peacock obtained the sole rights from the design engineer Herbert Garratt to manufacture Garratt engines using his patent for articulated steam locomotives. Beyer Peacock agreed to pay royalties to Garratt of two pounds sterling per ton weight of Garratt locomotives manufactured. Over a thousand Garratt locomotives were finally made with some of them weighing up to 250 tons!

Patent Licence transactions are recorded in the Register of Patents. Dawapurarathna's patents gave a contact address in Hulftsdorf, Colombo, which could either be the address of the family home or the address of his father's legal practice office. Any applicant who wanted a licence would have had to contact Dawapurarathna at this address but it appears that no such licence applications were received.

To get things in their proper perspective, at the time that Dawapurarathna applied for his patent, there were already over a hundred steam valve gear patents which were in force. Only a handful of these went into commercial manufacture. The vast majority of them used two links for driving the motion of the valve gear, only three or four designs used a single link like Dawapurarathna's design. The nearest to his design was the Southern valve gear.

Southern valve gear

Fig. 6: Southern Valve Gear *(Photo: Thiru Arumugam)*

This was designed by William Sherman Brown, an employee of Southern Railways (USA) and used on their locomotives. Fig. 6 shows this valve gear installed on a D55 2-8-0 Australian Consolidation locomotive built in 1918 which was used by the New South Wales Government Railway. The valve gear is driven off a single cranked drive bar off the driving wheel on the left. It is the rod below the main connecting rod. The rod is pivoted and hung by a bar, the left bar of the two vertical bars in the centre of the picture. The top of this bar is pivoted to a block. The position of this block can be varied by the engine driver by sliding it within the curved link. Note that this curved link is firmly bolted down to the engine frame at both ends. To the end of the cranked drive bar is linked a second vertical bar which is the right hand bar in the centre of the picture. The upper end of this bar is linked to a bell crank which translates the up and down motion of cranked drive bar to a horizontal motion to control the slide valve to give forward and reverse motion to the locomotive and also control the percentage steam cut off. An interesting working model of the Southern valve gear made up with Lego pieces can be seen at: youtube.com/watch?v=MqGdjvl71tg

To be continued in the next Article.

This Article was originally published in "The Ceylankan", Journal No. 64, November 2013.

12

Ceylonese teenager granted a Royal Patent – 100 years ago (Part 2)

by Thiru Arumugam

One wonders whether Brown's design of the Southern valve gear (see Fig. 6 of previous Article) was inspired by Dawapurarathna's design. The common factor is the single link drive, which was previously used mainly in Hackworth valve gear and Joy valve gear and that too was several decades earlier. The main differences are that Southern's curved expansion link is firmly bolted down at both ends and that the Southern gear uses a crank off a wheel whereas Dawapurarathna proposed an eccentric sheave on the axle. The latter difference is understandable because Dawapurarathna's design was for inside valve gear and steam cylinder i.e. within the engine frame and under the boiler, whereas the Southern gear is for an outside cylinder and valve.

The dates of the patents may be significant. Dawapurarathna's patent was granted on 09 June 1910. Brown applied for a US patent on 11 July 1911, just over a year later and US Patent No. 1,033,532 was granted to him on 23 July 1912. Brown then took the unusual step of applying for a British patent also and since there were sufficient differences between Dawapurarathna's patent, he was granted British Patent No. GB191407442(A) on 20 August 1914. We will never know for certain whether Brown's design of the Southern valve gear was inspired by Dawapurarathna's patent.

An interesting corollary was that many years later Atumaru Ayakazu an inventor from Japan was awarded US Patent No. 4404870(A) on 20 September 1983 for a *Reciprocator for Paint Gun*. The reciprocator had fixed and movable pulleys which could move the paint gun vertically and horizontally via a single cranked linkage off an electric motor. The US Patent Examiner seemed to think Dawapurarathna's patent was relevant to assessing whether the US patent was new and inventive in light of the published documents that already existed. It is likely the Examiner cited Dawapurarathna's patent as it is one of the first patents with the International Classification code of F01L29/02 (reversing gears by displacing eccentric), with only a dozen or so predating it. The US patent was eventually granted, so it seems the Examiner eventually decided that Dawapurarathna's disclosure did not anticipate the US patent application.

Engineering studies in the UK

When Dawapurarathna completed his schooling at Royal College, as there were no facilities for degree level studies in mechanical engineering in Ceylon, his parents arranged to send him to UK. They could afford to do so because his father had a good legal practice in Colombo. Dawapurarathna must have left for UK for further studies around 1912.

He did not waste much time because in the following year, 1913, we find him applying for a second patent. In this patent application he says that he is "*presently residing at 34, Blythswood Drive, Kelvinside, Glasgow*". Blythswood Drive no longer exists, its name was changed to Woodlands Drive many years ago. This Drive is relatively short and the entire length consists of near identical four storey town houses. These houses would have been occupied by extended families in Victorian days and any spare rooms rented to lodgers. It is seen that this Drive is just over five minutes walk from the University of Glasgow and therefore there is little doubt that this is where Dawapurarathna studied engineering. In 1913 the chief occupant of No. 34 was William B Robertson and it is possible that it was his wife who was the landlady who was in communication with Dawapurarathna's family in Colombo after the World War 1.

Choice of the University of Glasgow

The University of Glasgow was founded in 1451 and is the fourth oldest University in UK after Oxford, Cambridge and the University of St Andrews. With his intelligence he could have entered any University in UK that he chose to, but what reasons made Dawapurarathna choose the University of Glasgow for his higher studies? Perhaps one could conjecture that it was one or more of the following reasons: it was the University where James Watt was an Instrument Technician in the 18th century and he went on to develop the marginally efficient Newcomen stationary steam engine into the mechanically efficient steam engine that powered the industrial revolution, and his surname lives for evermore as the unit of electrical power, the "watt"; it was the University where Professor William Rankine in the 19th century developed the complete theory of the steam engine and propounded the Rankine Cycle as a mathematical model that can be used to predict the performance of the steam engine and text books written by him were in use when Dawapurarathna was a student; it was the University where considerable research was being conducted on steam engines; and finally, Glasgow was the home of the North British Locomotive Co., which was at that time the largest locomotive manufacturer in Europe. North British, together with its associated Companies, Dubs, Neilson Reid and Sharp Stewart, supplied 74 of the 410 steam locomotives purchased by the Ceylon Government Railway. No doubt Dawapurarathna would have seen and studied some of these locomotives in Dematagoda and Ratmalana when he was a schoolboy in Colombo.

The second Royal Patent

On 20 March 1913, a few months after Dawapurarathna commenced his engineering studies in UK, he submitted an application for a patent for *Improved Valve Mechanism for Internal Combustion Engines*. His application was successful and he was granted Royal Patent No. 6883 exactly a year later on 20 March 1914. The patent application is reproduced in Fig. 1 of this article and related drawings are reproduced in Fig 2.

The most commonly used valves in four stroke internal combustion engines are poppet valves. The minimum number of valves is two per cylinder, an inlet valve and an exhaust valve. Some high performance engines have more than this minimum number. Dawapurarathna's patent was a proposal to reduce the number valves from four for two cylinders to one valve for two cylinders. The two cylinders 'A' and 'B' have a common valve chamber 'c', in which there is a rotating tapered plug valve 'f', rotating at half the crankshaft speed. The air/fuel mixture from the carburettor enters from the top through the passage 'h' and is admitted to the cylinders when the gap 'g' is in line with the ports 'a' and 'b'. When the ports 'a' and 'b' line up with the gap 'k', the exhaust gases leave the cylinder through the passage 'j' to the exhaust outlet 'd'. Quite an ingenious idea to reduce the number of valves and the cost of the engine.

One of the points that requires further thought is the friction between the rotary valve 'f' and the chamber wall of the valve body 'c'. It may require valve rings to be fitted on the valve, similar to piston rings, but tapered. The other problem not mentioned is that of lubrication of the valve chamber wall. This was a major cause of failure of early rotary valve designs.

N° 6883   A.D. 1913

Date of Application, 20th Mar., 1913—Accepted, 20th Mar., 1914

COMPLETE SPECIFICATION.

Improved Valve Mechanism for Internal Combustion Engines.

I, BERTRAM ELIBANK DAWAPURARATHNA, Engineering Student, of 1, Hultsdorf, Colombo, Ceylon, at present residing at 34, Blythswood Drive, Kelvinside, Glasgow, do hereby declare the nature of this invention and in what manner the same is to be performed, to be particularly described and ascertained in and by the following statement:—

This invention relates to valve mechanism for internal combustion engines.

It has reference in particular to the known type wherein a single rotating plug or taper valve member having suitable inlet and outlet ports therein is adapted to co-act with ports in a valve casing common to two cylinders, the said valve being so formed and rotated as to permit of the function of the four stroke cycle being carried out at each revolution of the said valve, the exhaust port in the valve being formed in the same plane as the inlet port and having a transverse oblique passage to a side main exhaust. In this connection, the device also embodies known arrangement whereby the plug valve is adapted to be pressed within the casing by spring and collar means in order that any slackness due to wear may be automatically taken up and thus always maintains a tight joint.

The present invention consists in a specific arrangement of the above type substantially as illustrated in the accompanying drawings.

The accompanying drawings illustrate valve mechanism made in accordance with the invention in which:—

Fig. 1. is a part plan in section of a pair of cylinders.

Fig. 2 is an elevation of the valve with the casing in section.

Fig. 3. is a part similar view of Fig. 1 with the parts in a different position.

A, B, are two cylinders cast *en-bloc* with a common conical valve casing C, the one A communicating with said casing by the port a and the one B by means of the port b. d is the exhaust port leading from the casing C, said exhaust port being disposed at a lower level than the ports a b and said cylinders are water jacketed in the usual manner as at e.

f is a conical valve mounted in the casing c and adapted to be rotated at half engine speed by suitable tooth or other gearing by the spindle f^1 on which the valve is mounted. This valve f is provided towards the upper or wider end with an inlet port g communicating by the pipe h to the carburettor.

j is an exhaust passage formed through the body of the valve in an oblique manner the upper end opening into a gap k, similar to and in the same plane as the one g, and the other end j^1 opening on the opposite side of the valve in the same plane as that of the main exhaust d.

It will be seen that the ports a & b open into the valve casing at 90° apart and thus as the said valve is driven at half the speed of the engine shaft, the cranks of the respective cylinders must be disposed at 180 degrees. This arrangement of having the cranks at 180 degrees is preferable to ensure balanced or even running of the engine but if desired such as in the case where more than one pair of cylinders are employed in one engine, the cranks and consequently the position of the ports a & b could be varied. The position of the

[*Price 8d.*]

Improved Valve Mechanism for Internal Combustion Engines.

gaps or ports *g* & *k* would of course have to be formed in corresponding position.

In operation assuming that the parts are in the position of Fig. 1 it will be seen that the cylinder A is just commencing the suction stroke whilst the cylinder B is exhausting. Upon the continued movement of the valve in the direction of the arrow, the port *g* will fully open the inlet and then close same to allow of the compression. During the compression stroke the port *g* will have come opposite to the port *b* of cylinder B when its piston will be in the position to effect the suction stroke. When the valve has rotated one half revolution it is in the position shewn in Fig. 3, the charge in cylinder A is being fired and that in cylinder B being compressed. On further movement the cylinder B fires by which time the gap *k* and passages j^1 will be in the position to allow of the exhaust gases of A escaping. The cycle of operations is then recommenced by the valve moving into the position of Fig. 1.

For the purpose of taking up any slackness due to wear between the valve *f* and casing C the spindle f^1 is provided as has already been proposed with a collar *m* keyed thereon and a washer or ring *o* is rotatably mounted by ball bearings or otherwise, upon the lower end of said casing whereby an interposed spring *n* serves to maintain an efficient seating between the casing and valve and thus loss of power through leakage is obviated.

The spindle f^1 will be coupled to the driving mechanism through suitable means such as a slidable connection, as will permit the valve being always maintained closely against the seating without affecting the drive.

Having now particularly described and ascertained the nature of my said invention, and in what manner the same is to be performed, I declare that what I claim is:—

1. The improved valve mechanism for internal combustion engines constructed arranged and adapted to operate substantially as set forth.

Dated this 19th day of March, 1913.

CASSELL & Co.,
Registered Patent Agents,
Jessel Chambers, 88—89—90, Chancery Lane, London, W.C.

Redhill: Printed for His Majesty's Stationery Office, by Love & Malcomson, Ltd.—1914.

Fig. 1: Dawapurarathna's Patent Application for Valve Mechanism for I.C. Engines

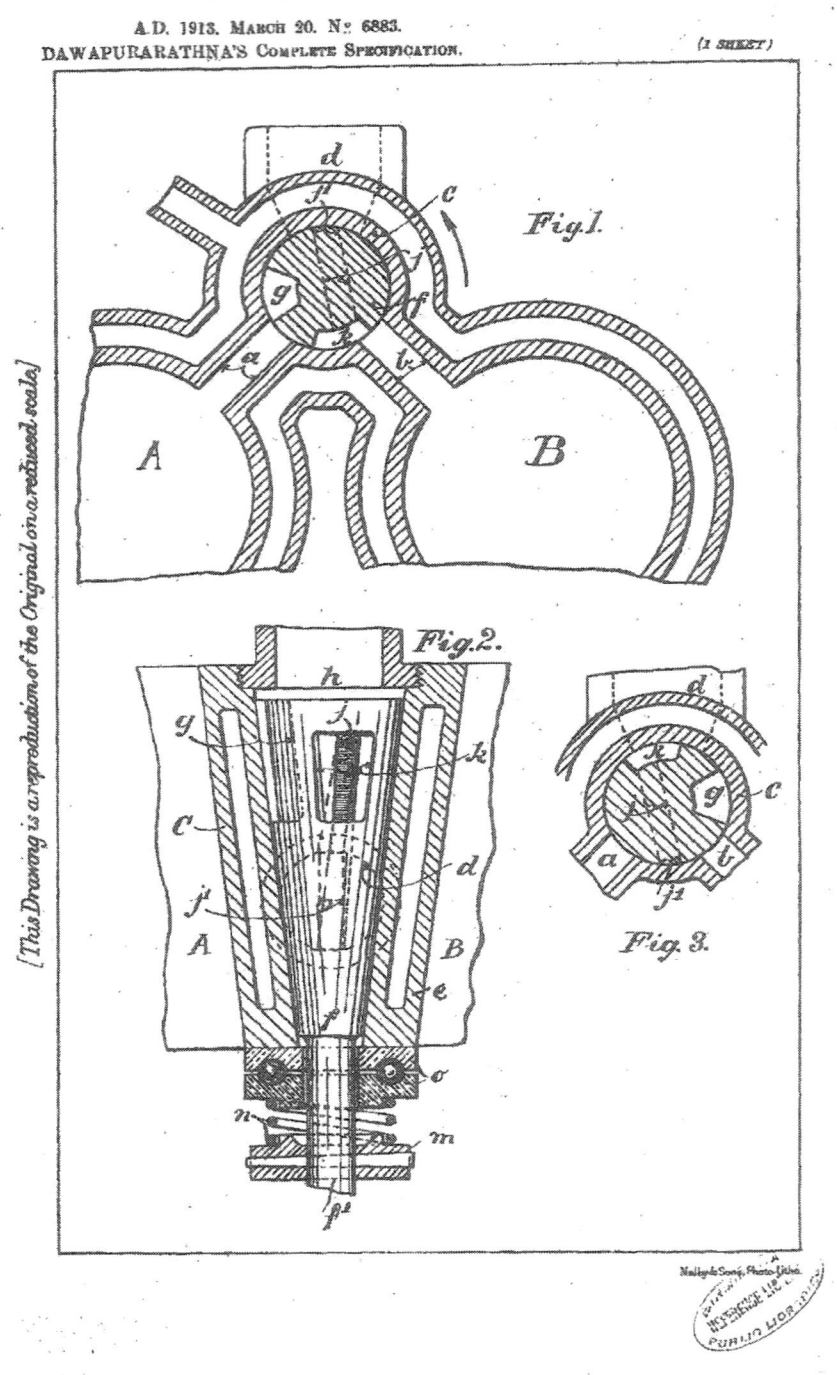

Fig 2: Drawing for Patent Application in Fig. 1

There was a lot of interest in rotary valves in the early part of the 20th century. Some of the experimental designs and associated patents which Dawapurarathna would no doubt have studied were by Frayer and Howard (1907), Italia (1911), Vallilee (1911), Darracq (1912) and Mead (1912). Later on Reverend Pearcy of Cheltenham (1926) and Frank Aspin (1933 onwards) proposed an arrangement of a tapered rotary valve above the cylinder, similar to Dawapurarathna's proposal, except that his was on the side of the cylinder. However, all of the other proposals were for one valve per cylinder whereas Dawapurarathna's proposal was for one valve for a pair of cylinders. Aspin did try out his valve on some motorcycle engines. By this time Dawapurarathna's Patent had already expired. It is not known whether Dawapurarathna's design went into commercial production.

Dawapurarathna's final years

After World War 1 started in 1914, communication between Dawapurarathna and his family in Colombo was intermittent and infrequent. Judge Weeramantry (page 174 of *Towards One World: The Memoirs of Judge C G Weeramantry*) says that there is a story that Dawapurarathna was flying a test plane during the war and that it crashed and he was seriously injured and that it was decided to send him back to Colombo to convalesce in a warm climate. Although functional parachutes were invented just before World War 1, the Allied forces did not issue parachutes to aircraft pilots because they felt that pilots would bail out during an emergency rather than try their best to save the aircraft! The value of human life has changed since then.

A check on the records of the Royal Flying Corps, the predecessor of the Royal Air Force in the World War 1, does not show his name. However, this does not necessarily mean that he was not in the Royal Flying Corps because on the night of 07 September 1940 during World War 2, a German incendiary bomb fell on the War Office Records Store in Arnside Street, London SE17, setting fire to the Store and destroying two-thirds of the World War 1 military service records of over six million service men and women. The other possibility is that he was employed by an aircraft manufacturer.

The story that he was injured in an air crash and was to be sent to Colombo to convalesce is probably correct because otherwise it is unlikely that he would attempt to sail to Colombo in mid-winter 1917 during the height of the war. The steamship *Nyanza* was a 6000 ton passenger liner built in 1907 and owned by the Peninsula and Oriental Steam Navigation Co. Fig. 3 is a painting of this ship. It could carry up to 94 passengers with a crew of 165. It sailed from the Port of London on 06 December 1917 under Captain C G Smith bound for Colombo, Madras and Calcutta and had on board cargo and 44 passengers, all of whom were adult males. Because of intense German U Boat activity in the seas around UK, the intended initial course was to follow the English Channel, hugging the coast of Southern England until it reached Plymouth Harbour in Devon.

Fig. 3: 6000 ton, P&O Liner "Nyanza" in which Dawapurarathna set sail for Colombo and was torpedoed

It left Plymouth in convoy on 09 December 1917 and later on the same day, while still in British territorial waters about ten miles south of The Lizard peninsula, Cornwall which is the southernmost point in England, the *Nyanza* was hit by a torpedo fired by the German U Boat *U53* under Commander Hans Rose. This submarine had a displacement of 715 tons and could carry up to six torpedoes driven by compressed air and during World War 1 it sank 87 Allied merchant ships with a total tonnage of over 200,000 tons. 6 passengers and 43 crew members of the *Nyanza* died immediately and many more were injured. Clearly the rules of war were not being followed. These required the submarine to surface, and send a boarding party to examine the merchant vessel's cargo manifest. If it was found that there was any cargo which would assist the enemy war effort, the Captain of the merchant ship was informed that it was going to be sunk, and time given for the passengers and crew to get away in lifeboats and abandon ship. The *Nyanza* was badly damaged but still seaworthy. The *U53* then went and torpedoed without warning and sank the 2000 ton British coal carrier *War Tune* which was nearby and presumably because of this diversion the *Nyanza* managed to escape and limp into Falmouth Harbour in Cornwall, the deepest harbour in Western Europe, which was about 25 miles away. The ship was later repaired and went back into P & O service until it was sold to a Japanese firm for scrap in 1927.

The typewritten passenger manifest of the *Nyanza* for this voyage records that Bertram Elibank Dawapurarathna, 22 years old, bound for Colombo, with future residence in Ceylon, occupied a second class cabin. His occupation is recorded as "Engineer" which confirms that he successfully completed his engineering studies in Glasgow. Another Ceylonese travelling on the same ship was 23 year old Walter de Silva. His profession is described as "Engineering".

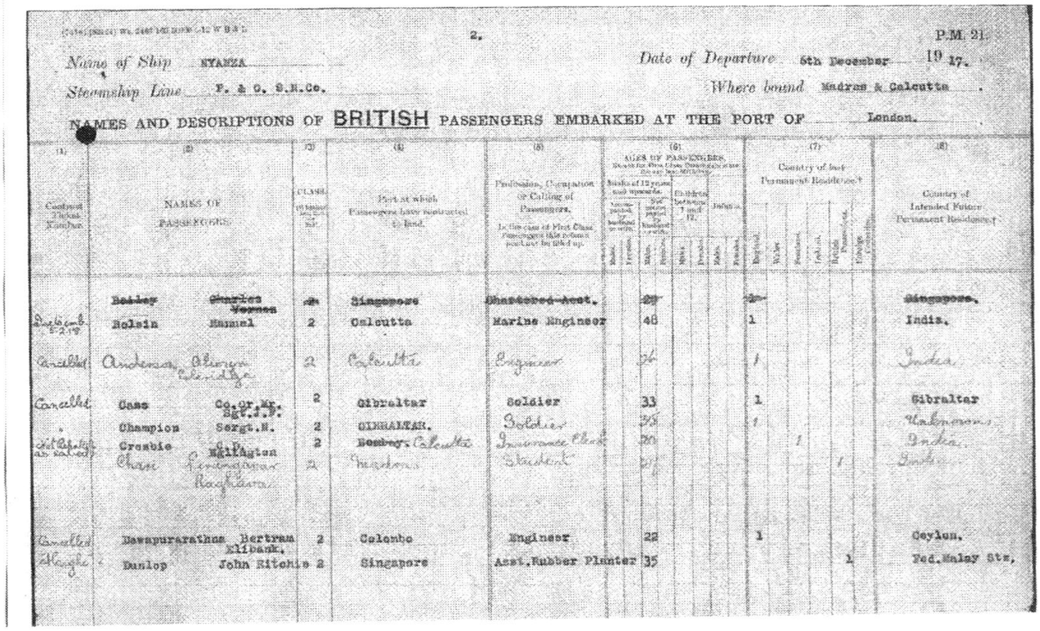

2. P.M. 21.

Name of Ship NYANZA — Date of Departure 6th December 19 17.

Steamship Line P. & O. S.N.Co. — Where bound Madras & Calcutta.

NAMES AND DESCRIPTIONS OF BRITISH PASSENGERS EMBARKED AT THE PORT OF London.

(1) Contract Ticket Number	(2) Names of Passengers		(3) Class	(4) Port at which Passengers have contracted to land	(5) Profession, Occupation or Calling of Passengers	(6) Ages of Passengers	(7) Country of last Permanent Residence	(8) Country of Intended Future Permanent Residence
	~~Bailey~~	~~Charles Vernon~~	~~2~~	~~Singapore~~	~~Chartered Acct.~~	~~29~~	~~1~~	~~Singapore.~~
[illegible]	Bolsin	Samuel	2	Calcutta	Marine Engineer	48	1	India.
Cancelled	Anderson	[illegible] Coleridge	2	Calcutta	Engineer	26	1	India
Cancelled	Case	Co.Qr.Mr. Sgt.J.F.	2	Gibraltar	Soldier	33	1	Gibraltar
	Champion	Sergt.H.	2	GIBRALTAR.	Soldier	35	1	Unknown
[illegible]	Crosbie	C.D.	2	~~Bombay.~~ Calcutta	Insurance Clerk	20	1	India.
	[illegible]	[illegible]	2	Madras	Student	[illegible]	1	India
Cancelled	Dawapurarathna	Bertram Elibank.	2	Colombo	Engineer	22	1	Ceylon.
Margha	Dunlop	John Ritchie	2	Singapore	Asst.Rubber Planter	35	1	Fed.Malay Sts.

Fig. 4: Extract from *Nyanza's* Passenger Manifest

On the margin of the passenger manifest there is a handwritten record of the fate of each of the 44 passengers due to the torpedo strike. Those passengers who were not seriously injured and were fit to continue their journey, were found passages on the P & O steamship *Margha* which sailed from Liverpool for the Far East eleven days later on 18 December 1917. These passengers have the word "Margha" written in the margin against their names in the passenger manifest. Those passengers who died in the torpedo attack have the entry against their names, with typical British euphemistic understatement, "Not recorded as saved". The passengers who were seriously injured and unable to travel on the *Margha* eleven days later, had the entry "Cancelled" against their names. Dawapurarathna's name and Walter de Silva's name are in the latter category, which meant that they were both seriously injured and unfit to travel on the *Margha* which sailed on 18 December 1917. Fig 4 is an extract from the passenger manifest of the *Nyanza*.

This time it appears that Dawapurarathna's injuries were terminal. We find that about four or five months later the UK Register of Deaths for April, May and June 1918, page 183, records the registration of the death in Leeds of Bertram E Dawapurarathna in Volume 9b, page 418, line number 91. This means that his remains were interred in any one of the 19 cemeteries which existed at that time in Leeds, West Riding, Yorkshire, England. Fig 5 is an extract from the Register of Deaths.

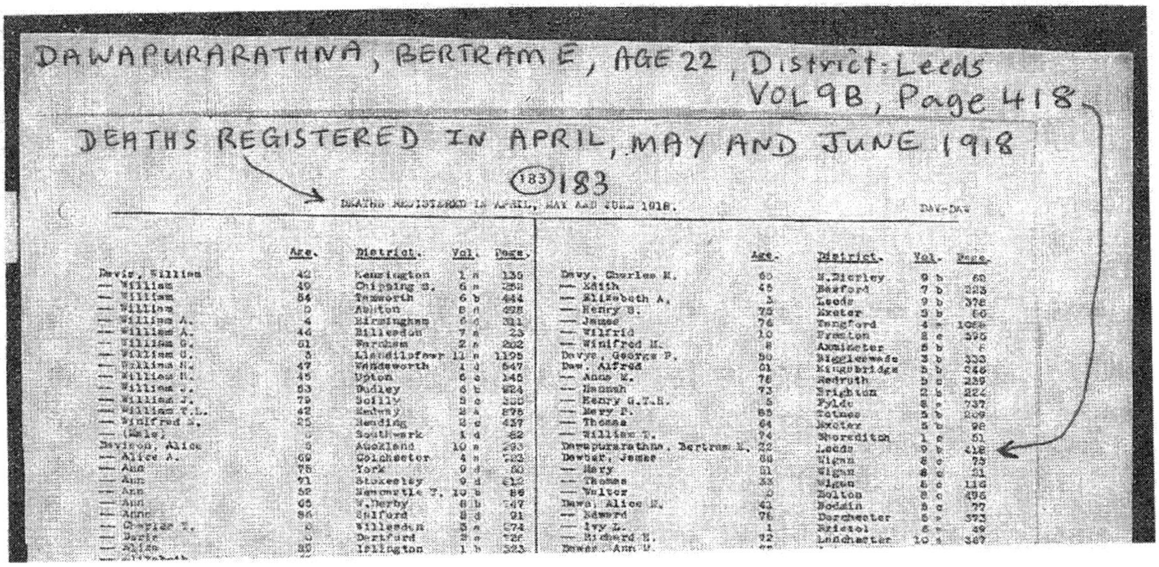

Fig. 5: Dawapurarathna's death record, aged 22 years, in a Leeds Cemetery, 1918

All these details of the final months of his life have been revealed here for the first time after a careful search of records. It will enable his relations to achieve closure about the end his life, which was open ended until now. This was the premature end of one who, if he had lived a normal life span, would without doubt have been one of Ceylon's greatest engineers. He would have been on a par with his illustrious relation D J Wimalasurendra, who had the vision to conceive the Laxapana Hydro-Electric Project about one hundred years ago. Around 1930, Wimalasurendra's daughter Marie, married Edwin who was Dawapurarathna's sister Enid's husband's brother. Judge Weeramantry was a four or five year old pageboy at this wedding (Weeramantry p. 92).

It is interesting to note that three people who were going to be connected by future marriages were studying in UK at the same time. They were Dawapurarathna who was in UK from 1912 to 1918; his future brother-in-law Gregory Weeramantry (father of Judge Weeramantry) who studied in London from 1913 to 1918; and his future close relation D J Wimalasurendra who studied electrical engineering in London from 1915 to 1917. They could never have guessed their future connections!

This Article was originally published in "The Ceylankan", Journal No. 65, February 2014.

13

BASIL WRIGHT and the film *SONG OF CEYLON* (1934)

by Thiru Arumugam

(This article is the text of an introductory talk given at the screening of two films at the 23 February 2014 meeting of CSA, Sydney.)

The program consists of two documentary films about Ceylon, directed and filmed by the Englishman, Basil Wright in 1934. The first film is *Negombo Coast* which runs for about 10 minutes and the second is *Song of Ceylon* which runs for about 37 minutes. Who was this Basil Wright and what were the circumstances under which these films were made? He was born in Dorset in 1907 and came from a well-to-do family. He studied in a private school and entered Cambridge University in 1926 where he studied classics and economics. He intended to become a creative writer and published a book of his poems while he was still a student. However, he became interested in films and when his parents asked him what he would like to have as a 21st birthday present, he had no hesitation in asking for a 16 mm movie camera.

In 1926 the British Government created the Empire Marketing Board. This was the time of the great depression and the prices and sales of primary products from the Colonies were falling and creating financial hardship. The function of the Board was to promote intra-Empire trade and as part of this promotion it had a Film Unit to make documentary films. John Grierson was appointed head of this film unit. He is considered to be the "father" of the British documentary and in fact he coined the word 'documentary' which he defined as "the creative treatment of actuality". In 1929 Grierson made the documentary film *Drifters* which is about herring fishing in the North Sea and this film kicked off the British documentary film movement.

Basil Wright saw *Drifters* and was very impressed and submitted some of his amateur films to Grierson who recognised his talent and immediately hired him as a trainee film director on a salary of eight pounds a week. Both Grierson and Wright were fans of the avant-garde Russian film movement, particularly Sergei Eisenstein who had made the feature film *Battleship Potemkin* in 1925. This film was named in the Brussels World Fair of 1958 as the greatest film of all time. This film has a scene in which the Tsar's Cossack soldiers march in unison down a flight of steps called the Odessa steps in Ukraine, firing at a crowd of unarmed civilian demonstrators. This scene has been described as one of the most influential scenes in the history of cinema.

In 1933, the Ceylon Tea Propaganda Board asked the Empire Marketing Board Film Unit to produce a four part film to promote Ceylon tea and about Ceylon in general, and were prepared to fund it up to two thousand five hundred pounds. Basil Wright was asked to proceed to Ceylon and shoot this film. He was accompanied by 19 year old John Taylor who was Grierson's brother-in-law. When Wright asked Grierson what his guidelines were in the shooting of the film, he was simply told to make something exceptional.

They arrived in Colombo on 1st January 1934. The Ceylon Tea Propaganda Board office in Colombo was responsible for all the local arrangements. The two of them were accommodated in the Grand Oriental Hotel and were provided with a chauffeur driven luxury Belgian Minerva car. They were also provided with a bus-caravan to carry their film equipment and six helpers. The Board had six of these vehicles which were used to go round the country distributing cups of plain tea to popularise tea drinking.

The Tea Board also engaged the services of a link-man with an extensive knowledge of Ceylon to accompany them and act as a guide and translator. That man was none other than Lionel Wendt who was born in 1900 and went to Cambridge and the Inner Temple in London to study law. When he was in London he also studied the piano in the Royal Academy of Music. On his return to Colombo he did practise law for a short while but spent more time giving piano recitals and also established himself as the leading still photographer in Ceylon. He died in 1944 at the age of 44 years and his memory lives on in the

Lionel Wendt Arts Centre.

Although Wright had read up all he could about Ceylon and Buddhism, he decided to spend his first month travelling around Ceylon with Lionel Wendt without doing any filming. The intention was to select sites for future filming. After doing that he decided to start shooting, which took about two months. Filming took place mainly at a tea plantation and factory, of Kandyan dancing, fishermen in Negombo, village life, Colombo Harbour, Gal Vihara in Polannaruwa and Adams Peak (Fig. 1). For the Adams Peak shooting he hired fifty extras including elderly men and women, to play the part of pilgrims ascending the mountain. The journey up and down took 36 hours because of the pauses for filming and because he wanted to film the shadow of Adams Peak which is visible for about twenty minutes at dawn on a clear day.

Fig.1: Aerial view of Adam's Peak

The cine camera that Wright used was a British made Newman-Sinclair. This was a relatively light weight camera designed for field use, not studio use, because it could only take 200 feet of film which would run out in two minutes at 24 frames per second. It had a clockwork spring wound drive mechanism and had interchangeable lenses. The zoom lens for movie cameras had yet to be invented. The light weight of the camera did however enable Wright to take the camera off the heavy wooden tripod and film shots from ground level and this was a new development in documentary film production.

Some of the problems that Wright had when filming were:

(1) Magnetic sound recording was invented about ten years later and there was no way he could record sounds in the field. Therefore all field shooting was on silent film and the sound track was added later in the studios in London.

(2) If Wright had been shooting in UK, at the end of the day he could send his films to the laboratory for overnight processing and see the rushes the next day and re-shoot if necessary. There were, however, no cine film processing facilities in Ceylon at that time. As a substitute, John Taylor took the same shots that Wright filmed, but with his Leica still camera, using the same film, filters, apertures and shutter speeds that Wright used and every few days John Taylor went to an English Tea Planter who had

in his bungalow a dark room, and processed the still prints there. This gave Wright some idea of the movie shots that he had taken.

(3) He had no portable generators or floodlights. He was thus totally dependent on sunlight and used a large number of aluminium reflectors to enhance the light level.

(4) He did not have a dolly to move the camera while shooting. The only moving camera shots in the film were taken from the observation car of the Kandy train.

When the field shooting was completed Wright and Taylor prepared to return to London. But as the sound track had to be recorded in London, they took with them to London the Kandyan dancer Ukkuwa and the drummer Suramba. Lionel Wendt also went with them as their chaperone and translator.

By the time Wright returned to London, the Government had closed down and wound up the Empire Marketing Board. Promotion of intra-Empire trade was thereafter done by all the countries of the British Empire having preferential customs duty rates for goods from other Empire countries. Fortunately the Film Unit of the Empire Marketing Board was taken over lock, stock and barrel by the Post Office and renamed as the GPO Film Unit and all existing contractual commitments were honoured.

It was during the process of editing of the film, when the 23,000 feet of shot film was edited down to about 3500 feet, that Wright began to have a clearer idea of the structure of the film. Technically, the edited film made significant advances in the use of combined dissolves and superimposition of images and was far ahead of its time.

The edited film consists of four parts. The first part was titled "The Buddha" and consists mainly of the ascent of Adams Peak. Part Two is titled "The Virgin Island" and shows village life. The third part was called "The Voices of Commerce" and shows commercial activity, including the harvesting, processing and shipping of tea. This part showed the impact of colonialism on Ceylon. The final part was titled "The Apparel of a God" and consists of extensive shots of the three huge Buddha statues carved out of an existing rock outcrop in the Gal Vihara in Polannaruwa, and of Kandyan dancing (Fig. 2).

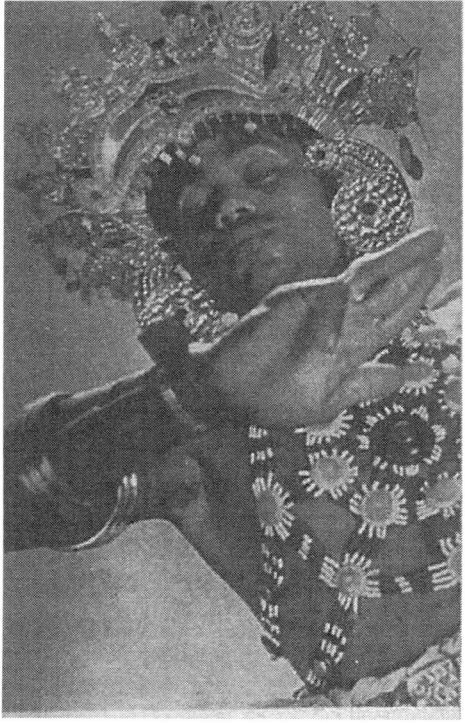

Fig. 2: Gunaya, Kandyan Dancer

In an article in the Summer 1934 edition of Cinema Quarterly, Basil Wright wrote:

"But in all the shooting our idea, apart from the production of certain one-reelers, was to achieve a co-ordination of all the primary elements of Ceylon into a construction which should carry a conviction, not merely of what Ceylon now superficially is, but of what Ceylon stands for in the line of that vital history which is measured in terms of statues, monuments, religion, and of human activity. It can easily be seen how the inter-relation of our three high spots forms the controlling factor of all the material."

The three high spots referred to are Kandyan dancing, Adams Peak and the stone images of Buddha in the Gal Vihara, Polannaruwa. A photograph of the standing Buddha in the Gal Vihara is reproduced in Fig. 3.

Fig. 3: Statue at Gal Vihara

The structure of the film is circular in keeping with the Buddhist mandala, and in the final part we come back to the start of the film and life in pre-colonial Ceylon. In the end is the beginning and in the beginning is the end. Wright was a socialist and an anti-colonialist. However, in deference to the colonial capitalism sponsorship of the film, he did not offer any overt criticism of colonialism. Instead, he presented the situation as it stood in Ceylon at that time and leaves the viewer to make up his or her mind.

Having edited the film, it now remained to add the sound track. Sound in films was relatively new at that time. The first feature film to have synchronised sound was the 1927 film "The Jazz Singer" with six songs sung by Al Jolson. Although cinemas soon installed sound systems because of their popularity with audiences, Film Societies and schools were slow to install them because of the high cost of sound projectors. The system used was optical. A variable density track corresponding to the sound signal was etched on the edge of the film. In the projector, a beam of light was focussed on to this strip and picked up by a photo-cell. This signal was amplified and converted to sound by loudspeakers.

The sound systems used by the feature film studios such as those at Ealing, Elstree and Shepperton used American systems made by RCA and Western Electric. These were expensive systems beyond the budget of the GPO Film Unit. Therefore a cheap British system called Marconi Visatone was purchased for three thousand pounds. This was an optical system but had the limitation that it could handle only two or three tracks simultaneously.

However E A Pawley who handled the audio recording for Song of Ceylon needed to record up to eight tracks which included the narration, background music, chanting, drumming and the various sound effects all of which were synthesised in the studio, such as dogs barking, bird calls, elephant trumpeting, train sounds, ship's sirens, gongs etc. This required repeated overlaid recording which led to sound synchronising problems.

Basil Wright had decided to do something unique and decided that it would be an avant-garde narration. He decided that the narration would not be a conventional commentary on the visual image, but that it would be contrapuntal to the visual image, with the two combining to form a pleasing montage. The sound track of *Song of Ceylon* should be compared with the sound track of *Negombo Coast* which has a conventional running commentary type of sound track.

Wright's original idea was to ask his friend from University days, the poet W H Auden to write poetry for the narration, but this arrangement did not materialise. Two years later this arrangement was done for another great documentary by Wright titled *Mail Train* in which the rhythm of Auden's poetry matches the clickety-clack noise of the train.

One evening when Wright was walking home from the British Museum down Tottenham Court Road, he saw in the shop window of a second hand bookshop a book titled *A Historical Relation of the Island Ceylon* by Robert Knox, which was originally published in 1681. He had never heard of this book and he bought it and when he read it he decided that that the sound track for Parts one, two and four of the film would be a narration of excerpts from this book. For the third part of the film "Voices of Commerce" the narration would be clips from business letters, stock market reports etc. When he found that British voices were inappropriate for the narration of the Robert Knox excerpts, the task of narrator was given to Lionel Wendt. Later on Basil Wright described the part played by Lionel Wendt in the making of the film and said that without Lionel Wendt there would have been no *Song of Ceylon*, and that he was one of the greatest still photographers in the world at that time.

The completed film, *Song of Ceylon*, was handed over to the sponsors, the Ceylon Tea Propaganda Board. They immediately pointed out that there must have been some misunderstanding because what they wanted was not one film of four chapters, but four separate one reel films, each with a running time of about ten minutes. So Wright had to go back to the cutting floor and edit four separate one reel films from the remaining footage. He titled them *Dance of the Harvest, Villages of Lanka, Monsoon Island* and *Negombo Coast* (Fig. 4). Of these, only the last one has been released to the public by the British Film Institute. The others seem to have gone into oblivion.

Fig. 4: Outrigger Canoes on sea shore

Song of Ceylon premiered in late 1934 as the second film in a program at the Curzon Cinema in the West End of London. The main film was *The Dark Angel* starring Merle Oberon whose mother was of

Ceylonese origin. Graham Greene was a prolific author and screenplay writer who wrote *The Third Man* and *Our Man in Havana* and many more novels. He was also the vitriolic film critic of the Spectator magazine and in his review of the evening's program he wrote that *The Dark Angel* was "one of the worst films of the year". However, Merle Oberon went on to win an Oscar for best actress for her role in this film.

As regards *Song of Ceylon,* Graham Greene wrote "it is an example to all directors of perfect construction and the perfect application of montage. Perfection is not a word one cares to use, but from the opening sequence of the Ceylon forest, the great revolving fans of palm which fill the screen, this film moves with the air of absolute certainty in its object and assurance in its method...... Mr Wright uses one of the loveliest visual metaphors I have ever seen on a screen. The sounding of a bell startles a small bird from its branch and the camera follows the bird's flight......"

The documentary film producer Martin Sheldon wrote "Beautifully photographed with an unorthodox and poetic sound track blending with an original score and an imaginative narrative, *Song of Ceylon* is a remarkably sensitive film that captures the beauty and remoteness of Ceylon and the Ceylonese heritage. It is the hallmark documentary that set the standard and by and large, solidified the documentary film as a recognised and accepted genre."

Robert Gardner, the Harvard documentary film maker spoke of the "spirituality that he evoked...... in the beginning of *Song of Ceylon* where stone, birds and water are joined to create an overwhelming atmosphere of holiness....... the effect is transfiguring. We are in his grip and we are changed forever."

Roger Manvell in his popular Pelican book titled *Film* says that "*Song of Ceylon* is possibly the greatest British produced film in any category up to 1935" and John Grierson the Producer of the film wrote that "Wright is now, I believe, the greatest lyrical documentary director in the country." Time magazine said that "Basil Wright's extraordinarily beautiful *Song of Ceylon* ...... bears about the same relation to ordinary travelogues that Keats *Ode to a Grecian Urn* bears to a cheap pottery catalogue."

Song of Ceylon was submitted to the International Film Festival in Brussels in 1935 where it won the award for the best documentary. The feature film *The Informer* which won four Academy Awards and was directed by John Ford, won the award for the best feature film in Brussels. John Ford was described by Orson Welles as the greatest director of all time. John Ford went on to direct films like *How green was my valley, The grapes of wrath,* and *The man who shot Liberty Valance.* It was expected that *The Informer* would win the award for best film in all classes in Brussels, but to everybody's surprise the Jury awarded this to *Song of Ceylon.* Unfortunately there were no Academy Awards at that time for Best Documentary Film, this category only started in 1941.

Winning these awards by *Song of Ceylon* had a tremendous impact on the documentary film movement in Britain. This resulted in the heyday of the British documentary over the next twenty years or so when British documentaries were world leaders.

We will give the last word to Basil Wright. In an interview in 1969 shortly after re-visiting Ceylon he said "*Song of Ceylon* was an experiment ......It's the only film I've made that I really loved, and it was in fact a religious experience....... it has the curious validity of being loved and admired and delighted in by the Ceylonese of today...... Well this was a magical film, you see."

Note: The two films can be viewed by following these two internet links:
Negombo Coast (10 min): **http://www.colonialfilm.org.uk/node/730**
Song of Ceylon (37 min): **http://www.colonialfilm.org.uk/node/486**

Fig. 1 is courtesy Insight Guide to Sri Lanka, APA Productions, Singapore, 1988.
Figs. 2, 3 & 4 are from Lionel Wendt's CEYLON, published by Lincoln-Praeger, London, 1950.

This Article was originally published in "The Ceylankan", Journal No. 66, May 2014.

14

Don Martino De Zilva Wickremasinghe (1865-1937) - Savant, Linguist and Epigraphist: and Notes about H C P Bell, Archaeologist (1851-1937)

by Thiru Arumugam

Introduction

Don Martino De Zilva Wickremasinghe was born in the Southern Province in 1865. He passed away in 1937. He was educated at Richmond College, Galle, which was originally called 'The Galle School'. It was founded on 25 July 1814 by the Weslyan Methodist Missionaries and is the oldest English medium school in the country. Although he did not have a Bachelor's degree, Wickremasinghe was appointed Lecturer in Tamil and Telugu by the University of Oxford. Subsequently he became Head of the Dravidian Department, University of London. He lectured at the School of Oriental Studies, University of London which was renamed in 1938 as the School of Oriental and African Studies. It has been described as the world's leading Institution for the study of Asia, Africa and the Middle-East. The jewel in its crown is the Library with over a million volumes. Wickremasinghe was completely fluent in the following languages and lectured in most of them at University level: English, German, Sinhala, Tamil, Malayalam, Telugu, Sanskrit, Pali and Prakrit.

Harry Charles Purvis Bell (1851-1937) was the son of a Major-General of Irish/Scottish descent, who was stationed in India. He was sent to England in 1864 for a public school education at Cheltenham College. After schooling, he did not enter University but spent two years tutored by a 'Crammer' who specialised in preparing students for the Civil Service examinations. He sat for the examination and passed it, being posted to the Ceylon Civil Service (CCS) in 1873. After several miscellaneous postings in the CCS, Governor Gordon appointed him in 1890 as the first Archaeological Commissioner and Head of the Archaeological Survey of Ceylon. Incidentally it was called a 'Survey' and not a Department as the Government then believed that all items of archaeological interest could be completely surveyed in about twenty years and after that all operations could cease! Bell continued in the post of Archaeological Commissioner until 1912 when he retired after nearly 40 years of service in the CCS. Although during this period of time he was entitled to several paid furloughs in Britain, he never availed of them, preferring to spend his leave in his beloved Ceylon. Even after his retirement he chose to live in Kandy.

Wickremasinghe's work in Ceylon

In 1884/5 Bell was stationed in the Southern Province and came to know Wickremasinghe, the young Pandit, and was impressed by his intellectual promise. In 1887 Wickremasinghe was appointed Assistant Librarian in the Colombo Museum Library where he worked under F H M Corbett. His main duty was to catalogue the Museum items. In 1887 Wickremasinghe compiled a "List of the *'Pansiyapanas Jataka', the five hundred and fifty Birth Stories of Gautama Buddha*" and this was published in the Journal of the Royal Asiatic Society, Ceylon Branch (RASCB), Vol. X, No. 35 of 1887, pp 205-218. To prepare this list, Wickremasinghe had to consult many ola manuscripts in temples all over the Island. Subsequently this was published as a 16 page booklet with Reinhold Rost named as a co-author. The latter was an Indologist who was the Librarian of the India Office, London.

Wickremasinghe's next publication was in 1890 when he edited *Nikaya Sangrahawa or Sasanawataraya,* which was a book written about the history of Buddhism in India and Ceylon. The original work in Sinhalese was written by Dewarakshita Dharmakirti Mahathera who lived during the reign of Bhuwaneka Bahu V (1378-1397 AD). Wickremasinghe dedicated the book to the Governor, Hamilton-Gordon, *"who, during the administration of the Government from 1883 to 1890, encouraged the study of Oriental Literature"*.

Wickremasinghe moves to Europe

By 1890 Bell was firmly established as the first head of the Archaeological Survey with his Office in Anuradhapura. He asked for Wickremasinghe to be released from the Colombo Museum to be his Native Assistant and Wickremasinghe arrived in Anuradhapura in March 1891 and was appointed Clerk/Interpreter. Meanwhile Corbett, the Head of the Colombo Museum, had arranged for his protégé Wickremasinghe to proceed on scholarship to study archaeology and philology at the German Universities of Erlangen, Munich and Berlin. Bell records in his Administrative Reports for 1893 and 1894 that Wickremasinghe left the Archaeological Survey "*on 28 February 1893 to proceed to Erlangen University to fit himself for advanced philological research. His loss has been very much felt by the Department, to which he rendered valuable service at the expense of his health*".

During his stay in Germany, the RASCB which Wickremasinghe had joined in 1889, deputed him to search the Libraries and Archives of Holland for certain Sinhalese MSS believed to have been taken from Ceylon by the Dutch during their occupation of the maritime provinces. Wickremasinghe left Germany in 1895 but had not spent sufficient time in any of the German Universities to qualify for a degree.

In 1895, Wickremasinghe moved to England and his first task was to catalogue Sinhalese material in the British Museum Library. Under the Colonial Copyrights Act, a copy of every book or manuscript published in the British Empire, in any language, had to be sent to the British Museum Library, which therefore had a comprehensive collection of Sinhalese books and manuscripts.

Wickremasinghe's book *Catalogue of the Sinhalese Manuscripts in the British Museum* was published by the British Museum in 1900. This 199 page book includes details of about one thousand Sinhalese Manuscripts. His next book was *Catalogue of Sinhalese printed books in the Library of the British Museum*. This 307 page book was published in 1901 by the British Museum and describes about 2000 titles.

During the period 1895 to 1908, Wickremasinghe published about nine articles in the Journal of the Royal Asiatic Society of Great Britain and Ireland. The tiles of the articles include "*The Thupavamsa*", "*The Avestic Ligature for hm*", "*Ceylon Epigraphy*", The Semitic origin of the Old Indian Alphabet", "*The several Pali and Sanskrit authors known as Dhammakitti*", "*Water (vatura) in Sinhalese*", "*Catalogue of the late Prof Max Muller's Sanskrit Manuscripts*", "*Sinhalese Copper Plate Grants in the British Museum*", and "*The Rev G U Pope DD*". The articles that he contributed to the Journal of the RASCB included "*List of Pansiyapanas Jataka*", "*Etymological and Historical notes on Ritigala*", "*Notes on a Sinhalese Inscription of 1745-46 AD*", and "*The antiquity of stone architecture in India and Ceylon*". He also wrote the Chapter titled *Ceylon 1215-1527 AD* which appeared in the *Cambridge History of India, Vol III*, which was published in 1928.

Richard Pischel (1849-1908) was a famous German Indologist and was Professor of Indology and Comparative Linguistics at the University of Halle, Germany from 1885 to 1902. In 1900 he published a 429 page book titled *Grammatik der Pratik-Sprachen* (Grammar of the Prakrit Languages). Prakrit is the Indo-Aryan language used for inscriptions from the time of Emperor Asoka in the 3rd century BC, and appears in literature in the form of the Pali Canon of the Theravada Buddhists. Wickremasinghe was thoroughly fluent in German following his two year stay in Germany. He studied Pischel's book and in 1905, Wickremasinghe published a book titled *Index of all the Prakrit words occurring in Pischel's Grammatik der Prakrit-Sprachen*. At 204 pages, Wickremasinghe's book was almost half the length of Pischel's book!

Epigraphica Zeylanica

Meanwhile in 1899, Bell's Administration Report says that the Report of the Committee reporting on the Archaeological Survey, chaired by Major-General F T Hobson, and appointed by the Governor, says that the "*Archaeological Commissioner considers an Epigraphica Zeylanica (publication in full with facsimiles and translations). The Committee adopts Mr Bell's suggestion that Wickremasinghe be appointed to do the epigraphical work in England and that B Gunasekera, Mudaliyar, Chief Translator to the Government be instructed to verify, or revise, Mr Wickremasinghe's conclusions. The Committee concludes that the work of the Archaeological Survey of Ceylon can be completed in 15 to 20 years"*. The last sentence is interesting. The Government of the day still believed that the Archaeological Survey of old Ceylon could be completed in a few years time and that there was no need to set up a permanent Archaeological Department!

Following the above mentioned Committee's recommendation, Wickremasinghe was appointed Epigraphist to the Government of Ceylon in 1899 and ceased to be a Colombo Museum employee. H C P Bell was very keen to publish a series of volumes of Epigraphia Zeylanica (hereafter referred to as EZ in this article) which was to be modelled on the Indian equivalent, Epigraphia Indica, the first volume of which had already appeared in 1892 and was printed in Calcutta. The EZ was to consist of reproductions of lithic and other ancient inscriptions, the text of the inscriptions, the transcripts and translations plus notes setting out the background and significance of each inscription.

Wickremasinghe was expected to work in England on the EZ, under the direct supervision of Prof A A Macdonell who was Boden Professor of Sanskrit and Keeper of the Indian Institute in the University of Oxford. Wickremasinghe moved to Oxford and started work, he was also appointed Librarian and Assistant Keeper of the Indian Institute. The arrangement was that Bell would send to Wickremasinghe 'estampages' or 'squeezes' of the inscriptions. Wickremasinghe would decipher the inscriptions and translate them and write notes about them. An estampage is a method of taking an inked impression of the inscription. The inscription is carefully washed clean and an inked paper is pressed on the inscription and an impression obtained, which is then 'mirror imaged' to provide a reproduction of the original.

The Bell sisters

Bethia Nancy Bell (born 1918) and Heather Margaret Bell (born 1920) were both daughters of C F Bell, the second son of H C P Bell. They were both employed as Library staff in the British Museum Library, and decided to write a biography of their illustrious grandfather which was titled *H C P Bell: Archaeologist of Ceylon and the Maldives*. It was published in 1993 and has 318 pages. This book will be described hereafter in this article as the 'Bell Biography'. As the sisters were both working in the British Museum Library they had access to the books and articles written by their grandfather and also to his annual Administration Reports. To complete their material for their book they decided to visit Ceylon.

When they visited Ceylon around 1990, it was already over fifty years since Bell had passed away in Kandy. They were therefore unable to meet anybody who had actually worked with Bell. However, they were cordially received by the staff of the Archaeological Department and invited to deliver a lecture about Bell at a meeting of the RASCB. As a result of subsequent newspaper coverage of the meeting, they made a totally unexpected discovery. It appears that Bell had a relationship in 1908 with Saveri Amma and had a daughter. He also had a relationship with Perumal Akka in 1916 and had a son. The descendants of these two branches of the Bell family were living in Ceylon and the Bell clan in England were totally unaware of the existence of these two branches of the family tree. Full details are included in the 'Bell Genealogy' section at the end of the Bell Biography.

Conflict between Wickremasinghe and Bell

The working relationship between Bell and Wickremasinghe regarding the production of EZ soon turned sour. Full details are given in Bell Biography Chapter 19 titled *Epigraphia Zeylanica*. Wickremasinghe complained that Bell was slow in sending estampages to him, and Bell complained that Wickremasinghe was far behind schedule in writing up EZ and hinted that this may be due to Wickremasinghe engaging in other more financially lucrative activities, meaning his lecturing duties and writing other books which will be mentioned later. The Bell Biography describes it as a *"contest by mail over thousands of miles between the Lion in the Anuradhapura jungle and the Unicorn in the Indian*

Institute, Oxford".

To these accusations by Bell, Wickremasinghe replied with dignity, enclosing letters about his work from seven scholars of worldwide reputation, including Dr J F Fleet, a retired ICS Officer and the most distinguished living Epigraphist of India. Wickremasinghe wrote to Bell, *"Allow me to submit respectfully my protest against the antagonistic attitude you continually take towards my work in spite of all my endeavours to work with you harmoniously, paying due regard to your official position as Head of the Department. It seems I can in no way please you now and I note with regret the want of that consideration which you showed me when I was your Assistant about fifteen years ago"*.

In 1907, a Clerk in the Colonial Office, London had entered a Minute in the file that *"Whatever the abstract merits of the controversy, it seems to me clear that with so offensive a Commissioner as Mr Bell, no qualified person can be expected to work as his subordinate Officer"*. Even Governor Henry McCallum entered the fray with the comment that *"Mr Wickremasinghe is an expert, Mr Bell is not. The best course will be to put a stop to unnecessary squabbling"*. Finally the Colonial Office resolved the issue by asking A B Keith to supervise the work of Wickremasinghe. Keith had three first class degrees from Oxford and was Secretary to the Crown Agents for the Colonies. Keith was later Professor of Sanskrit at the University of Edinburgh.

Wickremasinghe appointed Oxford Lecturer

Meanwhile in 1908, Wickremasinghe was appointed Lecturer in Tamil and Telugu by Jesus College, Oxford, and later promoted as a Reader. He was also an External Examiner for other Universities in the subjects of Sinhalese, Pali and Sanskrit. All this without having a degree, but this was adjusted by Oxford awarding him an Honorary Masters Degree. This must have been particularly galling to Bell, who had never entered the portals of a University.

In 1912, Bell retired from his post of Archaeological Commissioner, having reached the age of sixty years. His annual Administration Reports were some years in arrears when he retired. He completed writing these after he retired. He lived in Kandy until he died in 1937. *Epigraphia Zeylanica, being Lithic and other Inscriptions of Ceylon, Volume 1,* was finally published by Oxford University Press in 1912, the same year that Bell retired. EZ was edited by Wickremasinghe and consisted of reproductions of inscriptions, the deciphered text of the inscriptions, the English transliteration of the inscriptions, the translations of the texts and copious notes and comments on the inscriptions and their significance in charting the history of the country.

Wickremasinghe had also started on another venture. The London Publishers, E Marlborough & Co had started a 'Marlborough Self-Taught Series' of books for learning different languages. Wickremasinghe was commissioned to write for them and his first book of 120 pages was *Tamil Grammar Self-Taught* which was published in 1906. This was followed by the 96 page *Tamil Self-Taught* which was published in the same year. No doubt these books would have been popular with British Tea Planters wishing to learn spoken Tamil.

In 1916, Wickremasinghe followed up the above books with a 119 page book titled *Sinhalese Self-Taught*. The author is described as 'Lecturer in Tamil and Telugu in the University of Oxford, and in Pali and Prakrit for Jesus College, Oxford'. In the Preface to this book he refers to a separate grammar and an etymological and historical lexicon founded on the latest results of Prakrit philology being under preparation, but this was never published. Also in 1916 his 136 page book titled *Malayalam Self-Taught* was published. The author is described as 'Epigraphist Lecturer in South Indian Languages in the London School of Oriental Studies'. The only book missing in this series is Telugu Self-Taught. One wonders why he never got round to writing it, considering his knowledge of the subject.

Wickremasinghe moves to University of London

Wickremasinghe moved to London and continued to work on epigraphical studies. In 1928, the 348 page Volume II of EZ edited by him was published. Wickremasinghe is described as 'Reader in Tamil and Telugu in the University of London, Lecturer in Sinhalese and Head of the Dravidian Department at the London School of Oriental Studies'. Wickremasinghe generously dedicated this Volume to Bell "*as a small token of recognition of his eminent services to Ceylon epigraphical and historical studies*".

Volume II consists of reproductions of inscriptions and follows the same pattern as Volume I. A typical sample of the study of an inscription is given in Figure 1, and consists of the first ten lines of a slab inscription of King Nissanka-Malla (1187-1196 AD) at Ruvanvali Dagaba, Anuradhapura, with Sinhala text and translation. An English transcript of the text is also included in the original book but has not been reproduced here.

Parakrama Bahu I reigned in Polannuruva from 1153 to 1186 AD. He built many religious edifices and irrigation projects such as Parakrama Samudra (Sea of Parakrama). Wilhelm Geiger's translation of the Culavamsa devotes 124 pages to Parakrama Bahu's reign. He was succeeded by Vijayabahu II who reigned for only a year and then by Nissanka-Malla who ruled from 1187 to 1196 AD. The latter must have had an efficient publicity organisation because he left behind many inscriptions of which 18 were edited by Wickremasinghe in EZ Vols I and II. Nissanka-Malla does not seem to have been popular with the author of the Culavamsa because Geiger's translation devotes only two pages to his reign, compared with 124 pages for Parakrama Bahu I.

The content of the Inscription in Fig 1 is interesting. Culavamsa states that Vijayabahu II "*in his great mercy released from their misery those dwellers in Lanka whom his Uncle, the Sovereign Parakrama, had thrown into prison and tortured with stripes or with fetters*". However, according to the Inscription, Nissanka-Malla went further and rewarded these ex-prisoners with precious gifts and wealth so that they would desist from a life of robbery. In short, he bribed them! He also cancelled taxes for several years and permanently waived taxes on chena cultivation. It would be nice to have a Finance Minister like that!

His last days

By 1929 Wickremasinghe (Fig. 2) had failing health and eyesight problems and had to retire from his post in the University of London and return to Ceylon. He had, however, been working on material for Volume III of EZ, which was included when this Volume was published in 1933. This Volume was edited by S Paranavitana, the first Ceylonese Archaeological Commissioner, who says in the Preface that "*Dr Wickremasinghe in the first two Volumes of Epigraphia Zeylanica has set up a very high standard of scholarship*". Note that by this time Wickremasinghe had acquired a Doctorate. Volume III includes "*A Chronological Table of Ceylon Kings*" from Vijaya (483-445 BC) to the last King of Kandy, Sri Vikrama Rajasinha (1798-1815 AD). This Table was prepared by Wickremasinghe and runs to 44 pages. In comparison Geiger's list of Sinhalese Kings over the same period, in the Culavamsa, runs to only seven much smaller pages.

Anurādhapura: Ruvanvāli-dāgaba Slab-Inscription of Niśśaṅka-Malla.

TEXT.

1 ශ්‍රීමස්වූ තහග සත්‍ය ශෞය්‍යාදිගුණගණයෙන් අසාධාරණවූ ඔකාවස්රජපරපු
2 රෙන් ආ කාලිඟ චක්‍රවර්තිරාජවංශයට තිලකායමානවූ සිංහපුරයෙහි ස
3 ජාතවූ නිස්සංකමල්ල කාලිඟ පරාක්‍රමබාහු රජපාවහන්සේ ස්වවංශයට ප
4 රම්පරායාත ලංකාවිපයෙහි එක් සෙසත් කොටු මාළු පරාක්‍රමබාහුවහන්සේ දු
5 ක් රජවරිත ඉස්මැ කළ අන්දඳ අවිනයෙන් පීඩිතවූ දළිඳුවූ ගොස් සො
6 රකම් කොටු ජීවත්වන බොහො ජනයා ජීවිතාශා හැරැ සොරකම් කරන්නෙ ධනා

7 ශාවෙන් වේදැයි රන් රිදී මසුරන් මුතු මැණික් වස්ත්‍රාභරණාදිවූ උන් උන් කැමැති
   වස්තු හා
8 සරස් ගම් බිම් දී අභය දී සොරකම් හරවා සෙසු බොහො ජනයා ද ඒ ඒ
   දුඃඛයෙන් ගලවා මෙසෙ
9 මැ විවිධවිචිත්‍රවස්තුදාය‍නයෙන් සනාථකොටු මා දුන් දෙය ස්ථිරකොටු තවද
   වැඩියක් සමුදිව¹ ගතමනා
10 වේදැයි අවුරුදු ගණනාකට අය හැරැ වදරා තුන්රජයෙහිමැ හැමැ කලට කැනී
    අඩ හැරැ වදරා මා ද

TRANSLATION

The illustrious King, distinguished by a multitude of virtues, liberality, truthfulness, heroism, and the like, His Majesty Nissanka-Malla Kalinga Parakrama-Bahu, who was born in Simhapura as a tilaka ornament to the royal dynasty of Kalinga Chakravarti, descended from the line of kings of the Okkaka family, brought the Island of Ceylon, his family's heritage, under one canopy of dominion. And seeing many persons oppressed by the excessive and illegal punishments inflicted by King Parakrama-Bahu the Great, in violation of the customs of former sovereigns, and being impoverished, are eking out an existence by robbery and these men commit robberies, even at the risk of their lives, through their desire for wealth, he bestowed on them gifts of gold, silver, coins, pearls, precious stones, clothes, ornaments, and the like, whatever wealth each one desired, and also cattle, villages, and lands; and granting them security, he made them desist from stealing. He relieved a great number of other people also, each from his own misfortunes, and by similar manifold gifts of diverse kinds he gave them his patronage. Desiring that what he had given should not only be maintained but also be increased, he graciously remitted taxes for several years, and abolished the taxes on chena cultivation in the three kingdoms for all time.

Fig 1: Lines 1-10 of a Slab Inscription of King Nissanka-Malla (1187-1196) at Ruvanvali Dagaba, Anuradhapura, with Text and Translation, taken from Epigraphia Zeylanica, Vol. II, 1928, Pt. 18.

Fig. 2: D M De Z Wickremasinghe

Wickremasinghe and Bell both passed away in 1937, within a few months of each other. Volume IV of EZ was edited by Paranavitana and published in 1943. In the Preface he refers to Wickremasinghe's work on the EZ and says, of whom "*it can truly be said that he laid the foundations of the scientific study of Ceylon epigraphy on a firm basis. In the midst of his multifarious duties, first at Oxford University and later at London University, he edited and published, between 1903 and 1927, thirteen parts of this Journal, consisting solely of his own contributions. The scholarly and able manner in which Dr Wickremasinghe carried out this onerous task earned for him a first class international reputation among Indianists; but it is sad to reflect on the indifference of his own countrymen towards the great service he has rendered his country by his researches into the history, language, and culture of the Sinhalese people, incidentally bringing credit to Ceylon scholarship*".

Fig. 3: Harry Charles Percival Bell

In 1962 on the twenty-fifth anniversary of the deaths of Wickremasinghe and Bell (Fig. 3), D T Devendra wrote an article in the Journal of the RASCB (Vol VIII, Pt 1) in which he referred to the two of them and said that "*Of neither of these men has there been an obituary account worthy of their unforgettable labours in the Island's archaeology - a likely reason being that they remained in a sense, outside the world of those who later pursued the same studies*". This is particularly true of Wickremasinghe - the significant part of his work was all done in England. Since then homage has been paid to Bell by the Bell Biography, but an account worthy of Wickremasinghe is still awaited.

"*A prophet is not without honour, save in his own country ....*" (Mark 6:4)

This Article was originally published in "The Ceylankan", Journal No. 67, August 2014

15

Cocos Islands - and the Ceylon Garrison Artillery Mutiny (1942)

by Thiru Arumugam

Cocos Islands

Cocos Islands, also called Keeling Islands, is an Australian Overseas Territory in the Indian Ocean, almost exactly half-way between Ceylon and Perth. The nearest land mass to Cocos is Christmas Islands which is about 900 km to the north-east, with the Indonesian island of Java about a further 200 km north of Christmas Islands. Cocos Islands consists of two atolls and 27 coral islands, with a total area of only 14 sq km. The present population is about 600 of which about 500 are of Malay origin. Fig.1 is a map of the Islands.

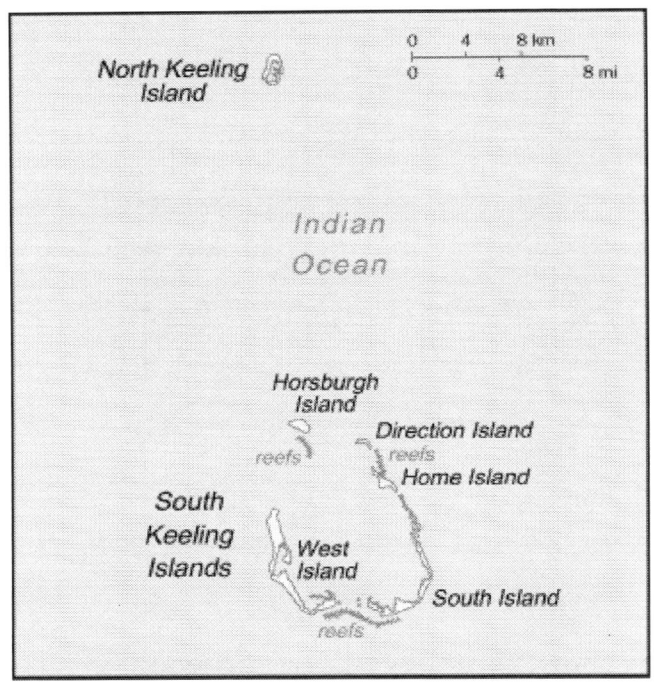

Fig. 1: Map of Cocos (Keeling) Islands
(*Courtesy Wikipedia*)

North Keeling Island consists of one atoll with a land area of only one sq km and is uninhabited. About 20 km to the south are the South Keeling Islands which consist of one atoll and 24 coral islands. Only two islands, Home Island and West Island are inhabited due to fresh water scarcity, although the locals have weekend shacks on some of the other islands. Coconut trees grow profusely on the sandy soil on most of the islands, originally sprouting from nuts carried by the waves but later commercially cultivated after the islands were inhabited.

In 1825, Captain John Clunies-Ross, a Scottish seafarer landed on the uninhabited Cocos Islands and decided to return later to make it his future home. He returned in 1827 to settle there but found that Alexander Hare, a British merchant had already settled on Home Island. Inevitably there were disputes between Hare and Clunies-Ross, leading to Hare leaving the islands permanently in 1831. Since then, seven generations of the dynasty of Clunies-Ross have lived on the islands.

The main income of the islands was from the export of coconuts, copra and coconut oil, mainly to Java. In 1857 the islands were annexed by Britain and John George Clunies-Ross was appointed Governor and Cocos was administered from the Straits Settlements (Malaya). In 1886 Queen Victoria granted the Cocos Islands in perpetuity to the Clunies-Ross family but reserved certain rights.

Telegraphy in Australia started in the nineteenth century. By 1858 there were telegraph lines connecting Adelaide, Melbourne and Sydney. It was decided to link Australia with UK. Charles Todd, the South Australian Superintendent of Telegraphs proposed that a 3200 km long, single wire, earth return, landline be erected from Adelaide via Port Augusta and through the relatively unexplored bush to Darwin. This line was completed in 1872. From Darwin an undersea cable was laid to the southern coast of Java, then a landline across Java to Jakarta. From there an undersea cable was laid to Singapore and Madras which was linked to Bombay and then on to UK. Australia now had news about events in Europe overnight without waiting for three months for news conveyed by the sailing ships.

By the turn of the century a duplicate cable route from Australia to UK was thought desirable. A route via Cocos Islands and Colombo was seriously considered. The final route selected was from Perth via Cocos Islands, Rodriguez Island, Mauritius, Durban and thence to UK following the west coast of Africa. This route would require a repeater station in Cocos. The contract was awarded to the Eastern Extension Telegraph Company who started work in 1901 and completed it in 1902. The Company leased from Clunies-Ross a portion of the uninhabited Direction Island in Cocos and built the repeater station there. In 1910 a wireless station was also built there to communicate with passing ships. This Cable and Wireless station operated until 1966 when it was closed down as it had become redundant due to satellite communications.

The German cruiser *Emden*

When World War I was declared on 28 July 1914, the German 3000 ton cruiser Emden with Captain Muller on board found herself a lone wolf in the Indian ocean. She immediately went on the rampage and sank nearly 30 British ships, mostly merchant vessels. On 22 September 1914 the Emden came within 3 km of the Madras shoreline and started firing at the massive fuel tanks of the Burmah Oil Company. A major fire started which was to burn for several days. The Emden's attack caused panic in Madras and a voluntary evacuation followed in the next few days.

The Emden then sailed round Ceylon but did not attempt to come close to Colombo as there were Allied warships in and around Colombo harbour. The Emden did however capture or sink five merchant ships which were on their way to or from Colombo Harbour. The Emden then decided to sail south to the British territory of Diego Garcia, which had no wireless or cable connections and would therefore be unaware that Germany and Britain were at war. The Emden spent a few days there and purchased provisions and fresh water while the crew stretched their legs on shore after several weeks at sea. The exploits of the Emden around Ceylon were well covered by the media and since then the word 'Emden' became part of colloquial Sinhala and Tamil languages to describe a crafty and resourceful person.

On the morning of 09 November 1914 the Emden arrived at Cocos Islands with the express intention of destroying the cable repeater station. A shore party was sent who set about destroying the cable and wireless repeater installation with gusto but before that the operators had sent out the wireless signal "SOS strange warship at entrance". This signal was passed on to the 5400 ton Australian cruiser HMAS Sydney which happened to be sailing near Cocos and was escorting the first convoy carrying Australian and New Zealand soldiers off to the war in Europe. Most of them ended up in Gallipoli.

Sydney broke off from the convoy and came to Cocos to investigate. Sydney had all the advantages over the Emden. She was faster with a top speed of 26 knots compared with Emden's 23 knots. More importantly she had six inch guns compared with the Emden's four inch guns, which gave her guns a greater range by a few thousand yards. All that Sydney had to do was to stay outside the range of the Emden's gun and pepper her with its own shells. The battle lasted a few hours and the Emden was terminally damaged. Captain Muller decided that Emden would not be a war trophy and ordered full steam ahead and rammed the ship into the coral reef surrounding North Keeling Island where she remained as a wreck for nearly forty years. The young Australian Navy had won its first naval battle.

Private Callistus Seneviratne who served in the Ceylon Light Infantry in Cocos Islands in 1942 recounted to Noel Crusz that one of his first tasks was to be a member of a group sent to North Keeling Island to destroy a petrol storage tank secretly built there by the Japanese. While he was there he boarded the wreck of the Emden and ripped off some brass items which he later got a Malay mechanic to turn into a shield with an inscription of the name of the ship.

For further details of the Emden see Douglas Ranmuthugala's article *The Last Voyage of the Emden* in the February 2008 edition of this Journal. The whole story is comprehensively covered in a recent 467 page book by Mike Carlton, *First Victory -1914- HMAS Sydney's hunt for the German Raider Emden*, William Heineman, 2013.

The Ceylon Garrison Artillery Mutiny

The years between the two World Wars was a quiet period in the Cocos Islands. All that changed, however, when Japan invaded Malaya at the end of 1941 and Singapore fell in February 1942. The British Government then transferred administrative control of Cocos from Singapore to the Governor of Ceylon, Sir Andrew Caldecott.

The cable link between Australia and UK via Java and Singapore was no longer available as these territories were under Japanese occupation. The only remaining cable link to UK was via Cocos Islands. Short wave radio communications can always be monitored by the enemy and codes cracked if the messages are coded, but cable messages cannot be eavesdropped by the enemy. It was therefore vital that the Cable Station in Cocos must be protected from damage or takeover by the Japanese.

As Australia was unable to spare troops for the defence of Cocos, troops were sent from Ceylon for this purpose. It was decided that a platoon of 32 personnel from the Ceylon Light Infantry (CLI) would be based on Direction Island where the Cable Station was located. It was also decided to install two six inch guns on neighbouring uninhabited Horsburgh Island. The gap between the two islands was the only entrance deep enough for ships to enter Cocos lagoon, and the guns would cover this entrance. The guns were installed and operated by the Ceylon Garrison Artillery (CGA). Fig. 2 shows one of the six inch guns as it stands rusted forlornly today on Horsburgh Island beach, pointing towards Direction Island which is on the horizon.

Fig. 2: Six inch Gun erected by the Ceylon Garrison Artillery in Horsburgh Island still stands
(Photo by Pip Giovanelli with permission from Australian Heritage Photographic Library)

In March 1942 the Officer commanding the Ceylonese troops in Cocos was Captain George Gardiner. He was a British Accountant working in Colombo who volunteered to join the Army when war broke out. His second in command was a Eurasian, Lieutenant Henry Stephens, a planter who was only nineteen years old. The two of them considered themselves racially superior to rest of the 37 CGA troops (Bombardiers and Gunners) who were Burghers, Sinhalese and Tamils, school leavers from leading Ceylon schools. In an independent Ceylon many of these troops would be considered Officer material. Lines of communication between the Officers and the troops were very poor and all this led to sowing the seeds of mutiny.

Noel Crusz was in Colombo in 1942 and was in personal contact with the Chaplains who were present at the execution of the mutineers. The subject of the mutiny engrossed his attention for the rest of his life and he later interviewed those soldiers who served in Cocos, and their relations. He trawled through the files in the Public Record Office in Kew, London and viewed the original records of the court martial. His lifetime of research culminated in the 248 page book *The Cocos Island Mutiny* published by Freemantle Press, 2001, and copies of the book are available from them. It is a fascinating read. This summary of the mutiny is based largely on Crusz's book reproduced with permission from the Publishers.

Gratien Fernando (Fig. 3) was born in 1915 of Buddhist parents. He studied at St Thomas College, Mount Lavinia. He was later converted to Roman Catholicism by Father Brennan of St Philip Neri's in Pettah. When war broke out he volunteered to join the CGA. He had no particular allegiance to the British and felt passionately about independence for Ceylon. In Cocos he would spend his off duty time listening to the short wave radio propaganda 'Tokyo Rose' broadcasts by the Japanese from Singapore and Manila. These broadcasts spoke of 'Asia for the Asians' and throwing off the yoke of European colonial rule. The Japanese proposed a "Greater East Asia Co-Prosperity Sphere" where heavy industry would be in Manchuria and Northern China and countries in the south would produce raw materials and foodstuff.

Fig. 3: Mutiny leader, Bombardier Gratien H Fernando
(Reproduced with permission from Fremantle Press, from "The Cocos Islands Mutiny" by Noel Crusz, 2001)

By March 1942, Malaya, Singapore and Indonesia were all under Japanese occupation. In the first week of April 1942, Colombo and Trincomalee were bombed by the Japanese. On 10th March 1942 the Indian troops in Christmas Island successfully mutinied, imprisoned the British Officers, hoisted a white flag and invited the Japanese in Java to come and take over, which they did. All this led Gratien Fernando to believe that the conquest of Ceylon by the Japanese was imminent. Added to this there was the resentment of the CGA troops to the racism of the Officers and the scene was set for a mutiny.

CSA Member Somasiri Devendra in his review of Crusz's book (Sunday Times, 20th May 2001) says that "There are fault lines in Ceylonese society that become deep fissures under the strain of homesickness, extreme youth, poor training, bad leadership and enforced solitude in a strange land."

Fernando believed that nearly half the Ceylonese CGA troops in Horsburgh Island would support the mutiny. The plan was to imprison the two CGA Officers, disarm the loyal soldiers, then train the six inch guns on Direction Island and call upon the CLI troops there to surrender and then send a radio message to the Japanese in Christmas Islands to come and take over Cocos Islands.

The mutiny was set for the moonless night of 8th/9th May 1942. The rifles of the five men sleeping in the guard room were taken away while they slept. However, Lt. Stephens woke up and came out of the Duty Officer's Room with his revolver to see Gunner Carlo Gauder standing six feet away with a rifle. An exchange of about ten rounds followed but amazingly neither was hurt even though they were only six feet apart, except for a leg wound for Lt. Stephens. Both studied at St Joseph's College at the same time and clearly neither could bring it among themselves to seriously harm a schoolmate.

Meanwhile Fernando climbed up the sixty foot high Observation Tower to get the Thompson (Tommy) sub-machine gun. He was, however, unable to attach the magazine in the dark. It is not known whether it was a box magazine or a drum magazine. He climbed down and went to the battery entrance to retrieve a gas powered Bren machine gun that he had previously hidden there.

Loyal soldier Gunner Samuel Jayasekera heard the telephone at the top of the Observation Tower ringing repeatedly and he started climbing up to answer it. Near the top of the Tower he was challenged by mutineer Gunner Benny De Silva. Hearing no answer, De Silva fired a single shot at Jayasekera fatally wounding him. Jayasekera was later given a funeral with full military honours on 10th May 1942. In 1958 the Commonwealth War Graves Commission recovered his remains from Horsburgh Island and re-buried them at the Kranji War Memorial, Singapore. A photo of his gravestone at Kranji is in Fig. 4. It is believed that this is the first time that this has been published.

Captain Gardiner had now woken up for the sound of firing and he came out and challenged the mutineers. Fernando had by now collected the Bren gun and he pointed it at Gardiner and pulled the trigger. Unfortunately for Fernando, and fortunately for Gardiner, the gun jammed at this vital moment probably due to a gas stoppage and the game was up. Fernando picked up a white towel and surrendered with the rest of the mutineers. They were rounded up and taken into custody.

Gardiner wasted no time in arranging for a court martial which was held from 12th to 16th May 1942. In view of the limited number of Officers at Cocos, it was set up as a Field General Court Martial. This enabled him to bypass the requirements of an Ordinary General Court Martial and appoint himself as the President even though he was the Commanding Officer of all the accused. It also meant that that he did not have to arrange for Defending Officers for the accused and they had no option but to conduct their own defence and cross-examine witnesses. These are travesties of natural justice. The other Members of the Court Martial were Lt. Henry de Sylva of the CLI and Lt S K Menon of the Ceylon Medical Corps.

The charges were (1) Causing a Mutiny, (2) Joining a Mutiny, and (3) Failing to inform the Commanding Officer of an intended Mutiny. There were fifteen accused and the names of those found guilty and the charges against each are given in Table 1. The Court Martial found eleven of them guilty and acquitted the remaining four accused. Death sentences were passed on seven of the accused and the remaining four were sentenced to varying terms of penal servitude or imprisonment.

Fig. 4: Gravestone of Gunner Samuel Jayasekera at Kranji War Memorial, Singapore
The Ceylon Artillery Coat of Arms is on top with the Latin motto *QUO FAS ET GLORIA DUCUNT* (Where right and glory lead). The inscription reads:
*2189 GUNNER
MAHADURA SAMARIS
DE SILVA JAYASEKERA
CEYLON GARRISON ARTILLERY
9TH MAY 1942 AGE 23*
(Photo by Sudhaman Arumugam)

Gardiner signalled the verdicts to Admiral Sir Geoffrey Layton, Commander-in-Chief, Ceylon, based in Colombo, and asked for confirmation of the sentences and permission to execute those on death sentence by firing squad at dawn the next day. To his surprise, he was told not to execute the prisoners and that arrangements would be made to bring the convicted soldiers to Colombo.

The convicted soldiers were brought to Colombo and the records of the Court Martial were sent to the Judge Advocate General in New Delhi for review. On 07 June 1942 the Assistant Judge Advocate General replied that all convictions on the first count (Causing a Mutiny) be set aside. The reasons for this were not clear, presumably they were procedural reasons. As regards the other charges, the death sentences on three of them, Gratien Fernando, Carlo Gauder and Benny de Silva were confirmed. The remaining eight were sentenced to varying periods of penal servitude or imprisonment.

There were many pleas for mercy by Ceylonese politicians and priests on behalf of those sentenced to death but Admiral Layton and Governor Caldecott were unmoved. Gratien Fernando accepted his fate and refused to plead for what he called "the White Man's clemency" and his last words when he was led to the gallows were "Loyalty to a country under the heel of a white man is disloyalty". He was hanged in Welikade Jail on 05 August 1942. His parents were distraught by the execution and both died of grief within a few weeks.

Benny de Silva was hanged two days later on 07 August. Carlo Gauder was hanged the next day 08 August, a few days after his twenty-first birthday. His last words were "Oh God, I don't deserve this".

Name	Where educated	Charges	Court Martial Verdict	Revised Verdict by Assistant Judge Advocate General
Bombardier Gratien H Fernando	St Thomas College	1, 2 & 3	Death Penalty	Death penalty on Charges 2 & 3
Gunner Carlo A Gauder	St Joseph's College	1, 2 & 3	Death Penalty	Death penalty on Charges 2 & 3
Gunner G Benny de Silva	St Sebastian's College	1, 2 & 3	Death Penalty	Death Penalty on Charges 2 & 3
Gunner R S Hamilton	Trinity College	1, 2 & 3	Death Penalty	Penal servitude for three years on Charge 3
Gunner G D Anandappa	St Anthony's College	1, 2 & 3	Death Penalty	Penal servitude for three years on Charges 2 & 3
L/Bombardier K W J Diasz	St Benedict's College	1, 2 & 3	Death Penalty	Penal servitude for four years on Charge 3
Gunner A Joe L Peries	St Joseph's College	1, 2 & 3	Death Penalty	Penal servitude for four years on Charge 3
Gunner A B Edema		1 & 3	One year imprisonment	No change in sentence. Charge 3 only
Gunner Mark A Hopman		3	Three years penal servitude	Commutation left to Confirming Officer
Gunner F J Daniels		3	Seven years penal servitude	Commutation left to Confirming Officer
Gunner Ken R Porritt	Royal College	3	One year imprisonment with hard labour	Commutation left to Confirming Officer

Table 1: Cocos Island Mutiny: List of convicted soldiers. The Charges were (1) Causing a Mutiny, (2) Joining a Mutiny, and (3) Failing to inform the Commanding Officer of an intended Mutiny. (Table collated from information in Noel Crusz *The Cocos Islands Mutiny*, 2001, with permission from the Publishers, Fremantle Press.)

All three were buried in Kanatte Cemetery in unidentifiable graves. They were not commemorated by the Commonwealth War Graves Commission. The three of them will go down in history as the only Commonwealth Serviceman executed for mutiny in World War Two. History will also decide on the impact of their actions in ushering in the independence of Ceylon which came less than six years later.

The Post-War Years

In 1955, the Cocos Islands were formerly detached from control from Singapore and officially became Australian Territory. Although the Australian Government had a permanent presence in the islands, John Cecil Clunies-Ross continued as the ruler of the Islands. However the Australian Government was not happy with the conditions of the workers, particularly because wages were paid by plastic tokens which could only be redeemed in the Company Store. Ultimately, in 1978 the Australian Government bought Cocos Islands from the Clunies-Ross family for six million dollars and the ruler, J C Clunies-Ross, was sent into exile to Perth where he moved into a modest house. His son and grandsons (the seventh generation of the Clunies-Ross dynasty), continue to reside in Cocos as ordinary citizens with no special privileges.

The copra industry ceased in 1980 and nowadays the main income is from government jobs and occasional tourists. However, the unemployment rate is much higher than the Australian national average. There is excellent scuba diving and snorkelling in the islands. Virgin Blue flies to Cocos from Perth three times a week via Christmas Islands.

Recently Cocos has been in the news because it is a favoured destination for asylum seeker boats from Ceylon. This is because it is several hundred kilometres closer to Ceylon than Christmas Islands and only half the distance from Ceylon to mainland Australia. There are no detention facilities on Cocos and the asylum seekers are housed in the Cocos Club which is taken over for the purpose, until arrangements are made to send them elsewhere a few days later. The Cocos Club Manager says that "It is just frustrating. We are a forgotten little dot of fly poo in the Indian Ocean". The Club sent a claim for $79,000 to the Australian Government for compensation for loss of use of the Club when asylum seekers arrive and for providing meals, sarongs, tee shirts and flip-flops to the asylum seekers. Due to a recent change in Australian Government policy no boats from Ceylon have succeeded in reaching Cocos in the last few months.

There are, however, two black clouds on the horizon. The first is a report in the Washington Post newspaper that the US Base in Diego Garcia, which is over 1000 km south-west of Ceylon, has outlived its usefulness as America winds down its military activities in the Middle East and Afghanistan, and will be mothballed in a few years time. But America will need a Drone Base in Australasia and Cocos Islands seems like a good bet. The Cocos Islanders worry is that if this happens they may be repatriated to the Australian mainland, in the same way that all the Diego Garcians were compulsorily repatriated to Mauritius and the Seychelles. This will be the end of their idyllic lifestyle on a tropical island.

The other black cloud is that by the end of this century due to global warming the Inter-Governmental Panel on Climate Change has forecast that the median level rise of the Indian Ocean could be 0.8 metres. If this happens, the Cocos Islands will virtually cease to exist. It may suffer the same fate as Kiribati (formerly Gilbert Islands) which is expected to be completely submerged in thirty years. Kiribati has purchased about 25 sq km of land in Fiji and the younger generation are being encouraged to emigrate while the going is good.

This Article was originally published in "The Ceylankan", Journal No. 69, February 2015.

16

Am I My Brother's Keeper? - the life and outline of four selected books by Ananda Kentish Coomaraswamy (1877-1947)

by Thiru Arumugam

"The artist is not a special kind of person; rather each person is a special kind of artist" Ananda Coomaraswamy.

Sir Muttu Coomaraswamy (1834-1879) was the first Ceylon Tamil Knight. He was a lawyer and Member of the Legislative Council of Ceylon. He was the first non-Christian Asian to be called to the English Bar. He married an English lady, Elizabeth Beeby, who was a Lady-in-Waiting to Queen Victoria. They had one child, Ananda Kentish Coomaraswamy (Fig. 1), who was born in Colombo on 22 August 1877. Sir Muttu's sister's sons were Sir P Ramanathan and Sir P Arunachalam. Sir Muttu passed away when Ananda was only two years old. He was brought up by his mother who never married again.

Fig. 1: Ananda K Coomaraswamy (1877-1947)

Ananda grew up in England where he studied at the newly established Independent School, Wycliffe College in Stonehouse, Gloucestershire. His name appears in the School's list of 25 'Notable Old Wycliffians'. In 1897 he entered the University of London, graduating in 1900 with first class honours in Geology and Botany. He returned to Ceylon and in 1903 was appointed as the first Director of Mineralogical Surveys. In 1904 he identified the mineral Thorianite found in gem pit gravel washings, and his work on this subject led to the award of a Doctor of Science degree from the University of London in 1906. He was the first Ceylonese to be awarded this degree, the highest degree of the University of London. He called the mineral Uraninite in an article in *Spolia Zeylanica*, but it was later identified as a new mineral and then followed an extended correspondence with double Nobel Prize winner Madam Curie about its radioactivity. She suggested that it be named 'Coomaranite' but he declined the honour.

In 1905 he founded the Ceylon Social Reform Society. The Society was *"formed in order to encourage and initiate reform in social customs amongst the Ceylonese, and to discourage the thoughtless imitation of unsuitable European habits and customs"*. The Society published a Journal at six monthly intervals which it continued to do for five years until it closed down.

After a few years he moved to India and studied Indian and South-East Asian Arts and Crafts, Religion and Metaphysics. He later wrote books on Buddhism such as 'Buddha and the Gospel of Buddhism', 'Elements of Buddhist Iconography' and 'Hinduism and Buddhism'. He described his work as *'research not only in the field of Indian Art but at the same time in the wider field of the whole of traditional theory of Art and of the relation of man to his work, and in the fields of comparative religion and metaphysics to which the problems of iconography are a natural introduction'*. Encyclopaedia Britannica describes him as a *'pioneer historian of Indian Art and foremost interpreter of Indian culture to the West'*. He set about dismantling Western prejudices about Asian Art through an affirmation of the beauty, integrity and spiritual density of traditional art in Ceylon and India. He claimed fluency in 36 languages, where his definition of fluency in a language is the ability to read a scholarly article without referring to a dictionary. Anthony Ludovici the famous British writer and philosopher says of Coomaraswamy *"Thanks to his command of Greek, Latin and Sanskrit, he was probably the greatest scholar of his age in the Scriptures of both East and West, and was therefore a formidable exponent of the philosophical and ontological foundations of his cultural doctrines"*.

He refused to join the British armed services in World War I on the grounds that India and Ceylon were not independent and declared himself a conscientious objector and publicly argued his position. As a result he was exiled from the British Empire and a bounty of 3000 Pounds placed on his head by the British Government and his house was seized. He therefore moved to USA in 1917 together with his extensive art collection. He was appointed Curator of Indian and Oriental Art at the Boston Museum of Fine Arts and worked there for the next thirty years until he retired in 1947. His entire private art collection was transferred to this Museum and the Asian collection there is described as *'among the finest in the Western world'*. The Museum's Catalogue presently lists 1419 artworks as originating from the Coomaraswamy Collection. Even today the Head of this Section is designated as the 'Ananda Coomaraswamy Curator of South Asian and Islamic Art', and the Ananda Coomaraswamy Annual Lecture is held every year.

In 2002 James S Crouch published 'A Bibliography of Ananda Kentish Coomaraswamy'. Crouch says that *'this book documents the remarkably productive career of one of the great minds of the 20th century'*. The book describes in detail American, English and Indian first editions of 95 books written by Coomaraswamy, plus descriptions of a further 96 books containing contributions by him and details of 909 contributions by him to periodicals and newspapers. What a prolific writer! In addition Crouch lists and describes 216 books and articles written up to 1992 by **others** about Coomaraswamy and his work. It is not surprising that it took Crouch 20 years to complete the Bibliography which runs to 430 pages. All this writing by Coomaraswamy was while he continued in his 'day job' of Museum Curator for 30 years and Visiting Lecturer at nearby Harvard University where he also supervised the work of PhD students.

Coomaraswamy reached the age of 70 years on 22 August 1947 and retired from his post in the Museum. He was given a felicitation dinner at which he gave his last public speech. He said *"This is my 70th birthday, and my opportunity to say: Farewell. For this is our plan, mine and my wife's, to retire and return to India next year; thinking of this as an 'astam gamana', 'going home' ."*

His plans were to go to India and work on a new translation of the principal Upanishads which Schopenhauer described as *"the production of the highest human wisdom"* after which Coomaraswamy planned to retire from worldly life and become a *Sannyasi* with renunciation of material desires. Alas, this was not to be. A few days later on 9th September he was working in his study on a revised edition of "The

Dance of Shiva" when his wife called him out to the garden. He went out to the garden and suddenly collapsed. An ambulance was called but it was too late. He had passed away peacefully in his beloved Japanese garden.

Roger Lipsey had this to say in his three volume book "Coomaraswamy": *"It is a very strange moment when a man of this kind dies. He had spent much of his time 'placing' death, understanding its role in the life of the world and the life of man, investigating all ideas concerning what part of man inevitably returns to dust and what part inevitably returns to the Lord, what the various conditions of the soul can be as it separates out from the body and moves, like an arrow released towards the sky"*. The remains were cremated and part of the ashes scattered in the Ganges and the rest scattered in a river in Ceylon.

It is not surprising that Ananda Coomaraswamy has been described as *'the most distinguished Sri Lankan of our time'*. Outlines of four selected books out of the 95 books written by him are given below.

Medieval Sinhalese Art

This was Coomaraswamy's first major book and it was published in 1908. The full title of the book is *"Medieval Sinhalese Art: Being a Monograph on Medieval Sinhalese Arts and Crafts, mainly as surviving in the eighteenth century, with an account of the structure of Society and the status of Craftsmen"*. It has 340 pages with 55 plates consisting of multiple photographs and 153 illustrations. The photos were selected from over a thousand relevant photographs taken by his English wife Ethel Mary Coomaraswamy (nee Partridge) on glass plate negatives which was the technology of the day.

To avoid going cap in hand to Publishers begging them to publish his book, Coomaraswamy did the next best thing and bought the ailing Essex House Press. Using his considerable inherited wealth he bought a small church called Norman Chapel in Broad Campden in Gloucestershire. He used part of the premises as his residence and moved the machinery of Essex House Press to the rest of the building. Hand printing of the book started in September 1907 and was completed in December 1908. The layout of the book, which is a work of art in its own right, and the printing of the 425 copies were supervised by him. Proof reading of the book was done by Don Martino De Zilva Wickremasinghe of the Indian Institute, Oxford, whose life and work have been described in the August 2014 edition of this Journal.

Copies of this first edition are quite rare in Australia, only two copies are traceable in libraries open to the public and the restricted access copy in the New South Wales State Library is numbered No. 313 of 425 copies. A copy of this first edition was available in the National Library, Canberra, but is now missing, perhaps it has gone walkabout. A copy of the third edition (1979) is available, but the reproduction of the illustrations is inferior. A similar numbering scheme was used, on the suggestion of the late Mike Udabage, for the 10th Anniversary "Collectors Issue" November 2007 edition of this Journal, when each of the 420 copies printed was individually numbered.

Coomaraswamy believed that in traditional societies there was no distinction between fine arts and other arts such as decorative arts, useful arts, handicrafts etc, nor between religious and secular arts. For him the most humble folk art and the loftiest religious creations were an outward expression not only of the sensibilities of those who created them but of the whole civilization in which they were nurtured.

He says in the book that rural arts and crafts are *"the only true art discoverable in Ceylon today. In a few years it may be gone forever. I have tried to make a picture of it, before it is too late"*. The reason for its probable disappearance he says is that *"In Ceylon as in India, the direct and indirect influence of contact with the West has been fatal to the arts. The two most direct causes of this adverse influence have been the destruction of the organisation of state craftsmen, following British occupation"*, and that this occupation *"has driven the village weaver from his loom, the craftsmen from his tools, the ploughman from his songs and has divorced art from labour"*.

Among the subjects discussed and illustrated in detail in this 340 page large sized (35 by 27 cm) comprehensive study of the subject are: Particular account of the Artificers, Elements of Sinhalese Design and Ornament; Architecture; Woodwork; Stonework; Figure Sculpture; Painting; Ivory, Bone, Horn and Shell work; Metal work - Iron, Brass, Copper and Bronze; Gold and Silver; Jewellery; Lac work;

Earthenware; Potter's songs; Weaving; Embroidery; Mat Weaving and Dyeing; and History of Sinhalese Art.

The release of the book created as much interest in UK as in Ceylon and Roger Fry the leading art critic and member of Virginia and Leonard Woolf's Bloomsbury set observed that Coomaraswamy *"is not concerned with the history of great masterpieces; his work is almost as much sociological as aesthetic; he seeks to investigate and explain the methods of Sinhalese craftsmen, to fix the outlines of an artistic industry and education before it finally disappears...... In this direction Dr Coomaraswamy's record is likely to be of great value"*.

As typical examples of illustrations from the book, Fig. 2 is the Flag of the Three Korales and the back cover of this book shows a 19th century Verandah Ceiling Painting from the Dalada Maligawa, Kandy. The original painting was in shades of brown and green and represents a forest scene with parrots, hares, squirrels and hunters. The illustration was copied by Ethel Mary Coomaraswamy but the original in the ceiling of the Dalada Maligawa no longer exists.

Fig. 2: Flag of the Three Korales
(from Medieval Sinhalese Art)

Bronzes from Ceylon, chiefly in the Colombo Museum

This book was first published in 1914 by the Colombo Museum as the first in a series of Memoirs of the Colombo Museum. It has 31 pages of text followed by 189 photographic reproductions of bronze sculptures, including a few from Coomaraswamy's private collection. Some of these sculptures he says are *'of spiritual and aesthetic rank nowhere surpassed'*.

Among the Buddhist Bronzes, eleven images of Buddha are illustrated. The largest of them is a 55 cm high sedentary statue and Coomaraswamy dates this as 5th or 6th century. It was found in Badulla and was presented to the Museum by G F K Horsfall, possibly a Government Agent. Coomaraswamy says that *'The existence of a Mahayana cult in Ceylon is abundantly supported by the discovery of many images of*

Bodhisatvas and Mahayana feminine divinities in Ceylon'. By far the largest of the Bodhisatva images is the 46 cm high bronze, probably of Maitreya, discovered in 1898 near the Thuparama Dagoba in Anuradhapura. Also illustrated are four small images of Avalokitesvara.

The largest of the Hindu bronzes are the eight images of Siva as Nataraja, all were found in Polonnaruva. The largest of these is nearly a metre high. However, Coomaraswamy does not rate these too highly and says that *'they are inferior as works of art to the best of the Buddhist images, the best images of Saiva Saints in Ceylon and the two splendid Natarajas in the Madras Museum'*. There are also eight smaller size images of Parvati, Siva's consort. There are seven images of Saiva Saints and Coomaraswamy describes the image of Sundara Murti Swami as having *'a touching quality of suddenly arrested movement and breathless wonder, and is one of the most remarkable works of all Indian art'*.

Also illustrated is the stunning bronze of the Goddess Pattini, nearly five feet (1.5m) tall, see Fig. 3. Coomaraswamy dates this as 7th or 8th century. It was found in the east coast of Ceylon and presented by Governor Brownrigg in 1830 to the British Museum in London where it is a prized exhibit, right at the entrance to the South Asian section. Coomaraswamy says that it *'is a most striking work; the face strong and thoughtful, and the modelling of the body and limbs most admirable'*. Since it has spent nearly 200 years in London, it is about time that it is returned to its country of origin.

Fig. 3: 1.5 m high 7th century Bronze Goddess Pattini from east Ceylon and now in the British Museum
(Photo: Thiru Arumugam)

The Dance of Shiva

This 196 page book was first published in New York in 1918 and is a collection of 14 essays, mainly about Indian art and culture. It is one of his best known books. In the title essay 'The Dance of Shiva', Coomaraswamy describes three dances of Shiva. He describes Shiva's dance as *'the clearest image of the activity of God which any art or religion can boast of'*. Of the three dances described, it is the third one that is most commonly expounded in Bharatha Natyam dance recitals. One of the names of Shiva is Nataraja, or Lord of the Dancers.

The legend is that a group of belligerent rishis endeavoured to destroy Shiva by incantations. They also created a monster (Muyalaka) in the shape of a dwarf but Shiva broke the creature's back by placing his foot on him. Shiva then proceeded to perform a mystic dance and it is in this form that he is portrayed as Nataraja in statues. In this form he has four hands and braided locks, he is adorned with jewellery, in his hair is a cobra and the mermaid figure of Ganga. One right hand holds a drum, the other is uplifted to indicate 'fear not'. One left hand holds fire, the other points down to the vanquished demon, Muyalaka. The left foot is raised. He stands on a lotus pedestal from which springs an arch (tiruvasi) which encircles him, fringed with flame. Fig. 4 is a 12th century bronze Nataraja statue exhibiting all of these features. It is about a metre in height and was excavated in 1907 at Siva Devale No.1 in Polonnaruva and is now in the Colombo Museum.

Fig. 4: 12th century, 1.0 m high Bronze Nataraja from
Siva Devale No. 1, Polonnaruva, now in the Colombo Museum
(Photo Thiru Arumugam)

All Nataraja statues are basically similar and differ only in detail. This is because the sculptor in making a statue of a Hindu God has to follow strictly the guidelines and principles laid down in the Shilpa Sastras (ancient texts on architecture and the arts).

The significance of the dance is described as follows, *"The Supreme Intelligence dances in the soul..... for the purpose of removing our sins. By these means, our Father scatters the darkness of illusion (maya), burns the thread of causality (karma), stamps down evil (mala), showers Grace, and lovingly plunges the soul in the ocean of bliss (ananda). They never see rebirth, who behold this mystic dance".*

Am I My Brother's Keeper?

This 110 page book is a collection of seven essays written by Coomaraswamy between 1943 and 1946 and was published by The John Day Company, New York, in 1947, which was the last year of Coomaraswamy's life. The book has an Introduction written by Robert Allerton Parker who was a Journal Editor and Critic. Publication of the book was arranged by Coomaraswamy's friends as part of their campaign to nominate him for the 1947 Nobel Prize for Literature. Alas, this was not to be, because Coomaraswamy died suddenly of a heart attack on 09 September 1947, a few days after his 70th birthday which was on 22 August 1947. That was the end of his nomination for a Nobel Prize because the prize cannot be awarded posthumously. It is a pity because Ceylon missed a chance of having its first Nobel Prize winner.

The 1947 Nobel Prize for literature was awarded to the prolific French writer Andre Gide whose work centres on a continuous search for intellectual honesty. Interestingly, Coomaraswamy quoted Andre Gide in his last speech which was on the occasion of a 70th birthday felicitation dinner for Coomaraswamy when he said *"Perhaps the greatest thing I have learned is never to think for myself; I fully agree with Andre Gide that 'toutes choses sont dites deja'* (everything has already been said) *and what I have sought is to understand what has been said"*.

The title of the book comes from the Bible (Genesis 4:9). Cain and Abel were the sons of Adam and Eve. Cain was a farmer and Abel was a shepherd. They both made offerings to God but only Abel's offering was accepted. This upset Cain and when they went to the fields, Cain killed Abel. Later when God said to Cain, "Where is Abel your brother?" he answered, "I do not know; **Am I my brother's keeper?**" Cain's words have come to symbolise people's unwillingness to accept responsibility for the welfare of their fellow human beings.

The first essay in the book has the same title as the book. It is a stinging attack on Occidental imperialism, especially upon the cultural imperialism which arrogates to itself a civilizing mission. He says that *"Systems of education* (in the East) *should be extensions of the cultures of the peoples concerned, but of these the Western educator knows little and cares less"*. He goes on to say that *"If West races are in future to do anything for the peoples whose cultures have been broken down in the interests of commerce and 'religion', they must begin by renouncing what has been aptly called their 'proselytizing fury'."* He says that he is *"speaking for those who once before 'bowed low before the West in patient, deep disdain'."* About Art he says that *"The disintegration of a people's art is the destruction of their life, by which they are reduced to the proletarian status of hewers of wood and drawers of water, in the interests of a foreign trader, whose is the profit"*. In other words, the West has failed to be the "brother's keeper" as far as the East is concerned.

One of the essays in the book is titled *'Spiritual Paternity' and the 'Puppet Complex'*. 'Spiritual Paternity' is described as the belief by some Australian Aboriginals and Pacific Islanders that during conception a spirit-child has entered the woman, and the 'Puppet Complex' is the Balinese view (inherited from their Indian genesis) that the body is like a puppet pinned together at the joints and that what pulls the string is that Being within us. This 14 page essay is an example of the prodigious depth of Coomaraswamy's self-taught scholarship, remembering that his University education and Doctorate were in Botany and Geology. The short essay is followed by 86 References and End Notes referring to this essay only. The References and End Notes run to 12 pages in a smaller font than the 14 page essay, and have a higher word count than the essay. Typical references are to Plato's Laws (his last Dialogue); Dante's Paradiso (the third part of his Divine Comedy); the Summa Theologica of Thomas Aquinas; a quote of Harvard Professor Ashley Montagu (*"in spite of our enormous technological advances we are spiritually, and as humane beings, not the equals of the average Australian aboriginal"*); and to India where he has numerous quotes from the Rigveda, Upanisads and Bhagavad Gita (*"Thy concern is with the action only, not with the result"*).

It shows the width and depth of his all-embracing self-taught scholarship.

On writing an Autobiography.

MUSEUM OF FINE ARTS
BOSTON, MASSACHUSETTS

May 1946

Dear Mr Durai Singam,

In reply to your various letters I enclose some information. I must explain that I am not at all interested in biographical matter relating to myself and that I consider the <u>modern</u> practise of publishing details about the lives and personalities of well known men is nothing but a vulgar watering to illegitimate curiosity. So I could not think of spending my time, which is very much occupied with more important tasks, in hunting up such matter, most of which I have long forgotten; and shall be grateful if you will publish <u>nothing but the barest facts</u> about myself. What you should deal with is the nature and tendency of my <u>work</u>, and your book should be 95 per cent on this. <u>I</u> wish to remain in the background, and shall <u>not</u> be grateful or flattered by any details about my self or my life; all that is <u>anicca</u>, and, as the "wisdom of India" should have taught you, "portraiture of human beings is <u>asvargya</u>". All this is not a matter of "modesty" but one of <u>principle</u>. For statements about the nature and value of my work you might ask the Secretary of the Bhandarkar Oriental Research Society, Poona 4, and Dr Murray Fowler, c/o G.and C. Merriam Co., Springfield, Mass., USA to make some statement, as both are familiar with it. I would not mind sending you press reviews of my books, but it would take more time than I have to hunt them up; I have no secretary who would do this sort of thing for me!

Very sincerely

Ananda K Coomaraswamy

When S Durai Raja Singam asked Ananda K Coomaraswamy for some information for inclusion in a Biography about AKC, his reply is given above and shows his modesty.

(Courtesy: "Who is this Coomaraswamy?" by S Durai Raja Singham, Malaysia, 1980).

This Article was original published in "The Ceylankan", Journal No. 70, May 2015.

17

Devinuwara - the City of Gods

by Thiru Arumugam

Introduction

Devinuvara, literally the City of Gods, is the southernmost point in Ceylon. It is just past Matara on the coastal road to Tangalle. During British days it was known as Dondra and its Tamil place name is Thondeswaram. The southernmost point on the sea-shore is called Dondra Head and Ceylon's tallest and most powerful lighthouse is located here. It was built in 1890 and it is 49m tall with its beams visible up to 50 km away. All materials for its construction came from UK, including the granite rock bricks. For further information on the lighthouses of Ceylon please see the November 2013 edition of this Journal for the Colombo Chapter Synopsis of Muhaj Hamin's talk on "Lighthouses in Sri Lanka and life in a Lighthouse".

Devinuwara has a historical connection with Gods. In 1917 the renowned historian, P E Pieris, who held a Doctorate in Literature from the University of Cambridge, wrote an article titled *Nagadipa and Buddhist remains in Jaffna* which was published in the Journal of the Royal Asiatic Society (Ceylon). In the article he wrote that (p 17/18) *"Long before the arrival of Vijaya there were in Lanka five recognized Isvaram of Siva which claimed and received the adoration of all India. These were Tirukketisvaram near Mahatittha, Munissaram dominating Salawata and the Pearl Fishery, Tandesvaram near Mantota, Tirukkonesvaram opposite the great Bay of Koddiyar and Nakulesvaram near Kankesanturai."* Tandesvaram near Mantota (Matara) is his reference to Thondeswaram or Devinuwara.

Local legends believe that Ravanna (circa 2500 BC), the King of Lanka had his main palace near the Dondra lighthouse in an area which is still known as Kovil Watta. Ravanna was a Brahmin and an ardent worshipper of Siva and it is therefore probable that he would have built a temple for Siva here. Local belief is that the final epic battle between Ravanna and Rama also took place in Devinuwara.

Around 110 AD the Greek cartographer Ptolemy drew a map of Ceylon which is probably the oldest known map of Ceylon. In this map he identifies the southernmost tip of Ceylon as *Dagana, civitas sacra luna* and has drawn an icon of a temple at this point. Ptolemy did not personally visit Ceylon but relied on information and sketches from Greek sailors who visited the Island. As a result there has been some corruption in place names in his map. For example, Anuradhapura is marked as *Anurogramum*. It is therefore likely that his *Dagana* is a corruption of the place-name Deva-nagara, an alternative name for Devinuwara. As regards *civitas sacra luna* this means 'city sacred to the moon'. An alternative name for Siva is Santhirasekarer, because he is depicted with a crescent moon in the locks of his hair. It is therefore possible that Ptolemy's icon and reference was to a Sivan temple in this location. Ptolemy's map of Taprobane is reproduced as Fig 1.

Fig. 1: Ptolemy's 110 AD Map of Taprobane
(Courtesy Wikipedia)

Devinuwara today

The artefacts that exist today at Devinuwara include the 7th century AD *Galge* (a stone temple), a Pansala, the Othpilima Vihara, a Dagaba, a recent standing statue of Buddha, a three storey Vishnu Devale, an elaborately carved 14th century stone archway large enough for an elephant to pass through during the perahera (the only archway remaining of four that were here originally), about 200 stone pillars over three metres tall, a Kataragama Devalaya, seven Devalayas in a row in one building, the *Simhasana* shrine of Skanda, and a four metre high lamp post with four relief carvings which have been identified by Paranavitana, the first Ceylonese Archaeological Commissioner, as Siva, Ganesha, Karthikeya and Brahma.

The *Galge* is a small all-stone temple about a kilometre north of the main temple complex. It is about eight metres long and five metres wide. It consists of two rooms, a *garbha-grha* (or holy of holies), with an ante-chamber in front. There are no windows and ornamentation is limited. It has been studied in detail by Paranavitana. He is of the opinion that this temple is pre-Chola in style and is therefore of the Pallava period, and he dates it at around the 7th century AD. This would probably make it the oldest existing all-stone temple in Ceylon, and make it contemporaneous with the Pallava Shore Temple in Mahabalipuram, Tamil Nadu, which is considered to be among the earliest all-stone temples in India. There are no inscriptions in or near the *Galge* to enable us to identify what deity was enshrined in the 'holy of holies'. Local legends are that Rama stood on this spot and fired the fatal arrow which killed Ravanna who was standing at the location of the present Vishnu Devale in the valley below. A picture of the *Galge* can be seen in Fig. 2.

Fig. 2: Galge: 7th century AD Stone Temple, Devinuwara
(Photo: Thiru Arumugam)

The three storey Vishnu Devale is probably about hundred years old and is in the Kandyan style of architecture. The Vishnu Devale can be seen in Fig. 3. The Kataragama Devalaya of Skanda is a separate small shrine and the seven Minor Devalayas are in seven rooms in one building. The seven deities are Valli Matha (Skanda's consort), Pattini, Saman, Gana Deviyo (Ganesha), Aluth Deviyo (Dadimunda?), Basnaiva Deviyo and Devol Deviyo.

Fig. 3: Three storey Vishnu Devale, Devinuwara
(Photo: Thiru Arumugam)

Administrative control of the Devales is the responsibility of the Basnayake Nilame. He is neither appointed, nor is it a hereditary post. He is elected for a five year term by the votes of the 650 Grama Niladharis (formerly called Village Headmen) in the region. The persons responsible for the religious services in the Devales are called Kapuralas. It is a hereditary position and the Devinuwara Kapuralas can trace their lineage back over ten generations or more. The Kapuralas act as intermediaries between the devotees and the deities. The devotee gives a tray containing the offering of betel leaves, flowers, fruits, rice etc. to the Kapurala and tells him the nature of his problem e.g. health, financial, employment, downfall of enemies etc. The Kapurala then goes into the inner sanctum sanctorum and implores the help of the deity in solving the devotee's problem. The Kapurala chants an appropriate *yatika* (petitionary prayer) addressed to the deity. The deity being a Bodhisattva (enlightened being) also gains merit by helping the devotee. The Kapurala retains a part of the offering and returns the rest to the devotee.

Another God associated with Devinuwara is Skanda. Local belief is that Skanda (son of Siva) crossed the Indian ocean in a *Gal-pahura* (granite raft) and landed at Devinuwara. He rested on a stone slab near the beach, called the *Simhasana,* while local residents paid obeisance to him. A shrine has been built to enclose the stone slab, which is close to the beach and about a kilometre directly south of the main temple complex. A 1950s picture of the *Simhasana* shrine with a thatched roof is shown in Fig. 4. Two stone pillars which formed part of the original temple here can be seen in the front of the picture. The thatched building has since been replaced by a permanent building. From Devinuwara, Skanda made his way overland to Kataragama where he courted and married the Veddah Princess, Valli, and he is venerated as the Kataragama Deviyo.

Fig. 4: The Simhasana where Skanda rested, Devinuwara
(Courtesy: Archaeological Dept.)

Fig. 5 is a picture of a Siva Lingam which was unearthed by a gardener digging a flower bed in the garden of the Othpilima Vihara about twenty years ago. The proportions of the Lingam which is tall and slender, and the fact that it only has a base and no pedestal seem to indicate that it is not of the Chola period and could be early Pallava period or around 7th century AD or earlier. At the top there is recess where there would originally have been a large precious stone. The recess is surrounded by a carving of a crescent moon pointing upwards. The crescent moon is found in the locks of Siva's hair, and this Lingam may have been the holy of holies of an ancient Sivan temple and could have been the reason for Ptolemy's description of this place as a 'city sacred to the moon'.

Fig. 5: Ancient Siva Lingam Found near Othpilima Vihara, Devinuwara
(Courtesy: Inst. of Fine Arts)

Time line of past events

The earliest reference in the Mahavamsa to the building of a Vihara here is that it states that about 659 AD King Dappula 'erected the Khadirali-Vihara and offered to the God'. In the year 790 AD King Dappula Sen had a vision that a red sandalwood log would land at Devinuwara floating across the sea. He had this log carved into an image of Vishnu and built a temple here and installed it as the principal deity. This image remained here for about two centuries and was later moved, finally to the cave temple in Dambulla.

The reason for the veneration of Vishnu by Ceylon Buddhists arises from events arising during the passing away of the Buddha as described in Mahavamsa Chapter VII, Verse 5. He called upon Indra, King of the Gods to protect Vijaya and Lanka. *"When the lord of gods heard the words of the Tathagata he from respect handed over the guardianship of Lanka to the god who is in colour like a lotus"*. Geiger, the translator of the Mahavamsa, adds a footnote at this point *"Devass' uppalavannassa, that is Visnu. The allusion is to the colour of the blue lotus (uppala)"*. Over the subsequent centuries, it would appear that the gods Vishnu and Upulvan had independent identities in Ceylon until about the 15th century, when the identity of Upulvan was subsumed into that of Vishnu. As a result the Devales in Devinuwara, Kandy, Alutnuvara, Hanguranketa, Gadaladeniya, Lankatilaka, Dambulla, Aluthgama, etc., are now described as Vishnu Devales.

There are many subsequent references to Devinuwara in the Mahavamsa including the restoration of the Vihara by Vijayabahu in 1058 AD, the building of a monastery named 'Nandana' (The Delight) by Vira Bahu in 1244 AD, the restoration of the temples by Parakrama Bahu II in 1250 AD and the building of an image house and four stone gateways (one of which still exists) by Parakrama Bahu IV in 1325 AD.

Ibn Battuta was a Moroccan who lived in the 14th century. He was the world's greatest traveller, travelling continuously for nearly thirty years and visiting the countries of the world where Muslims lived, including Ceylon. He came to Ceylon in 1344 AD and visited Devinuwara and wrote that in the temples *"there are about a thousand Brahmins and Yogis, and five hundred young women, daughters of the nobility of India who sing and dance all night before the image. The idol is of gold, and as large as a man.*

In place of eyes it has two large rubies".

A stone inscription found in the district dated 1410 AD, which is now in the Colombo Museum, has similar text in three languages Chinese, Persian and Tamil. The Tamil text describes gifts from the Ming Dynasty Chinese Emperor Yung Lo to the God of the Tenavaram (another name for Devinuwara) Temple. The gifts include 1000 kalancus (5 kg) of gold, 5000 kalancus of silver (26 kg), 50 rolls of silk, copper vessels, gold stands, scented oil and sandalwood. The Chinese Emperor wanted to curry favour with the Ceylonese as he was desperately anxious to acquire Buddha's tooth relic.

Sandesa Poems

In the 14th and 15th centuries the popular genre for Sinhala poems was the Sandesa poems. In these lengthy poems a bird flies carrying a message from somebody at a starting point to a recipient at its destination. During its flight the bird describes the starting point, the sights it sees along its route and finally describes the destination. Sri Rahula Thera, the leading scholar of his day, was an exponent of this style of poetry. The Sandesa poems which describe Devinuwara are the Paravi Sandesa, Kokila Sandesa, Mayura Sandesa and the Tisara Sandesa. The following verse from the Paravi (Dove) Sandesa written by Sri Rahula Thera in 1445 AD describes the temple dancers of Devinuwara. Paul Pieris, who had a Doctorate in Literature from Cambridge, said that this is the finest description of temple dance in Sinhala poetry. The translation is as follows:

With flowers entwined in the tresses of their hair,
And garlands pendant from their necks,
The women dance, as dances the budding leaf
Of the mango twig to the music of the breeze.

The Kokila (Cuckoo) Sandesa, was written by a poet who was a 15th century Principal of the Irugalkula Pirivena in Dondra. The verse which commences the description of Dondra, the starting point of the Cuckoo's flight has been translated as follows:

Know Dondra is this place, this city fair,
Where stately mansions, bright as Meru, shine;
Where gems and coral show in plenteous store,
In princely shops adorning lively streets;
Where lotus blows in orchards e'er in bloom,
And strains of music fill the balmy air.

Based on the information provided in the Sandesa poems and in the stone inscriptions, Archaeologival Commissioner Paranavitana concluded that Devinuwara had four categories of holy places:
1) Viharas (Buddhist monastic establishments)
2) Devales (Shrines of Sinhalese Gods)
3) Kovils (Shrines of Hindu Gods)
4) Agrahara (Area for residence of Brahmins)

Tragic event

In 1587 AD, King Rajasiha I laid a siege of the Portuguese Fort in Colombo. In retaliation the Portuguese despatched Thome de Sousa with a fleet to create a diversion by ravaging the southern coast of Ceylon. The fleet arrived at Devinuwara and the Portuguese historian Diogo do Couto describes *"the pagoda of Tanavarem half a league from this city, the most celebrated and most resorted to by pilgrims of all in the Island, excepting that of Adam's Peak"*. On seeing the arrival of the Portuguese ships, the inhabitants of Devinuwara fled leaving a ghost town. Diogo do Couto described the action of Thome de Sousa and his men in the following words:

"The first thing in which they employed themselves was to destroy the idols, of which there were more than a thousand of diverse forms, some of clay, others of wood, others of copper, and many of them gilt. Having done this they demolished the whole of that infernal structure of pagodas, destroying their vaults and cloisters, knocking them all to pieces, and then proceeded to sack the storehouses, in which they found much ivory, fine clothes, copper, pepper, sandalwood, jewels, precious stones, and ornaments of the pagodas, and of everything they took what they liked, and to the rest they set fire, by which the whole was consumed. And for greater insult to the pagoda, they slaughtered inside several cows, which is the most unclean thing that can be, and for the purification of which are required great ceremonies. And they also set fire to a wooden car made after the manner of a towered house of seven stories."

When the destruction was completed all that remained were only some of the stone structures: the Galge stone temple up on the hill; one of the four stone gateways; and about four hundred stone pillars, some standing, some fallen and some broken, and all of these still exist.

The recovery

Then followed a bleak period for Devinuwara, until the middle of the 17th century when King Rajasiha II regained control of this area by driving out the Portuguese. He built a simple Vishnu Devale. In 1807 Cordiner visited Devinuwara and reported that there was a Vishnu Devale and a humble Vishnu Kovil of mud and thatch. The 20th century saw considerable rebuilding activity with the construction of a three storey Vishnu Devale, Pansala, Viharas, Dagaba and a standing Buddha statue the height of a coconut tree. Improvements to the temple complex are still ongoing.

In the thirteenth century Parakrama Bahu II inaugurated an annual Esala Perahera which is since held every year in July/August. Archaeological Commissioner H C P Bell claims that this "was the origin of such processions in the Island" and this would therefore considerably pre-date the Kandy Perahera. The Devinuwara Vishnu Devale authorities claim that over 750 such annual peraheras have been held. The organisation of the Perahera is the major annual task for the Basnayake Nilame and the Devinuwara Perahera is second only to the Kandy Perahera in grandeur and popularity.

Anuradha Seneviratna was formerly a Professor in the University of Peradeniya and Head of the Department of Sinhala. What he wrote about Polonnaruva in the introduction to his book *Polonnaruva: Medieval Capital of Sri Lanka* applies equally appropriately to Devinuwara: *"With Buddhist and Hindu shrines in the same grounds embracing a common architectural tradition……….. (it) was a city that symbolised the unity and integrity of the island as well as the religious and ethnic harmony which prevailed in medieval Sri Lanka."*

This Article was originally published in "The Ceylankan", Journal No. 71, Aug 2015.

Excerpt from a lecture given to the Tamil Seniors Association, Sydney on 28 May 2015 on *Thondeswaram*

By Thiru Arumugam

We would next like to share with you a specially commissioned short Dance Drama about Thondeswaram. In 1999 Shruthi Laya Sangam, London, decided to stage *Pancha Ishwaram,* a Bharatha Natyam Dance Drama about the five ancient Sivan Temples of Ceylon.

Sanmugam Arumugam was asked to provide background information about the temples. This was sent to Madras to Padma Bushan Lalagudi Jayaraman, arguably the foremost violinist in South India, to write the lyrics. This was done by him in conjunction with Prof V V Subramaniam. Lalgudi composed the music for this dance drama. He was later awarded the National Film Award for the best Music Director for his music for the Tamil film *Sringaram*.

The choreography for the dance drama was by Vijayalakshmi Krishnaswamy, Professor of Dance at Kalakshetra. She also trained the dancers who were mainly Kalakshetra Graduates. The Vocalist was S P Ramh, an "A" Grade Carnatic Vocalist of All India Radio, New Delhi. The concert was held on 16 October 1999 in the Great Hall of the University of London. At end of concert, Lalgudi gave the vote of thanks, came to down to the audience and draped a *Pon Aadai* (Golden shawl) on 94 year old Sanmugam Arumugam.

A free verse translation of the words of the lyrics of the Thondeswaram segment of the dance drama is given below.

Thondeswaram Dance Drama

A free verse translation of the Tamil Lyrics

Scene: Thondeswaran Temple courtyard.

Narrator: An old devotee laments about the destruction of the temple and shares this nostalgic memory with a sympathetic listener. At the end the listener consoles the old lamenting devotee with the hope that the temple will be restored to its former glory.

Old Devotee: Oh God, may I pray at your holy shrine?
You, who bless those who homage pay to you,
Tripura Sundari's consort divine.

I'm yearning for your compassion, so you
Must pay heed to my endless suffering,
And will you not grant me some graces few?

You are the Lord, I am your devotee,
Turn not a deaf ear to my humble plea,
When will you shower blessings onto me?

Listener: List'ning to your sad song, Oh devotee,
I was so moved, my heart was deeply touched.
Share with us your mournful melancholy.

The devotee looks up with affection,
And rising slowly to his full height, starts

                    Praising the glory of Thondeswaran.

Note: *A sequence of pure dance by the Listener follows*

Old Devotee: Haven't you heard of Thondeswaram of yore?
               The Sivan temple with towers beauteous
               And it's sacred, sprawling buildings galore.

               Our ancestors here prayed in ancient days.
               Six times daily were poojas held, and they
               Sang and danced, lauding you in many ways.

Note: *A short dance sequence by the ensemble,*
       followed by a Siva pooja are enacted at this point.

Old Devotee: The storm tossed sailors safely guiding light,
               The sea-shore temple's mighty gopuram,
               Beacon for vessels on the ocean's might.

               Now hear the story of how this temple,
               Was destroyed by men zealously evil,
               And then your heart will surely tremble.

               The sturdy Lingam, full of tranquil grace,
               The Nandhi patiently chewing the cud,
               Mute witnesses in this sacrosanct place.

               The stories we have heard resemble dreams.
               One day surely these dreams will come true,
               The lost glory will be restored, it seems!

Listener: Faith can't be ignored, it's not a surprise
          Say the four Vedas; you can be sure that
          Thondeswaram will, like a phoenix rise.

          That much is truly certain. So until then,
          Devoted holy one, peace be unto you,
          And by His grace this must surely happen.

          Amaithee, Amaithee.

(The assistance of Mrs P Sundaralingam in this translation is gratefully acknowledged.)

18

The first Ceylonese family in Australia – revisited

by Thiru Arumugam

The subject of the first Ceylonese family in Australia has been previously discussed in this Journal in the February 2002 issue by Sydneysider Glennys Ferguson in her article *The first Ceylonese family in Australia*. She is a direct sixth generation descendant of William O'Dean who arrived in Sydney as a convict with his family from Colombo in the Brig *Kangaroo* on 07 February 1816, about 28 years after the First Fleet, and they were the first Ceylonese family to settle in Australia. CSA Member M D (Tony) Saldin has also written about O'Dean in the February 2013 issue of this Journal in his article *Malay Mercenaries in the Military Service of Kandyan Kings*.

No apology is offered for revisiting this subject for the following reasons. Firstly, a rough survey of current CSA members shows that about two-thirds of them joined CSA after February 2002 and are therefore unlikely to have read Ferguson's article. Secondly, this year marks the 200th anniversary of O'Dean's court martial in Colombo on 04 May 1815 and his banishment for life to Australia, he left Colombo with his family on 19 August 1815. Thirdly, the digitisation of some records by the National Library of Australia, the State Library of New South Wales (NSW) and State Records NSW has given easy access to finding more information about O'Dean without having to pore over reels of microfilm. Finally, Paul Thomas is a Lecturer at Monash University, Melbourne and has recently done considerable research on the life of O'Dean and his work as a Malay Interpreter in Australia. This research has resulted in his publication of a twenty page article titled *Oodeen, a Malay Interpreter on Australia's frontier lands* which was published in May 2012 in the Journal "Indonesia and the Malay World", 40:117. He has also written five pages about O'Dean under the sub-title *Oodeen: Diplomacy and trade in the north* in the book "Macassan History and Heritage: Journeys, Encounters and Influence" edited by Marshall Clark and Sally K May, ANU, 2013. This article draws on all of the above mentioned sources, together with much additional material.

O'Dean in Ceylon

As Ferguson has pointed out, one of the difficulties in searching for information about O'Dean are the many variations in the spelling of his name in official records. The variations include O'Dean, O'Deane, Odean, Odeen, Oodeen, Hoodine and Wooden. His first name as used by him in Australia is William, but towards the end of his long life he used the first name of John, and the name on his tombstone in St Stephens Church, Camperdown, Sydney, is John Odean. The Blogspot "Vinod's Places" gives his original surname as used in Ceylon as Jainudeen, which could very well have been his original surname, which was later anglicized to John O'Dean. This propensity towards name variation also extended to his six children who used different first names at different times. In this article he will be referred to as William O'Dean.

William O'Dean was born about 1775, either in Ceylon or possibly in Ambon Island. This small island is in the Maluku Archipelago in Indonesia and is near New Guinea. Ambon was the original headquarters of the Dutch East India Company until the founding of Batavia, now called Jakarta. There is some evidence that O'Dean may have served with the Dutch Ambonese Regiment in Ceylon.

When the British took over Ceylon from the Dutch, O'Dean was appointed a Drum Major, a non-commissioned officer in the British 1st Ceylon (Malay) Regiment. In 1803 Governor Frederick North decided to attack Kandy, but the war turned out to be a disaster for the British who had to surrender. Meanwhile according to sources quoted by Thomas (2012), O'Dean had already become concerned about deteriorating conditions in the Malay Regiment including poor wages and decrease in the opium allowance and he deserted the British Army and he was soon followed by 50 or 60 others. O'Dean joined the King of Kandy's troops and actively fought against the British. He married a Kandyan lady, whose first name is given in subsequent Australian records as Eve, and they had three children born in Ceylon, a girl followed by two boys, and they lived peacefully in Kandy until 1815.

In 1815, Governor Robert Brownrigg launched an attack on Kandy. This time the British campaign was successful. O'Dean was taken prisoner by the British near Gannoruwa on 23 February 1815. He was court-martialled in Colombo under Case No. 72 on 04 May 1815 on charges of desertion and sentenced to be hanged. However, the sentence was commuted to transportation for life to Australia and he was also allowed to take his family with him, a rare privilege for convicts at that time. Thomas (2012, p.127) says that: *"The commander of the Malay Regiment had successfully argued against a sentence of capital punishment for Odeen, but the court made it clear it was not for 'any feeling of the Traitor Odeen' that it offered the pardon; the primary motivation for the change in sentence being consideration of the sentiments within the Malay regiment."* Perhaps it was felt that execution of O'Dean would affect the morale of the Malay regiment.

The voyage of the Brig *Kangaroo*

HM Colonial Brig *Kangaroo* was a two masted sailing ship with square sails which was launched in 1812. It was an armed Brig which was based in Australia from 1814 to 1817. Lachlan Macquarie was the fifth Governor of NSW and held the post from 1810 to 1821. He oversaw the transition of NSW from a penal colony to a free settlement. Previously he had served the British Army in India and Ceylon and commanded the 73rd Regiment of Foot. In 1796 he was directly responsible for the capture of Colombo and Galle Fort from the Dutch, the latter with barely a shot being fired.

He has ensured that his name will never be forgotten in NSW by naming many places after himself. Bill Bryson in his travelogue *Down Under* makes a droll dig at the Scotsman Macquarie:

"You really cannot move in Australia without bumping into some reminder of his tenure. Run your eye over the map and you will find a Macquarie Harbour, Macquarie Island, Macquarie Marsh, Macquarie River, Macquarie Fields, Macquarie Pass, Macquarie Plains, Lake Macquarie, Port Macquarie, Mrs Macquarie's Chair (a lookout point over Sydney harbour), Macquarie's Point and a Macquarie town. I always imagine him sitting at a desk, poring over maps and charts with a magnifying glass, and calling out to his first assistant 'Hae we no' got a Macquarie Swamp yet, laddie? And look here at this wee copse. It has nae name. What shall we call it, do you think?'

And that's just some of the Macquaries by the way. Macquarie is also the name of a bank, a university, the national dictionary, a shopping centre and one of Sydney's principal streets. That's not to mention the forty-seven other Roads, Avenues, Groves and Terraces in Sydney that, according to Jan Morris, are named for the man or his family."

In early 1815 Macquarie instructed Lieutenant Jeffries who commanded the Brig *Kangaroo* to sail from Port Jackson, Sydney to Colombo and back. The *Kangaroo* set sail on 19 April 1815 from Port Jackson. According to the 11 May 1816 issue of *The Hobart Town Gazette and Southern Reporter* on board were about 100 members and families of the 73rd Regiment. The *Kangaroo* sailed along the east coast of Australia following the route taken by Captain Cook barely 35 years earlier. However before reaching Cape York the ship grounded on a sand bank and could only be set free by jettisoning some of her fresh water stocks and part of the passenger luggage. The ship sailed through the Torres Straits and reached Timor where she anchored for a week and took on board fresh supplies. The *Kangaroo* finally reached Colombo Roads on 24 July 1815.

On 02 August 1815 the Governor of Ceylon, Sir Robert Brownrigg, instructed Jeffries to sail to the Gulf of Mannar to help free the Arab ship *Shaw Aram* which was stuck in a shoal with detachments of His Majesty's 22nd and 87th Regiments on board. The mission was successfully completed and the *Kangaroo* returned to Colombo, setting sail for Sydney on 19 August 1815. On board were O'Dean, his wife and three children and also eight convicts who had escaped from Australia as stowaways on ships but had been apprehended in Ceylon and India. The *Kangaroo* on her return voyage called at Point de Galle, Trincomalee, Penang, Acheen in Sumatra, Prince of Wales Island in the Torres Straits and finally reached Sydney on 07 February 1816.

O'Dean in Sydney

The arrival of an Asian convict family was considered an interesting event and was recorded on page 1 of the Sydney Gazette of 17 February 1816 in an article written by the Editor (see Fig. 1). The article comments that "*The appearance of this little family is truly interesting: and the more so, when the feeling mind considers that misfortune has brought them to a part of the world in which it is scarcely conceivable that they can find any means of contributing to their own support. Their native country abounds in fruits, and all natural luxuries of the East, which are attainable almost without the necessity of human exertion*".

The Kangaroo has brought hither from Colombo several convicts, some of whom are prisoners who had escaped from this Colony, and who, from the strict attention of the Police throughout all the British ports in India, could not possibly escape the vigilance of the Government.

One of the prisoners brought by the Kangaroo is a Malayan, who was drum major of the 1st Ceylon regiment in the memorable Kandyan war in 1802-3; & having gone over to the enemy, was upon the late capture of the Kandyan country taken prisoner, and condemned to be shot; which sentence was commuted to transportation for life to this territory; whither he is accompanied by his wife and three fine children. The man, who appears to be intelligent, gives an account of the death of several officers who were made prisoners by the Kandyan Monarch; among whose unfortunate number were Major Davey, of the 1st Ceylon, and Captain Romley, of the 73d Regt. He is dark complexioned, approaching to a black, and is about 5 feet 10 inches in height. His wife, who is a Cinglasse, being a true descendant of the aboriginal inhabitants of the island, is of a small stature, handsomely formed, of a dark olive complexion, and agreeable features, as are also her three children, of whom the two youngest are boys.—The appearance of this little family is truly interesting; and the more so, when the feeling mind considers that misfortune has brought them to a part of the world in which it is scarcely conceivable they can find any means of contributing to their own support. Their native country abounds in fruits, and all the natural luxuries of the East, which are attainable almost without the necessity of human exertion.

Fig. 1: The O'Deans arrive in Sydney
(The Sydney Gazette, 17 Feb 1816)

O'Dean, however, was soon able to contribute to his own support by obtaining a job as a Watchman in the Sydney Dockyards. He had a record of good conduct and as a result he was able to get a Ticket of Leave from Governor Macquarie, who was known to be lenient in these matters, even before he completed the minimum period of service for a Lifer which was 8 years service under one Master. The Ticket of Leave permitted him to work or be self-employed within a given district of the Colony, and to acquire property. Church attendance was compulsory, as was appearance before a Magistrate when required. The Convict Index Citation 4/4430, Reel 774, page 174 (State Records NSW) states that on 28 November 1821, the Governor granted O'Dean a Conditional Pardon (CP). This meant that he was now free, the only condition was that he could not return to his home country. In March 1826, O'Dean successfully petitioned the Governor and obtained employment as a Constable of the Government Domain.

An extract from a register of ex-convicts and their families prepared about late 1824 is in Fig 2. The family name is stated as Hoodine. There is no first name for the head of the family, his status is given as CP (Conditional Pardon), arrived in Sydney in the ship *Kangaroo* with a life sentence and presently employed as a Watchman in the Sydney Dockyards. His wife's first name is given as Eve, with status CF (Certificate of Freedom). A total of six children are listed. The first is an unnamed two month old infant with status BC (Born in the Colony). She was subsequently named Esther. The oldest is the 18 year old daughter Sarah (CF). Next is a 16 year old son Sancho (CF) followed by 14 year old son Cameron. The three oldest children were all born in Ceylon, and the three younger children were born in Sydney. Next is a daughter Cooper, although her age is given as 14 years she cannot be the same age as Cameron and must be younger. She is followed by a two year old daughter named Moore.

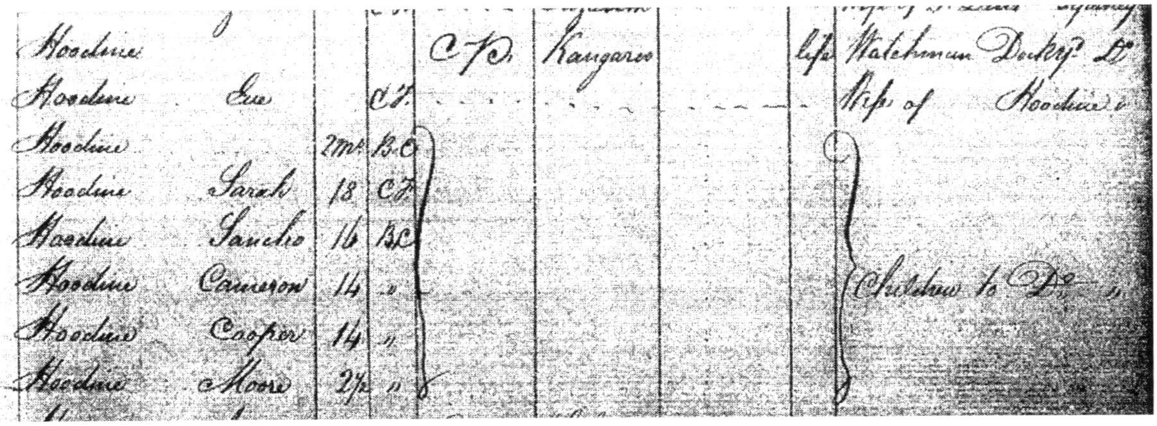

Hoodine			CP	Kangaroo	life	Watchman Dockyd Do
Hoodine	Eve		CF			Wife of Hoodine
Hoodine		2m	BC			
Hoodine	Sarah	18	CF			
Hoodine	Sancho	16	BC			
Hoodine	Cameron	14	"			Children to Do
Hoodine	Cooper	14	"			
Hoodine	Moore	2½	"			

Fig. 2: The "Hoodine" family, 1824
(Courtesy: State Records NSW 1787-1859 and findmypast.co.uk)

O'Dean in Fort Wellington

At that time (1825) the western border of New South Wales was the 129 degree longitude line (Thomas 2012, pp 129/130). At present this line is the eastern border of Western Australia. The States of Queensland, Victoria, South Australia, Western Australia and the Northern Territory and the settlements of Brisbane, Darwin, Melbourne, Adelaide and Perth did not exist at that time. Tasmania was a penal colony named Van Diemen's Land. New South Wales therefore covered nearly two-thirds of the country and present day Western Australia was known as New Holland.

The Government was aware that Indonesian fishermen were seasonally visiting the northern coast of Australia to fish for trepang (sea cucumber) which they dried in temporary campsites on land and exported to China. The Government was anxious to establish contact with these fisherman to trade with them and also obtain information from them about Dutch activities in Dutch East Indies. The establishment of a Fort would also to discourage the Dutch from getting ideas about settling in New Holland (i.e. Western Australia). There were also vague hopes that this settlement would one day become a second Singapore. The latter had already been founded in 1819 by Stamford Raffles and was a successful trading post.

A settlement was therefore established in 1824 called Fort Dundas in Melville Island which is due north of present day Darwin. It was found, however, that this location was outside the sea route of the Indonesian fishermen and it was not possible to establish contact with them. It was therefore decided to found a new settlement in Raffles Bay (Fig. 3) in the Coburg Peninsula which is about 300 km north-east of present day Darwin. This was called Fort Wellington after the Duke of Wellington because it was founded on 18 June 1827, the twelfth anniversary of the Battle of Waterloo.

Fig. 3: Sketch of Raffles Bay, 1827, site of Fort Wellington

An interpreter was required for communication with the Indonesian fisherman, and O'Dean fitted the bill perfectly. He was of Malay ancestry, spoke the Malay language and was a Muslim. All this would help build confidence with the Indonesians. O'Dean was offered the job on a princely salary of 70 Pounds per annum. To get this amount in its proper perspective, the Fort's Surgeon, Dr Davis, was paid 90 pounds per annum. O'Dean was also given permission to build a home at Fort Wellington and was provided with rations. The weekly rations of a colonist at that time were 4lbs salted pork or 7 lbs beef, 7 lbs flour, 3 pints dried peas, ½ lb rice and 6 oz. butter. O'Dean accepted the offer and reported at Fort Wellington with one of his sons in July 1827, one month after the settlement was founded. The rest of the family remained in Sydney for the time being.

Conditions at Fort Wellington were far from congenial (Fig. 4). The problems included: loneliness; total isolation, with the only other European settlement in the northern region being Fort Dundas about 300 km to the west; scurvy due to lack of fresh vegetables and fruits; night blindness often caused by Vitamin A deficiency; and conflict with the indigenous Iwaidja people. Meanwhile O'Dean continued with his work as an Interpreter conveying much useful information from the visiting Indonesians to the Fort Commandant, Captain Henry Smyth. However Captain Smyth soon fell ill with scurvy and returned to Sydney. His position as Fort Commandant was temporarily filled by Lieutenant Sleeman. By mid 1828 O'Dean had built a cottage for the family, and obtained permission to return to Sydney on the *Mary Elizabeth* to bring his family, arriving in Sydney on 20 August 1828 (Thomas, 2012, p. 133).

In Sydney, O'Dean was devastated to find that his family had already left for Fort Wellington. He must have crossed his family on the high seas. His resourceful wife, Eve, had taken with her five children, furniture, household utensils and also a goat. The same ship that took O'Dean's family to Fort Wellington also took the new Fort commandant, Captain Collet Barker.

Fig. 4: Problems at Fort Wellington, 1827
(Courtesy: John Ross "Chronicle of Australia", Viking Publishers, 1993)

To make matters worse, the new NSW Governor, Ralph Darling, refused to sanction O'Dean's return passage to Fort Wellington on the grounds that he was reconsidering the future of the settlement. Governor Darling was an enlisted man who rose to the rank of General. He is remembered in the history of Sydney for preventing the establishment of theatres. He passed a law banning the performance of drama and did not allow music concerts to take place.

O'Dean submitted a petition to the Governor pointing out that he was separated by half a continent from his family and even offering to work on half wages. Darling finally relented and allowed O'Dean to return to Fort Wellington. O'Dean left Sydney in January 1829 in the *Lucy Anne*, arriving in Fort Wellington on 17 February1829. Also travelling on the same ship was a 22 year old Ceylonese convict Jean Herman Maas who had just arrived in Sydney and was posted to Fort Wellington. No doubt O'Dean and Maas would have had long conversations about their former lives in Ceylon.

Jean Herman Maas

Jean Herman Maas was of Ceylonese origin, the son of a public servant, and of Dutch-Sinhalese descent. As an eighteen year old he was convicted of forgery in Ceylon and sentenced to transportation for seven years to Isle de France (i.e. Mauritius). He arrived there in June 1825 travelling from Colombo on the same ship *Alexander* which carried Ehelapola Maha Nilame who was also banished to Mauritius. (See pp 142-3 of CSA Member Prof Raja C Bandaranayake's book *Betwixt Isles*, 2006. The book was reviewed in the August 2007 edition of this Journal.)

In Mauritius, due to his literacy and part European parentage, Maas was not put on a road gang but was attached as an assistant to a British Engineer. Within a year he was again arrested trying to pass off a forged coin. A search of his belongings found coining equipment and 47 forged coins. (See pp 44-6 of *Subaltern Lives* by Clive Anderson.) He was charged and sentenced to transportation to Sydney for 15 years.

Maas embarked as a convict on the ship *Celia* and reached Sydney in early 1829. He was assigned to Fort Wellington as copying clerk and to assist O'Dean, because he had some knowledge of Malay, but not as extensive as O'Dean. In the latter part of 1829 Maas was sent back to Sydney where he was assigned to the Liverpool Commissariat's Office as a clerk. At that time there was an extensive road building program as new roads were being built to the Blue Mountains. Maas had to assist John Lambie, the Assistant Surveyor of Roads. Maas had the task of preparing Invoices for work done by Contractors which were certified by Lambie and payment made. In July 1830 Maas decided to do some creative accounting and prepared two spurious invoices for 137 pounds and 51 Pounds, forged Lambie's signature and payment from the Commissariat Pay Office was collected.

The fraud was detected and the case heard in the Campbell Town Assizes on 13/14 August 1830. According to The Sydney Gazette of 17 August 1830 when Maas was asked to address the Court he said: *"I have been accused of the heinous crime of fraud and forgery and found guilty; I know I am doomed to die and expect no pardon."* He was found guilty and sentenced to death and hanged on 01 September 1830. Fig 5 reproduces extracts from The Sydney Gazette report of his trial. He was the last person to be hanged for forgery in NSW. After 1833, forgery and cattle theft were no longer hanging offences. In his short life of 24 years, Maas had the dubious distinction of being convicted for forgery in three countries, Ceylon, Mauritius and Australia.

O'Dean returns to Fort Wellington

O'Dean arrived back in Fort Wellington on 17 February 1829 to be re-united with his family, but to his dismay he found that the new Fort Commandant, Captain Collet Barker, had already arranged for his family to return to Sydney in the same ship, *Lucy Anne*, that had brought O'Dean. This was on the grounds that he did not have the resources to provide rations for the large O'Dean family. The *Lucy Anne* left for Sydney on 25 February 1929, the family had been re-united for only eight days, after a separation of eight months.

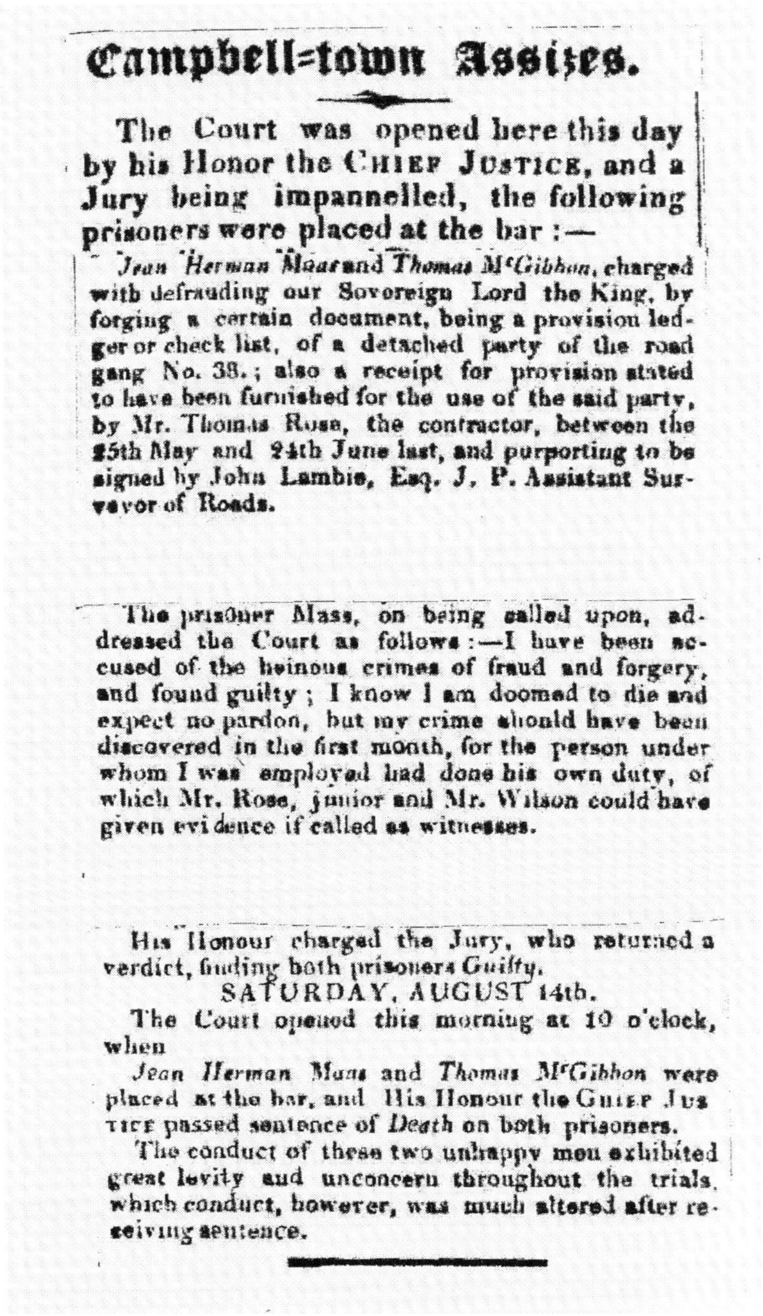

Campbell-town Assizes.

The Court was opened here this day by his Honor the CHIEF JUSTICE, and a Jury being impannelled, the following prisoners were placed at the bar :—

Jean Herman Maas and Thomas M'Gibbon, charged with defrauding our Sovereign Lord the King, by forging a certain document, being a provision ledger or check list, of a detached party of the road gang No. 38.; also a receipt for provision stated to have been furnished for the use of the said party, by Mr. Thomas Rose, the contractor, between the 25th May and 24th June last, and purporting to be signed by John Lambie, Esq. J. P. Assistant Surveyor of Roads.

The prisoner Mass, on being called upon, addressed the Court as follows :—I have been accused of the heinous crimes of fraud and forgery, and found guilty ; I know I am doomed to die and expect no pardon, but my crime should have been discovered in the first month, for the person under whom I was employed had done his own duty, of which Mr. Rose, junior and Mr. Wilson could have given evidence if called as witnesses.

His Honour charged the Jury, who returned a verdict, finding both prisoners Guilty.

SATURDAY, AUGUST 14th.

The Court opened this morning at 10 o'clock, when

Jean Herman Maas and Thomas M'Gibbon were placed at the bar, and His Honour the CHIEF JUSTICE passed sentence of Death on both prisoners.

The conduct of these two unhappy men exhibited great levity and unconcern throughout the trials, which conduct, however, was much altered after receiving sentence.

Fig. 5: Trial of John Herman Maas (Extracts from Sydney Gazette, 17 August 1830.)

O'Dean continued his work as an Interpreter obtaining information from the Indonesian trepang (sea cucumber) fisherman. They would arrive in fleets of *praus* (sailing vessels) capable of carrying a crew of about 30 sailors. They set up camps on the beaches, harvested trepang at low tide, dried and smoked them and took them back for export to China. They mostly came for Makassar which is the capital of South Sulawesi and is now the fifth largest city in Indonesia. One of the problems that O'Dean had in interpreting was that only some of the fishermen spoke Malay, their mother tongues were the Sulawesi languages of Makassarese or Bugis, with which O'Dean was not familiar. The other problem was that these fishermen did not use maps or charts, navigating by a simple compass. They were therefore unable to identify places which were shown to them on maps and charts.

Captain Collet Barker

The new Fort Commandant, Captain Barker, kept a detailed personal Journal of daily events during his one year stay at Fort Wellington. This has now been reproduced in the book *'Commandant of Solitude: The Journals of Captain Collet Barker, 1828 – 1831'*, by John Mulvaney and Neville Green, 1992. The section about Fort Wellington covers about 200 pages, with many references to O'Dean and the work they did together.

However, Sir George Murray, the Secretary of State for the Colonies who was based in London, gave instructions to NSW Governor Darling to close down the Fort. The reasons he gave were: *"lack of any substantial trade with the islands of the Eastern archipelago, the sickness suffered by the settlement residents, and the difficulty in supply of provisions to the settlement."* On 28 August 1829 Fort Wellington was abandoned.

Captain Barker sailed off the next day anti-clockwise round Australia in the ship *Governor Phillip* to his next assignment, to found a settlement in King George Sound, presently the site of the town of Albany in Western Australia. On 29 March 1831 he was ordered by the NSW Governor Darling to hand over the King George Sound settlement to the Governor of Western Australia and return to Sydney. On his way back he was instructed to stop at the mouth of the Murray River in South Australia and explore the possibility of a settlement there. He anchored and proceeded up the river bank on foot with six others. In both of his previous settlements, Barker had built up the trust of the indigenous people and would go their camps unarmed. This proved his undoing here. He saw a high sand bank on the opposite side of the river which he wanted to explore. He was the only swimmer in the group so he stripped to his underwear, swam alone across the two hundred metre wide Murray River and was seen climbing the sand bank. He was never seen again.

Subsequent investigations revealed that on the other side of the sand bank he was confronted by three indigenous people armed with spears. Because he was not in uniform, they did not know that he was an Army Officer. They assumed that he was a member of a sealing party that had caused them much harassment. Sealing parties had abducted indigenous women and killed as well. He was speared to death and his body was thrown into the Murray River and never seen again.

Perhaps Captain Barker had a premonition of his death because the very last entry in his Journal are lines from Alexander Pope's poem *Ode to Solitude*, written by Pope in 1700 when he was only twelve years old. The last verse in this poem is particularly poignant:

Thus let me live, unseen, unknown,
Thus unlamented let me die;
Steal from the world, and not a stone
Tell where I lie.

There is a stone, but not where he lies. His brother Officers of the 39th Regiment led by Colonel Lindesay did leave a stone. They built a tomb five feet long and installed a tablet nearly three feet high in St James Church in the heart of Sydney. (*The Australian*, 13 July 1832; Mulvaney and Green, pp 3, 22-26.)

Today the site of Fort Wellington in Raffles Bay is uninhabited and access is only possible by boat. It is now part of the Garig National Park in the Coburg Peninsula. The only reminder of its existence is the Cairn and inscription in Fig. 6. This was erected in 1977 to commemorate the 150th anniversary of the founding of the settlement. The text is repeated below as some words in the inscription are no longer readable:

Fig.6: Cairn marking the site of Fort Wellington
(Source: Prof Jenny Edwards, UTS, Sydney)

"This Cairn marks the site of Fort Wellington, the second British Settlement in North Australia from June 1827 to August 1829, garrisoned by men of the 39th Regiment of Foot and Royal Marines. It was unveiled by the Hon. Mr Justice W E S Forster, Acting Administrator of the Northern Territory, on Monday 26th September 1977 to commemorate the 150th anniversary of the founding of the Settlement. It also honours the Aboriginal and White peoples who lived here."

O'Dean back in Sydney

With the closure of Fort Wellington in August 1829, O'Dean returned back to Sydney and to his former job in the Sydney Dockyards. At that time the population of Sydney was about equally divided between those of convict background and free settlers. In order to maintain law and order, strict sentences were imposed as this incident reported in the Sydney Gazette of 24 November 1836 shows:

"On Sunday morning as John O'Dean, the Cingalese priest and interpreter, was standing at his gate, a woman of colour named Jane Cox, a native of King's Island, who had been sixteen years in the Colony, came up and said she was out of place, he asked her what she could do, she replied washing, ironing and needlework, he then engaged her as a servant; shortly after nine o'clock O'Dean's daughter saw a ring belonging to her father valued at nine pounds, safe in the till of a chest in his bedroom, at ten o'clock it was missing, Cox went into the room at this time; at five o'clock in the evening Cox went out on a plea of getting a clean gown, but did not return. On Monday morning O'Dean saw her in Prince Street, when she ran into a public house, he followed her and gave her into custody. She delivered up the ring to the Constable."

The case was heard a few weeks later and Jane Cox was found guilty and sentenced to transportation to Van Dieman's Land (i.e. Tasmania) for five years. On the other hand O'Dean was perhaps fortunate to get off lightly when he had a minor brush with the law as this incident reported in the

Sydney Monitor of 12 September 1838 shows:

"Yesterday, O'Dean, the Cingalese interpreter, was charged by a Lascar [i.e. seaman] named John Williams with robbing him under the following circumstances. Williams stated that on Monday, as he was proceeding along Kent Street, with his bedding and baggage to join ship, he encountered O'Dean, who alleged that he was indebted to him for 12 shillings for board and lodging; this Williams denied, when O'Dean seized upon the baggage, and carried it off. O'Dean's defence was that when the prosecutor was last in Sydney, he resided with him, but went away in his debt, and now meeting him, and he refusing to pay, he thought he had a right to make a reprisal by seizing his property. The Bench discharged O'Dean, but cautioned him not to take the law into his own hands – if Williams owed him any money, he could obtain his remedy in the Court of Requests."

He supplemented his income by taking in boarders and also interpreting for Indonesian Lascars appearing in court cases. He also claimed to have the only copy of the Koran in Sydney and charged the princely sum of five pounds for a Muslim who had to swear an oath in court. However this lucrative income ceased when a rival turned up with a copy of the Koran and charged only ten shillings for swearing an oath.

Eve O'Dean died in 1839 aged about 50 years. She was buried in the Devonshire Street Cemetery, Haymarket (Ferguson). In 1901, this cemetery space was required for Sydney's Central Railway Station and Belmore Park. All remains were exhumed and transferred to a number of other cemeteries and Eve's final resting place has not been traced.

Over the next few years four of his children passed away and O'Dean died in 1860 at the ripe old age of 87 years, after living in the Colony for 44 years. He was survived only by his second daughter Cooper who died in 1867 and his youngest daughter Esther who died in 1861. He was buried in the 18,000 grave St Stephens Church Camperdown Cemetery, Newtown where his tombstone still stands (Ferguson).

Thomas (2012, pp 138-9) offers this assessment of the life of O'Dean:

"Oodeen's arrival in Australia and his eventual employment as a Malay Interpreter appears unexpected in the context of popular narratives on Australian history.... As a historical figure, Oodeen was undoubtedly a pioneer in terms of his profession, his religion, and as a settler of an Indonesian/Sri Lankan heritage. In this context he has a place at the beginning of each of these histories.... However, it is as an interpreter that Oodeen provides an understanding into the motivation and context in which an English-speaking colonial bureaucracy felt it necessary to ensure it could communicate with the cultures in its periphery."

Thus ended the saga of the first ever Ceylonese family to settle in Australia, but their numerous direct descendants live on in Australia.

This Article was originally published in "The Ceylankan", Journal No.72, November 2015.

19

Ceylon Cricket Team nearly had Australia, led by Don Bradman, on the ropes in 1948!

by Thiru Arumugam

The Ceylon Cricket Team nearly had Australia, led by the legendary Don Bradman, on the ropes in 1948! Those were the halcyon days of sponsor-less amateur cricket in Ceylon. The Australian Cricket team led by Don Bradman toured England in 1948. They played 31 first class matches, including five Test matches. They won 23 matches, many by large margins, 8 matches were drawn and they did not lose a single match. They were the only unbeaten side to tour England. Because of their unbeaten record the team was called "The Invincibles". Bradman had already announced that this would be his farewell tour, and many records for crowd attendance were broken.

Australia's strong batting line up included Don Bradman, Arthur Morris, Lindsay Hassett, Neil Harvey and Sid Barnes. The formidable bowling line up included Ray Lindwall, Keith Miller, Bill Johnston and Ernie Toshack. In their warm up matches played before leaving Australia for their tour, the team scored 538 for 5 against Tasmania and 442 for 7 against Western Australia.

The team set sail for England from Fremantle on 19 March 1948 in the P & O liner Strathaird. The ship arrived in Colombo on 27 March and a one-day match (not limited overs) had been arranged against Ceylon to be played at the Tamil Union cricket grounds in Wanathamulla. Word had got around that Don Bradman was definitely playing and a record crowd of over 20,000 turned up.

Australia won the toss and decided to bat first. Sid Barnes, who had a Test batting average of 63, opened the batting and scored 49. The other opener, Bill Brown was out cheaply for only 3 runs, lbw to Sathi Coomaraswamy, and then the great Don Bradman came in to bat, with a great roar from the crowd. The bowler, Russell Heyn, probably had the greatest moment of his life when he had Bradman caught off his bowling by R L de Kretser for only 20 runs.

At lunch time the Australian bowler Ian Johnson had his doubts about the length of the pitch and demanded that it be measured. It was found that the pitch was only 20 yards long, not 22 yards! It is surprising that this was not spotted until then. Thereafter the bowlers delivered the ball from two yards behind the crease.

Australia declared at 184 for 8 with Sathi Coomaraswamy the most successful bowler taking 4 wickets for 45 runs. Ceylon went into bat and were 46 for 2 with F C de Saram (who had played for Oxford University) and M Sathasivam (who later scored a double century against South India) at the crease when a monsoonal downpour resulted in play being called off. Who knows what could have happened if rain had not curtailed play?

Some photos from the match, courtesy of Michael Roberts, are appended below.

Article has been submitted for consideration for publication to the Editor of The Ceylankan.

Standing (L to R) – F.C. de Saram, S.S. Jayawickreme, S. Coomaraswamy, M. Sathasivam, B.R. Heyn, C.I. Gunasekera.
(On ground) – B. Navaratne, H. Perera, M. Rodrigo, S. Nagendra, H.S. Oorloff.
Some of the players selected to play against the Australia.

Fig. 1: Ceylonese Cricketers against Australia, 1948
(Photo courtesy Michael Roberts)

Fig. 2: Bradman and Sathasivam walk out to toss
(Courtesy: Julian Oakley of the Art of Cricket)

Fig. 3: Ceylon Team walks out to field *(Courtesy: Padmini Coomaraswamy Album)*

Fig. 4: Sathi Coomaraswamy beats the legendary Don Bradman, Ben Navaratne collects.
(Courtesy: Padmini Coomaraswamy Album)

20

A Tale of Two Bridges: over the River Kwai in Thailand and over the River Kelani in Ceylon

by Thiru Arumugam

This article is about two bridges. The first bridge is over the River Kwai in Thailand and is part of the railway line built by the Japanese in 1942 during World War Two, linking the railway networks of Thailand and Burma. The second bridge was over the River Kelani at Kitulgala and was built by Columbia pictures in 1957 as a set for the film *The Bridge on the River Kwai*. It was the largest film set ever built up to that time.

Part 1: The Bridge over the River Kwai

Malaya and Singapore fall to Japan

On 07 December 1941, Japan declared war on the United States, Britain and the Netherlands. By this date, Japan had already occupied Manchuria, Korea, Formosa, the coastal regions of China and French Indo-China (Vietnam, Laos and Cambodia). Thailand was not a European colony and claimed neutrality but Japan told Thailand that unless it collaborated with the Japanese, Bangkok would be carpet bombed, and Thailand reluctantly agreed to collaborate with the Japanese. The Japanese troops immediately landed in Bangkok and started moving rapidly southwards, invading Malaya on 08 December 1941.

Meanwhile, Winston Churchill had already ordered the 30,000 ton battleships *Prince of Wales* and *Repulse* together with the aircraft carrier *Indomitable* to proceed to Singapore. However, the latter ran aground in the West Indies and only the two battleships arrived in Singapore. When Admiral Phillips heard about the Japanese invasion of Thailand, he proceeded in the two battleships, without air cover, towards Bangkok but the battleships were spotted by the Japanese and were attacked by 34 bombers and 51 torpedo carriers operating from Saigon. The *Prince of Wales* and *Repulse* were quickly sunk with the loss of 840 British lives. This sinking now gave Japan virtually total command of the seas around Malaya and Singapore, with devastating consequences for British morale.

As regards air cover, the original request was for 582 aircraft for the defence of Malaya and Singapore but the Chiefs of Staff in London had cut this down to 336 aircraft because priority was given to the Battle of Britain and the Western Front. In the event, when the Japanese invasion of Malaya took place, only 158 RAF aircraft were in Malaya, and the fighter aircraft were not Hurricanes and Spitfires but the obsolete American Brewster Buffalo fighter planes. These were no match for the Japanese Mitsubishi Zero and Nakajima Ki-43 planes and 60 Buffaloes were shot down, 40 were destroyed on the ground and 20 destroyed in accidents. The net result was that within two weeks of the Japanese invasion there was virtually no air cover left for the Allied forces in Malaya.

On the ground, the Japanese had a total of 190 tanks whereas the Allied forces had hardly any tanks, only Bren-gun carriers and armoured cars. The net result of all this was that the Allied forces had to retreat southwards in the face of the Japanese advance. It took only five weeks for the Japanese to occupy the whole of northern and central Malaya. Finally the Allied troops retreated to the Johore Bharu causeway which links Malaya and Singapore. After all the Allied troops had crossed over into Singapore on 31 January 1942 the causeway was blown up to hinder the Japanese advance. But in so doing, the Allies had shot themselves in the foot. 50,000 Allied troops had been killed or captured in Malaya.

Singapore does not have any rivers. The bulk of its fresh water supply came from Johore, Malaya, via a massive pipeline which crossed over to Singapore under the causeway. When the causeway was blown up by the Allies the pipeline was also blown up and Singapore's water supply was cut off. The

Japanese troops invaded Singapore on 07 February 1942 and intense artillery battles took place in Singapore for a week. On 15 February, the Japanese General Yamashita called upon the Allies to surrender. General Percival, the General Officer Commanding, was faced with a quandary. Due to the pipeline being blown up there was only enough fresh water in Singapore for a couple of days. Also about half a million Chinese civilians had fled from Malaya to Singapore, doubling the population of Singapore overnight. If the Japanese carried out their threat to carpet bomb Singapore City there would be many civilian casualties.

Percival had no option but to surrender and 80,000 more Allied troops became prisoners of war, in addition to those who had surrendered in Malaya. Churchill described the fall of Fortress Singapore as *"the worst disaster and the largest capitulation in British history"*. On the other hand, General Yamashita has written in his diaries that his call to the Allies to surrender was the biggest successful bluff of his military career as he had only 30,000 men and was outnumbered three to one by the Allies and street fighting would have ended in disaster for the Japanese. Furthermore he had ammunition left for only one day.

The Allied forces surrender gave a new unforeseen problem to the Japanese. They now had about 130,000 prisoners of war whom they had to house and feed. The Bushido code of conduct for a Japanese Samurai (warrior) expects him to fight unto death and not surrender *"One's main purpose in throwing away his life is to do so either for the sake of the Emperor or in some great undertaking of a military general. It is that exactly that will be the great fame of one's descendants"*. Following this code, there were only about six Japanese soldiers who surrendered in Malaya, whereas the Japanese were now responsible for 130,000 additional men.

Japan invades Burma and bombs Ceylon

Japan's next target was Burma because of her oilfields and rice surplus. Burma was invaded in January 1942 by the Japanese following jungle tracks through North Thailand and also from the south. The Allies retreated and the Japanese attacked and captured Rangoon in March. The Japanese continued their northward thrust and Mandalay soon fell into their hands. By May, the whole of Burma was under Japanese control and the Allied forces had retreated across the Indian border to Imphal.

On 04 April 1942, Squadron Leader Leonard Birchall was flying a PBY Catalina flying boat from his base in Koggala on a routine reconnaissance flight in the seas surrounding Ceylon. He was about 400 miles south-east of Koggala when he saw something that made his eyes pop out. A Japanese fleet of six aircraft carriers (carrying a total of 300 planes), four battleships, three cruisers and three destroyers were steaming at full speed towards Ceylon. This was the same fleet that had previously attacked Pearl Habour, with the same fleet commander, Admiral Nagumo. Birchall's Radio Officer quickly sent a message back to base about the approaching fleet before the Catalina was shot down.

On the next day, Easter Sunday, 36 Japanese fighter planes, 54 dive bombers and 90 level bombers flying in formation attacked Colombo. They were led by Commander Fuchida who had previously led the first wave of attacks on Pearl Harbour. Their target was the Eastern Fleet of ships based in Ceylon including the 23,000 ton aircraft carriers *Formidable* and *Indomitable*, but expecting a Japanese attack Admiral Somerville, Commander-in-Chief of the Eastern Fleet, had ordered his fleet a few days earlier to set sail for Addu Atoll in the Maldives. The only naval ships left in Colombo harbour were the cruiser *Hector* and the destroyer *Tenedos* which were promptly bombed and sunk. The Japanese planes also spotted the 10,000 ton heavy cruisers *Cornwall* and *Dorsetshire* about 200 miles south-west of Ceylon and sank them with the loss of 424 lives.

On 09 April the Japanese attacked Trincomalee. One of the Japanese pilots in a kamikaze suicide flight dived his plane straight into one of the massive oil storage tanks which burned for days. The Japanese also spotted the 10,000 ton aircraft carrier *Hermes* off Batticaloa and sank it with the loss of 307 lives. This was the only aircraft carrier lost by the British in World War Two. The Australian destroyer *Vampire* which was accompanying the *Hermes* was also bombed and sunk.

The Japanese fleet then turned round and returned to Singapore. Although the Japanese air raids were partially successful, they had failed in their main mission which was to seek and destroy the Eastern Fleet. Perhaps it was for this reason that the Japanese decided not to invade India via Ceylon but to invade India through Burma.

Construction of the Thailand-Burma Railway

To invade India through Burma, the Japanese would have to move thousands of tons of military hardware and tens of thousands of their troops into Burma. The easiest method would be to move this by sea to Rangoon but Japan was already short of merchant ships and American submarines were already taking a heavy toll of Japanese ships. Furthermore the distance from Bangkok to Rangoon by sea was about 2000 km. There were no roads between Thailand and Burma capable of carrying this amount of traffic, therefore the only alternative was to construct a railway between the two countries, linking the existing railway systems. Fortunately the railway systems of Singapore, Malaya, Thailand and Burma all used the same metre gauge for the rail tracks and the same train could run through all these countries. The route of the railway line (see Fig. 1) would start from Ban Pong in Thailand and go over relatively flat land for the first 50 km to Tamarkan where it would have to cross the River Kwae Yai.

A note about nomenclature. The word 'Kwai' in the Thai language means 'River'. There was no such thing as 'River Kwai' since this means 'River River'. Pierre Boulle wrote a book and gave it the title of 'The Bridge on the River Kwai' presumably because it sounded nice, and the film of the book also had the same title. After the war, thousands of tourists came to Tamarkan to see the 'River Kwai' and the bridge referred to in the book and the film and so the Thai Government renamed the river as 'Kwai'. Furthermore, the book and the film describe Allied commandos being parachuted into Burma and trekking over the Thai border to blow up a wooden bridge. Tamarkan is very far from the Burmese border and so the bridge referred to in the book and the film must be the bridge at Songkurai which is about 250 km further up the railway line. This part of the railway line has been abandoned since the war and is now covered by the jungle tide.

There are two rivers in this region flowing roughly from north to south. On the west there is the Kwae Noi (which means Little River) and on the east there is the Kwae Yai (which means Big River). The confluence of the two rivers is at Kanchanaburi, about five km south of Tamarkan. The route selected for the railway was to cross the Kwae Yai north of the confluence and then follow the banks of the Kwae Noi all the way to its origin near the Burmese border, then cross the border at the Three Pagodas Pass and join the existing Burma railway system at Thanbyuzayat. The total length of the line was 415 km of which about 350 km was through thick tropical rain forest with a total of 688 bridges, big and small. 63 of the bridges were more than 50 metres long. Of these bridges, all but eight bridges were made of timber, which was plentiful in the surrounding forests. Most of the Japanese railway engineers had qualified in USA and they used as a guide the American Merriman-Wiggin standard for timber bridges. However the American engines were much heavier than the Japanese engines that were used on this line, so the timber bridges were over-designed.

Two Japanese Railway Regiments with a total of 12,000 Japanese were entrusted with the task of completing the railway in just over a year. In mid-1942 the 5th Regiment started work at the Burma end and the 9th Regiment started work at the Thai end. They were faced with a problem in that the Japanese military could not spare any machinery for the project such as bull-dozers, excavators, cranes etc., therefore the entire job had to be done by manual labour using hand tools. They therefore decided to use the Allied prisoners-of-war in Singapore to work on the railway, and in addition conscript labourers from Burma and Malaya. The latter were mainly Indian Tamils who had worked in the rubber estates. It is possible that a few Ceylonese were also included.

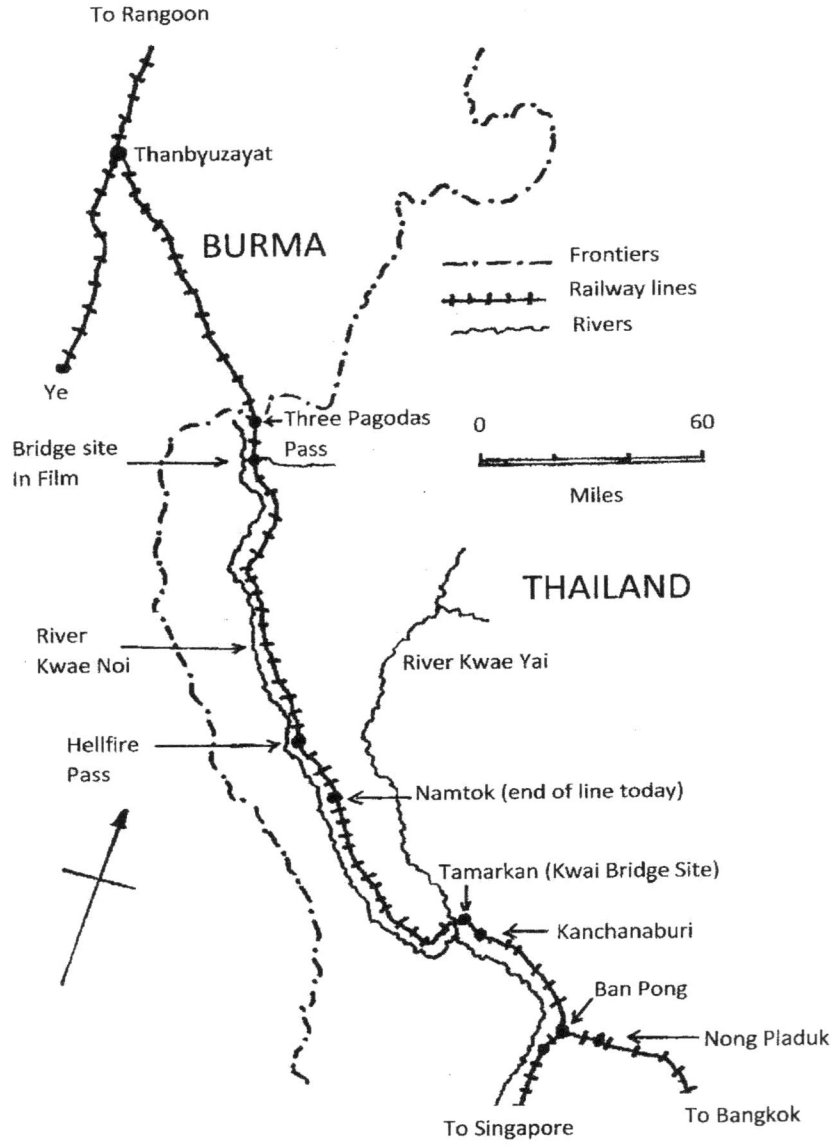

Fig.1 Japanese Railway line from Ban Pong (Thailand) to Thanbyuzayat (Burma)   1942 - 1945

The Japanese Government had sent low-level delegates to the Geneva Convention held in 1929. These delegates signed the Convention but the Japanese Government never formally ratified the Convention and therefore they did not consider themselves bound by it. According to the Convention, prisoners-of-war cannot be used to do work that directly helps the war effort of their captors. Also, Officers cannot be asked to do manual labour. The Japanese disregarded these conditions and in any case they thought that they would win the war and there would not be War Crimes Trials after the war.

Construction of the Bridges at Tamarkan

The Kwae Yai is about 350 metres wide at Tamarkan and the river rises to high levels during the monsoonal rains. This meant that a permanent timber bridge could not be built here and the permanent bridge would have to be built with concrete piers and steel trusses. The Japanese found some steel trusses at the site of a proposed bridge in Java and these were brought here. These trusses were sufficient for eleven 20 metre spans of the concrete bridge. At the northern end, where the river is shallow, the bridge was completed with nineteen 5 metre timber spans.

The major engineering difficulty was the construction of the concrete piers. The bed rock in the river here was underneath two to three metres of soft over-burden in a fast flowing river. The piers were built by first constructing a temporary circular earth coffer dam. A concrete ring was then lowered into the river bed. Divers would then remove the earth under the ring which gradually sank to the bed-rock. Successive rings would then be slotted on top as the concrete structure went down. The building of the approach works was undertaken simultaneously with the concrete works and the whole bridge was completed by May 1943, taking about ten months in all.

However, as there was no road access to the route of the railway up-river, the Japanese could not wait for the concrete bridge to be completed to transport rails up-river. Therefore they decided to construct a temporary timber bridge also at Tamarkan so that trains could start transporting rails up-river. Construction of the temporary timber bridge, which was about 100 metres away from the concrete bridge, commenced in August 1942 and it was completed by January 1943. Light trains were able to start crossing the Kwae Yai four months before the concrete bridge was completed. This wooden bridge was constructed by driving vertical wood piles into the river bed. As there was no pile driving equipment, ropes were tied on to a concrete block or a heavy piece of timber and passed over a pulley overhead. Scores of POWs would then slowly haul the ropes so that the weight moved upward. When it had reached a given height, the ropes would be released and the weight would freefall on to the cap of the pile driving it down inch by inch. Fig. 2 shows a train passing over the temporary wooden bridge at Tamarkan. Two spans of the concrete and steel bridge can be seen in the background.

With the completion of the Tamarkan wooden bridge, work on the line up-river progressed faster and by May 1943 the railway was operational up to 130 km from the starting point. The monsoon broke in May and there were torrential daily showers which then slowed down the pace of work. By October the line had passed Konkuita which is 263 km from the starting point and was ready to join up with the line being constructed southwards from the Burmese end. On 17 October 1943 the two lines were linked up and the 415 km long Thailand - Burma railway was fully operational.

Living conditions of the workforce

It is generally accepted that this railway was one of the great engineering achievements of World War Two. But it was achieved at a great human cost. About 61,000 Allied POWs, including 13,000 Australians worked on the railway. Physical beatings and torture by the Japanese soldiers and Korean guards were commonplace forms of punishment. The POWs were not provided with hats, boots or clothes as required under the Geneva Convention. They were only given a piece of cloth about two feet square which they wore like a span cloth around their waists. That is all they wore when they worked on the line, in rain or sun. As regards food, they were given some rice porridge for breakfast, a ball of rice for lunch and another ball of rice for dinner which would sometimes have a few beans and leafy vegetables. The daily diet had a calorie content of about 1000, whereas a man doing manual labour requires well over 2500 calories. The net result was that a POW who started off weighing 150 lbs at the beginning of the war, weighed about 90 lbs at the end of the war, literally skin and bone.

Fig. 2: The Wooden bridge at Tamarkan. Two spans of the steel bridge are in the background.
(Courtesy: Australian War Memorial)

Living accommodation consisted of huts made of bamboo with leaky thatched roofs. Inside the hut there was a raised bamboo sleeping platform with a space of only 18 inches width allocated per person. Toilets consisted of deep open pits across which bamboos were laid. One had to use these toilets squatting in the open air with no privacy. Separate huts were provided for the sick, but for those who were sick the food ration was reduced to half. Doctors were available, there were about 100 Australian Doctor POWs, but no medical equipment or medicines were provided. As a result there were many casualties due to sickness and malnutrition. The common diseases were cholera, cerebral malaria, dysentery and beri-beri. About 13,000 POWs, including about 2700 Australians, died in the construction of the railway. This was about 21 percent of the POWs who worked on the railway.

The Japanese also used about 200,000 conscripted Asian labourers as part of the workforce. They were mainly Indian Tamil labourers from the rubber plantations in Malaya and also Burmese nationals. Their living conditions were worse than the POWs. There were no sick bays or medical personnel. No toilets were provided. They had to go into the bush to ease themselves. As a result, when it rained all the streams which provided the camp's water supply got polluted and cholera was rampant. It is estimated that about 80,000 or 40 percent of the Asian labourers died in the construction of the railway. At the War Crimes Trials held after the war, 111 Japanese and Korean soldiers were convicted for war crimes committed on the Thai-Burma railway and 32 were executed.

Operation of the Railway

The railway was operational from October 1943 to mid-1945 and during this period about 300,000 tons of military supplies and tens of thousands of Japanese troops were transported from Thailand to Burma. About two or three trains ran daily, usually at night to avoid being bombed by the Allies. By early

1945 the Allied Eastern Air Command based in eastern India used B-24 Liberator Bombers to attack the Burma-Thailand railway. The wooden bridges were regularly bombed but the Japanese were able to repair them fairly quickly. On 24 June 1945 B-24 Liberator Bombers flown by 159th and 356th Squadrons of the RAF were designated with the task of permanently destroying the steel and wooden bridges at Tamarkan. When the aircraft left the bridge sites they reported that three spans of the steel bridges had been broken and that the wooden bridge had been breached in two places. (See Fig. 3) This air raid marked the end of the wartime careers of the two bridges across the Kwae Yai at Tamarkan. On 06 August 1945 the atom bomb was dropped on Hiroshima and nine days later Emperor Hirohito announced Japan's formal surrender.

Fig. 3: Steel Bridge at Tamarkan after RAF bombing raid of 24 June 1945
(Courtesy: Australian War memorial)

Immediately after the war the Japanese Government was asked, under war reparations, to provide replacement steel trusses for the damaged trusses in the concrete bridge. The concrete bridge was repaired, but the wooden bridge was abandoned and hardly any trace of it remains today. The railway line is still operational up to Namtok which is about 125 km from the Thailand starting point of the line. The rest of the line, nearly 300 km, was abandoned after removing the steel rails. The jungle tide has now overgrown this part of the line. Nowadays Tamarkan and the nearby town of Kanchanaburi are visited by about four million tourists annually who come to see the site of the bridge made famous by the film *The Bridge on the River Kwai*.

Part 2: The film *The Bridge on the River Kwai* and the Bridge over the River Kelani in Ceylon

The Book

Pierre Boulle was a French engineer working in rubber factories in Malaya. When the war broke out he was arrested and was a POW but did not work on the Thai-Burma railway. After the war he listened to stories about the wartime experiences of British rubber planters who had worked as POWs on the Thai-Burma railway. The net result was the publication of his semi-fictional French book in 1952, *Le Pont de la Riviere Kwai*. This was translated into English in 1954 as *The Bridge on the River Kwai* and was a multi-million copy best seller. The character Col. Nicholson in the book is purportedly based on Col. Toosey who was the senior British Officer in the POW camp at the bridge site in Tamarkan. The difference is that Col. Nicholson is portrayed as a collaborator whereas Col. Toosey argued long and hard with the Japanese to improve the conditions of the POWs and was often assaulted for his pains. Also the entire section in the book about commandos parachuted into Burma to go and blow up the Kwai bridge is pure fiction because as we have seen, the bridge was demolished by Allied bombers.

The film

In 1956, Horizon Pictures of UK decided to make a film of the book. They had the backing of Columbia Pictures of Hollywood who financed the film and were also responsible for world-wide distribution of the film. Sam Spiegel was selected as the Producer and David Lean was the Director. The main members of the cast were William Holden, the Hollywood No. 1 box office draw at that time, Alec Guiness, and Jack Hawkins. The Japanese, Sessue Hayakawa, was selected to play the role of Col. Saito. He was a famous 68 year old veteran actor from the silent film days.

Sam Spiegel sent Donald Ashton, the Art Director, to Thailand to have a look at the bridge site and select locations for filming. Ashton found that the Tamarkan bridge site was on flat land and was not scenic, whereas the book describes a bridge site in a mountain gorge. Furthermore, it was the dry season and the flow in the river was a trickle. Ashton was married to the daughter of a British tea planter working in Ceylon. He remembered seeing, on his way to his father-in-law's estate, the River Kelani in a picturesque mountain gorge in Kitulgala. He suggested to Spiegel that the location for shooting the film be shifted to Ceylon and Spiegel agreed.

The Bridge

Sam Spiegel did not want the bridge in the film to be a mock-up. He wanted a full size solid timber bridge. Husband & Co. was a firm of Civil Engineering Consultants based in Sheffield, England. They had a roads contract in Ceylon and had an office in Colombo. Keith Best was the Chief Engineer and he was commissioned with the task of designing the bridge. All the wooden bridges in the Thai-Burma railway were trestle bridges, based on a standard American pattern. However at Kitulgala the bridge would be up to 70 feet above the river bed and it would be difficult to build a trestle bridge. Keith Best therefore decided to design a cantilever bridge using the shape of the Firth of Forth cantilever railway bridge in Scotland as a guide. The bridge would be 425 feet long and would be the largest film set built up to that time. Keith Best had completed his bridge design when there was a new development.

In the 1890s the rubber planters in the Kelani Valley complained to the Governor that whereas the up-country planters could send their tea to Colombo by rail, they had to send their rubber to Colombo by bullock cart. The Governor approved the construction of the Kelani Valley railway line and construction work started in 1900. It was a narrow gauge 2ft 6in railway compared with the 5ft 6in broad gauge railways in the rest of Ceylon. By 1912 the line was completed from Maradana to Yatiyantota with a branch line from Avisawella to Opanayaka. The first batch of seven steam engines for this line were ordered from Hunslet, an engine manufacturer in Leeds, UK. The engines were numbered 102 to 108. In 1957 a Board of Survey in the Ceylon Government Railway had recommended scrapping the 55 year old Engine No. 104 as it was no longer economical to run. The Minister in charge of the railways contacted Sam Spiegel and told him that they were prepared to give him Engine No. 104 and a few carriages and that they could be blown up with the bridge in the climax of the film.

Fig. 4: Kitulgala Wooden Bridge under construction *(Courtesy: Columbia Pictures)*

Sam Spiegel jumped up at the idea and informed Keith Best about this new development. This required a total re-design and strengthening of the bridge. Originally it was designed to take the load of a company of soldiers marching across the bridge. It would now have to carry a 30 ton train travelling at about 20 mph. The bridge was re-designed and the contract to build the bridge was awarded to Equipment and Construction Co. (ECC), a leading local construction company.

ECC started work on building the bridge at Kitulgala. They used over 500 workers. Trees were felled in the jungle on the opposite bank and dragged by 35 elephants to a saw mill and from there to the river bed. It was a difficult job dissuading the elephants from flopping down to have a bath every time they crossed the river. Fig. 4 shows the construction of the bridge by ECC. Wooden piles were driven into the river bed to support the cantilevers. Concrete foundations were also used. Fig. 5 shows the completed bridge.

Fig. 5: The completed Bridge at Kitulgala *(Courtesy: Daily Mail)*

Filming details

Apart from the bridge at Kitulgala, other locations in Ceylon were used for the shooting of the film. Scenes were shot on the beach at Mount Lavinia Hotel, at the Peradeniya Botanical Gardens, the POW camp site was at a quarry believed to be near Mahara, and at various jungle locations. There were no studio shots, it was filmed entirely in Ceylon. The parts of the British soldiers were played by Ceylonese. They were young Burghers, the Bambalawatte boys. They were paid hundred rupees a day, which was quite good because it would take them about a week to earn that money in an office job. Chris Greet of Radio Ceylon played the role of a British Officer and spoke a few lines. Chandran Rutnam, straight from school, was an assistant to the Props Manager. He appears briefly in the film pushing a boat in which William Holden is riding. Rutnam subsequently made the film industry his career. Denis Flamer Caldera has a similar build to William Holden and he was Holden's stunt double.

Sir Malcolm Arnold was the Music Director, with music played by the Royal Philharmonic Orchestra. The Colonel Bogey March was a popular march in the British Forces dating from World War One. Arnold wanted this to be the theme music but Columbia objected and wanted to have 'Bless them all' as the theme but Arnold finally had his way. Arnold wanted the troops marching into the camp to sing the song, but it was pointed out that the words would never get past the Censors because the words included a comparison of a part of the anatomy of Hitler, Himmler, Goebels and Goering! It was finally decided that the troops would whistle the song. The disc of the music was in 'Top of the Pops' for several weeks.

With the completion of the bridge, everything was ready for the climax of the film which was the blowing up of the bridge. Unlike the other scenes, there could be only one 'take' as the bridge could be blown up only once. Many VIPs including the Prime Minister, S W R D Bandaranaike, were present to witness the scene. The contract to supply the explosives and blow up the bridge was given to Imperial Chemical Industries (ICI). The explosion was filmed by four cameras, two on either side of the bridge. A switch was installed near each camera and this was connected to a bulb on David Lean's desk. When the train approached the bridge, the cameramen had to start the camera rolling, turn on the switch and run away to a safe distance. A fifth switch was fitted at the beginning of the bridge. This switch was to be turned on by the engine driver who had to jump off the moving train. David Lean was to give the signal to ICI to blow up the bridge only when all five bulbs lit up.

Fig. 6: Engine No. 104 steamed up for her last journey, like a condemned man led to the gallows
(Courtesy: Columbia Pictures)

When all was ready, the engine driver was signalled to start the train. Fig. 6 shows 55 year old Kelani Valley Engine No. 104 steamed up and ready for its final run, like a condemned man waiting to be led to the gallows. As the train approached the bridge, one by one the bulbs lit up. But only four bulbs lit up. What could have gone wrong? Was one cameraman still at his post, or worse still, was the engine driver still on the train? David Lean had to make a split second decision. He decided to play safe and he decided not to signal ICI to blow up the bridge. The train thundered across the bridge at speed. At the far end, the railway line ended in a sand bag wall which the driverless engine would have hit at full speed, head on and get badly damaged. Fortunately, somebody had carelessly parked a mobile generator on the railway track. The engine hit the mobile generator which went flying. The engine was derailed, but damage to the engine was minimal except to the cow-catcher.

What had happened was that one of the cameramen in his eagerness to run away to a place of safety, had forgotten to turn on his switch. The engine was jacked up back on to the track and two days later the blowing up scene was shot, this time without any ceremony or VIPs present. Everything went well, the bridge was blown up and the train fell into the river, and it was a dramatic climax to the film. Fig. 7 shows the bridge being blown up.

Fig. 7: Kitulgala Wooden Bridge blown up with the train *(Courtesy: Columbia Pictures)*

Film release

The film was completed and released in UK on 02 October 1957 and in USA on 14 December 1957. The film cost about three million dollars to produce. During the initial release alone, the Box Office takings were over 30 million dollars. It had the highest Box Office takings of any film in the USA in 1958. The British Film Institute rated it the 11th greatest British film of all time. At the 1958 Academy Award ceremony it won seven Oscars, a record for a British film. The Oscars were for Best Picture (Sam Spiegel), Best Director (David Lean), Best Actor (Alec Guinness), Best Screenplay, Best Music, Best Editing and Best Cinematography – it was among the first films in Cinemascope. Sessue Hayakawa was short-listed for Best Supporting Actor but failed to win the award.

Latest development

The stretch of the River Kelani near Kitulgala has five major rapids and four minor rapids. Kitulgala has become the base for white water rafting in Ceylon within the last few years. Many tourists flock to the place and the tourist infrastructure has been established i.e. restaurants, cafes, guest-houses etc. However, as pointed out in the article *D J Wimalasurendra – Pioneer Ceylonese Engineer* in the November 2011 edition of this Journal, the Broadlands Hydro-electric Scheme is being constructed. When it is completed next year, the water flowing through the Kitulgala rapids will be reduced to a trickle as it will be diverted through the hydro power station, and that will be the end of white water rafting here. The white water rafting associations protested and as a compromise the Ceylon Electricity Board agreed to release water down the river during daylight hours for rafting, even though it would be a loss of revenue to the CEB. The rafting associations were still not satisfied and said that there would be a drop in tourist visits. As a further concession, the Minister of Power and Energy announced a few months ago that *"Steps will be taken to restore the bridge, which was used for the film Bridge on the River Kwai, to its original state to attract the attention of tourists"*. So the Bridge at Kitulgala is going to rise again to its former glory.

Article has been submitted for consideration for publication to the Editor of The Ceylankan.

21

A Fighter Plane called "The Jaffna" fought against the Germans in World War One!

by Thiru Arumugam

Introduction

Towards the end of the 19th century, Ceylonese started migrating to Malaya to seek their fortunes. The majority of the migrants were from the Jaffna Peninsula and most obtained employment in Government Departments. In fact, at one stage it is estimated that 40 percent of the administrative staff of the Malayan Railways were Ceylonese. Others made their mark in the professions, and a few ventured into business.

When World War One started and aircraft construction was in its infancy, the British Government assumed that aircraft would only play a limited part in the war effort and would be limited to being used as observation aircraft. As the war progressed, it became apparent that aircraft could also be fitted with machine guns to be used as fighter planes and could also be used to drop small bombs.

The problem facing the British Government was funds. The war effort was already costing five million pounds a day. A decision was therefore made to ask the residents of the British Empire to contribute financially to the war effort. As a spin off to this, a request was made to fund the cost of aeroplanes. A person who responded enthusiastically to this request was Charles Alma Baker who was born in New Zealand to British parents in 1857 and died in Malaya in 1941. He trained as a Surveyor and went to Malaya to work for the Government where he carried out the earliest cadastral surveys. He also cleared large tracts of jungle on his own account and planted rubber trees which earned him a considerable fortune.

Alma Baker set about encouraging individuals, groups and state governments to contribute towards the cost of purchasing airplanes. By the end of the war, he had been personally responsible for encouraging groups to raise funds required for 94 planes, out of which 53 planes were funded from Malaya and 41 planes were funded from Australia. Of the 53 planes funded by Malaya, 16 planes were paid for by His Highness the Sultan of Johore, at that time one of the richest men in the world. Baker himself met the cost of four planes. For his efforts, Alma Baker was made a Commander of the British Empire (CBE). In all, about 350 planes were paid for by fund raising in the British Empire.

An example of the rhetoric used by Alma Baker in his fund raising is this extract from a letter from him to the *Times of Malaya:*

It cannot be possible that at this stage in our history there is a single subject of our King, and a member of the most glorious Empire the world has ever seen, who can pause and think whether he or she is called upon to do all they can to help to hold it, by saving the lives of the brave men who have given their all for our great cause.

Fundraising for "The Jaffna"

One of the groups that responded to the appeal to fund the cost of aeroplanes was the Ceylon Tamils resident in Malaya. A public meeting was held at the Town Hall, Kuala Lumpur which was well attended. A Committee was elected to carry out the fund raising. Dr E T MacIntyre was elected Chairman and W F Wijayaratnam of the Federated Malay States Railways was elected Secretary. Representatives from other States were also elected to raise funds in their States. The writer's grandfather, Sitiawan Ganapathypillai, was responsible for collection in the Taiping area and also gave a significant personal donation.

Dr E T MacIntyre, the Chairman of the fund raising Committee, qualified as a Doctor at the Colombo Medical College in 1895 and decided to migrate to Malaya in 1896 to practise as a Doctor. He was the son of Dr C N MacIntyre, who qualified as a Doctor in the Medical School run in Jaffna by the American Missionary, Dr Samuel Fisk Green, see *The Ceylankan,* May 2009 and August 2009. In 1904/05, Dr E T MacIntyre travelled to Edinburgh and obtained the medical degree of MD. On his return to Malaya he was never promoted above the low grade of Medical Officer, on the grounds that his initial medical qualification was not from a British University. Dr E T MacIntyre's grandson is the Sydneysider Playwright, CSA Member and frequent contributor to *The Ceylankan*, Ernest Macintyre.

At the inaugural meeting, the Committee decided on a target of raising 2250 Pounds (19,300 Straits dollars) to meet the cost of a fighter plane. A Ceylonese businessman, M Cathiravalu, offered to contribute 1000 Straits dollars to the fund and also said that if there was a delay in the Committee raising the target amount, he agreed to take the responsibility of underwriting the shortfall. The success of the project was therefore assured.

Within five months the Secretary of the Committee announced that the sum of 14,500 Straits dollars had been remitted to the British War Office. A few weeks later the balance amount of 4800 Straits dollars was remitted, to form a total of 2250 Pounds. The funds were used by the British War Office to purchase a FE.2B fighter plane which they named "The Jaffna". The plane was handed over on 22nd December 1915 and can be seen in Fig 1a and Fig 1b.

Fig 1a: The FE.2B Fighter plane "The Jaffna" funded by Ceylonese in Malaya
(Courtesy: C Alma Baker)

The Committee informed the British Government of their intentions and what happened next is described in the *Whitehall Gazette* of March 1920:

"And, more than this, when the Jaffna Tamils, residents of the Malay States – not possessed of too much wealth – were asked whether they would rather give an observation-plane, which would be less costly, their anxiety to know whether this would actually cause destruction to the enemy and their insistence on paying the full sum for a first class battle-plane looked rather as if the German propaganda not only failed to convince even those who were not bound to the British flag by ties of birth, but came out

in an inverse ratio to what was expected."

Fig 1b: Close up to show the lettering on the fuselage

The contents of a letter dated 27 April 1916 in which the thanks of Bonar Law, Secretary of State for the Colonies, are conveyed is reproduced in Fig 2. Bonar Law subsequently became the Prime Minister of UK.

> FROM THE RIGHT HON. ANDREW BONAR LAW, SECRETARY OF STATE FOR COLONIES.   **Letters of Appreciation**
>
> Downing Street,
> April 27th, 1916.
>
> SIR,—I am desired by Mr. Bonar Law to acknowledge receipt of your letters of the 3rd and 11th of March relating to the completion of the Malayan Air Squadron.
>
> The thanks of His Majesty's Government for your own generosity and for that of the other subscribers are being conveyed officially through the High Commissioner for the Malay States, but Mr. Bonar Law desires in addition to take this opportunity of expressing to you his special interest in the work which you have so successfully brought to a conclusion and his appreciation of the patriotic spirit shown by the Jaffna Tamils from Ceylon in subscribing for an aeroplane out of their comparatively small resources.
>
> I am, Sir,
> Your obedient servant,
> F. G. A. BUTLER.
>
> C. Alma Baker, Esq.

Fig 2: Letter from Bonar Law, Secretary of State for the Colonies
(Courtesy: C Alma Baker)

World War 1 aircraft were built primarily of wood and fabric and were very flimsy. The net result was that aircraft life averaged months rather than years. In fact, about 40 percent of the nearly 10,000 Allied aircrew fatalities in World War 1 were during training exercises and not during combat. Although the parachute was invented, they were not issued to pilots on the grounds that the pilots may use the parachutes when in difficulties, rather than try their utmost to save the plane. In view of the short life of planes, the War Office gave the assurance quoted below, which ensured that throughout the entire duration of the war there would always be a fighter plane called "The Jaffna".

"The War Office further decided to replace any subscribed aeroplane that was damaged or lost, and will affix a new nameplate, bearing the original name plate, so that the generous gifts of His Majesty's subjects from all parts of the Empire, towards helping to build up the Empire's air forces during the Great War, will remain imperishable and permanently recorded both during the war and after, of the donors' generosity."

A few months later the residents of all nationalities of Kuala Kangsar also raised sufficient funds to meet the cost of an aeroplane. Prominent among the fund raisers was a prosperous Ceylonese businessman, Solomon Ramanathan, who donated 1000 Straits dollars. The plane was named "The Kuala Kangsar" and was handed over on 20th February, 1917.

Meanwhile in Ceylon, the newspaper the *Times of Ceylon* invited all nationalities to contribute to a fund to pay for the cost of aeroplanes for the British War Office. Sufficient funds were collected to meet the cost of four aeroplanes and the names of the planes and the amount raised were as follows: Ceylon No. 1 *"A Paddy-bird from Ceylon"* (1500 Pounds); Ceylon No. 2 *"A Devil-bird from Ceylon"* (2250 Pounds); Ceylon No. 3 *"A Nightjar from Ceylon"* (2250 Pounds); Ceylon No. 4 *"Flying Fox"* (2250 Pounds). Separately, F J de Saram contributed 1500 Pounds for the full cost of a plane. Judging by the amounts raised, it is likely that Ceylon Nos. 2, 3 & 4 were Vickers FB.5 fighting biplanes. Ceylon No. 1 and the F J de Saram plane were probably BE.2C reconnaissance aircraft built by the Royal Aircraft Factory.

The FE.2B Fighting Bi-plane

"FE" is an abbreviation of Farman Experimental. The aircraft was designed by the Farman brothers, Maurice and Henri, working in France. The FE2Bs were built either by the Royal Aircraft Factory or by sub-contractors. It was a relatively large aircraft in its day with a wing span of 48 feet and was 13 feet tall. It was built of wood, fabric and wire, and had a maximum all up weight of 3300 lbs. It was initially fitted with a 120 hp Beardmore engine made in Scotland, but as it was found to be underpowered, the engine size was soon increased to 160 hp, with a top speed of 1300 rpm. The slow running engine required a four bladed propeller. There was heavy steel armour plating on the floor to protect against machine gun fire from the ground. A fixed observation camera was fitted on the outside of the aircraft fuselage. The maximum bomb load was 350 lbs. The top speed was a leisurely 75 mph and the rate of climb a sedate 300 feet/min. It had a crew of two, a pilot and an observer/gunner.

Fairly early in WW1, the Germans had developed interrupter gear which enabled their fighter planes to fire through the arc of the propeller without damaging the propeller. This was done by driving a cam off the propeller shaft. A follower was riding on the cam and this was linked to interrupt the firing of the machine gun when the muzzle of the gun was in line with the propeller blade. Any incorrect adjustment or jamming of the interrupter could result in the propeller blade being shot off with disastrous consequences. This was fitted to their Fokker E III Eindecker mono-planes which inflicted carnage on the British planes which did not have interrupter gear and were handicapped by having to fire outside the propeller arc.

Fig 3: A FE2B Gunner lines up an approaching Fokker Eindecker in his gunsights.
(Courtesy: Wikimedia Commons)

The British responded by developing 'pusher' aircraft like the FE.2B where the engine and propeller were facing backwards and were fitted behind the pilot. The observer/gunner sat in front of the pilot and below him, right in front of the plane and had a magnificent view forward, upwards and downwards. He had two machine guns, one facing forward and the other facing to the rear. The latter had a restricted field due to the obstruction by the plane, and the FE.2Bs were vulnerable to attack from the rear. To avoid restricting the movement of the gunner, he did not have a seat. He had to crouch down when firing forwards and stand up when firing backwards, making sure that he was not thrown out of the cockpit as he was not belted down. Needless to mention, the observer/gunner was a sitting duck as far as oncoming enemy aircraft line of fire was concerned. Fig 3 shows a FE2B gunner lining up an approaching Fokker Eindecker in his gunsights

The German Flying Aces: Max Immelmann and Manfred von Richthofen

Max Immelmann (1890-1916) was the first German flying ace of WW1. An 'ace' is defined as a pilot who has destroyed at least five enemy aircraft. Immelmann is credited with destroying at least 15 enemy aircraft. On 18 June 1916, Immelmann flying a Fokker E 111 Eindecker encountered a flight of FE.2Bs flown by the 25th Squadron of the Royal Flying Corps (the predecessor of the Royal Air Force). Immelmann was shot down by a FE.2B piloted by McCubbin with Waller as the gunner. Immelmann died when his plane hit the ground. It appears that Waller's gunfire damaged Immelmann's propeller. The taking out of the Germany's leading flying ace of the time was considered a major triumph for the Royal Flying Corps and for the FE.2Bs. Who knows, perhaps "The Jaffna" may well have been part of that historic squadron of FE.2Bs.

Later in the war Manfred von Richthofen (1892-1918), better known as the 'Red Baron' became the German 'ace of aces' and was credited with destroying 80 enemy aircraft. On 06 July 1917 while flying an Albatross DV he encountered a formation of FE.2Ds flown by the 20th Squadron of the Royal

Flying Corps. The FE.2D is an improved version of the FE.2B with a more powerful Rolls-Royce engine developing 250 hp. Richthofen was hit in the head by a single bullet but managed to land the plane safely. He underwent major surgery and was out of action for several months, and was never the same again. On 21 April 1918 he was engaged in a low level dogfight in northern France with two Sopwith Camels and crashed and died. It has never been definitely established who fired the fatal shot, but it is most likely to have been from machine gun fire from the ground by a gunman from the Australian 24th Machine Gun Company.

A Reproduction FE.2B Aircraft

A presentable vintage aircraft can be made in one of three ways. Firstly, it can be a restored aircraft. The starting point here is an original aircraft, usually in a dilapidated condition, which is then carefully restored as far as possible to its original condition using either modern or original components, and to look like the original. Secondly, it can be a replica aircraft. A replica aircraft is built to look like the original. It does not necessarily use an original engine or airframe and components. The original dimensions and appearance are maintained, but modern simplified construction methods are used. Replica aircraft are commonly used in movies. Finally, we have reproduction aircraft. A reproduction aircraft is built from scratch using the exact specification and drawings of the original aircraft. Original materials are used in its construction and original components made. It is exactly like an aircraft rolling out of the original production line, but many decades later.

An example of a reproduction FE.2B is the one built by The Vintage Aviator Ltd (TVAL) of Hood Aerodrome, Masterton, New Zealand. About ten years ago TVAL were commissioned to build a reproduction FE.2B. They were fortunately able to procure an original Beardmore 160 hp engine, interplane struts, radiator shutter controls, oil and fuel tanks and wheels. These were overhauled and reconditioned and brought up to as-new condition. Everything else, including the complete air-frame, controls, instruments etc. were built up from scratch using the original blueprint drawings which were converted to CAD drawings. The same materials and processes used in the original design were used e.g. Irish linen fabric, ash and spruce timbers, hand spliced cables etc. Using the original drawings, special jigs had to be built. The whole process of hand-built construction took about three years. TVAL describes the cockpit appearance of the reproduction aircraft as follows:

"This one of a kind airplane hasn't been seen in the skies for nearly a decade. In the pilot's cockpit the colours and textures bring you back to a time when plastic and vinyl didn't exist; shiny copper tubing is carefully routed all over, brass control stick, air valve, fuel valve and magneto switches glisten, rich brown leather cushion and Sutton harness catch your eye, aluminium seat frame and nickel plated control levers dot the space and the big glass toped liquid filled compass becomes the centrepiece."

Construction of the aircraft was completed on 25 April 2009 and the NZ Certificate of Airworthiness was awarded. A second reproduction FE.2B was completed by TVAL in 2012 and the two aircraft are often seen flying in tandem on flying days. A picture of the aircraft can be seen in Fig. 4.

A Farman Shorthorn in Melbourne

The Point Cook airfield is the birthplace of the Australian Flying Corps (AFC) and the Royal Australian Air Force (RAAF). It is the oldest continually operating military airfield in the world and has been operational since 1914. It is located in the outskirts of Melbourne. Within the premises there is an RAAF Museum which is open to the public.

Fig 4: A reproduction FE2B built by The Vintage Aviator Ltd, Masterton, NZ in 2009
(Courtesy: Phillip Capper, Wellington, New Zealand)

The Farman Shorthorn is a World War I biplane which has many similarities to the FE.2B, and it was the first armed aircraft to engage in aerial combat in WW1. It was first built in 1914 and a total of about 300 planes were built. It was designed by the designers of the FE.2B, the Farman brothers. Like the FE.2B it is a pusher aircraft with the engine behind the pilot and the propeller facing backwards. It is powered by a Wolseley-Renault air-cooled V8 engine developing 80 hp, giving it a top speed of about 66 mph. It is predominantly made of wood and fabric and a maze of struts and wires hold the two wings in place and prevent them from warping in flight. As in the FE.2B, the observer/gunner sits in front of the pilot, but the two sit at the same level, and therefore the observer/gunner does not get as clear a view forward as in the FE.2B. Also the pilot's view forward is obstructed by the observer/gunner.

Fig 5: A restored Farman Shorthorn in the Point Cook Aviation Museum, Melbourne.
(Photo: Thiru Arumugam)

The AFC purchased a total of five Shorthorns in 1916/17 and used them for flight training at Point Cook. After the war they were sold to a private individual who used them extensively for joy-flights, advertising and barnstorming. In 1981 one of the five aircraft, CFS-20, was donated to the RAAF in a dilapidated condition, in which only about 30 percent of the parts were re-usable. It was painstakingly restored and is now on display in the RAAF Museum at Point Cook. This aircraft is shown in Fig. 5.

A Centenary Sky

Although there were three attempted flights in the preceding twelve months which ended in crashes, the first safe aeroplane flight in Ceylon was on 7th December 1912 when two Frenchmen, Georges Verminck and Marc Pourpre, flew two Bleriot planes with 25 hp engines at the Colombo Racecourse. Towards the end of 2012, the Civil Aviation Authority, Sri Lanka, made a belated decision to publish a book titled *A Centenary Sky* to commemorate 100 years of civil aviation in the country.

Captain Elmo Jayawardena was given the task of researching, editing, designing and publishing the book within only three months so that the book could be released on the 100th anniversary of safe powered flight in Ceylon, which was on 7th December 2012. It is difficult to conceive how he achieved the herculean task of completing this 223 page hardcover book, with almost every page in colour. It appears that he worked 18 hour days during the three months.

Captain Elmo, as he is mostly known, flew for Air Ceylon, Air Lanka and for 20 years in Singapore Airlines where he was an Instructor on Boeing 747s. Apart from flying, he is an accomplished writer in very lucid prose. His novel *Sam's Story* was awarded the Gratiaen Prize in 2001 for the best work of literary writing by a Sri Lankan in English.

When Captain Elmo was collecting material for *A Centenary Sky* he sent out emails requesting those who had access to relevant materials and photographs to help him in the task of writing the book. The writer of this article, who in the halcyon days of his youth held a Private Pilots Licence, responded by sending Captain Elmo information and photographs of the plane called "The Jaffna". This formed the nucleus of a chapter titled "An Aeroplane called Jaffna" in Captain Elmo's book *A Centenary Sky*. The copy of the book held by the writer of this article has this hand-written inscription by Captain Elmo: "*To Thiru: Thank you for giving me the information and the photo to write about the aeroplane named 'Jaffna'. Blue skies. Elmo Jayawardena.*"

Captain Elmo concluded his Chapter about the 'Jaffna' with the following words:

"*Having the choice to name the plane, the Tamil community in Malaya elected to call it 'Jaffna'. It was in remembrance of a birthplace in a faraway land, where the heartstrings often resonated nostalgic bells...... But the first gift to the sky, was the little fighter plane 'Jaffna'. Certainly less known, but very much in the annals of aviation. It did fly in some war-torn sky, in formation or in dogfight, but it flew. Then she went into oblivion till someone decided to resurrect her.*

That is what I write, and that is what you read, and that is how memories stay alive for the generations to come."

To be submitted shortly for consideration for publication, to the Editor of The Ceylankan.

22

Was there a Ceylonese in the First Fleet?

by Thiru Arumugam

Introduction

Wickrema Weerasooria studied at Royal College and graduated with a First Class Honours degree in Law from the University of Ceylon. In 1971 he obtained a PhD from the London School of Economics and from 1972 to 1977 he lectured at Monash University, Melbourne. He returned to Australia in 1986 as High Commissioner for Sri Lanka. In 1988 he published a 368 page book titled *Links between Sri Lanka & Australia.*

In page 219 of his book, Weerasooria states that Al Grassby, a former Labour Minister for Immigration has stated in his book *The Tyranny of Prejudice* that there was a Ceylonese in the First Fleet.

Albert Jamie Grassby (1926-2005) was appointed in 1972 as Minister for Immigration in the Whitlam Labour government and he made several reforms in immigration policy and is referred to as the founder of 'multi-culturalism'. He was responsible for dismantling the White Australia policy and he promoted immigration from non-English speaking countries. What he wrote in page 54 of his book *The Tyranny of Prejudice* (AE Press, 1984) was:

"One of the typical examples is the constant reference to the First Fleet bringing 1000 Englishmen to settle in Australia. This is the beginning of the homogeneous myth. In fact, in the First Fleet, as I have mentioned, there were twelve nationalities and they included, of course, Englishmen, people from other parts of the United Kingdom, and also people from Germany, Ireland, Italy, Spain, Poland, Ceylon, and West Indian blacks among seamen, soldiers and prisoners."

The search for the elusive Ceylonese was on ……..

The situation in UK in the late 18th century

There was considerable lawlessness in the UK in the late 18th century. To try and control this, long periods of imprisonment were imposed for relatively minor offences e.g. seven years imprisonment for stealing a lace handkerchief. As a result, the prisons were overcrowded and some prisoners were accommodated in floating hulks in harbours. The solution was to send off some of these convicts to America where they were sold for twenty pounds each as indentured servants. About 50,000 convicts were sent off in this way, but this came to an end in 1784 when the newly independent United States refused to accept any more convicts. An alternative destination had to be found and a few convicts were sent to West Africa, but this was a total failure as almost all of them died within a few months due to malaria and other tropical diseases. Finally, it was decided to send convicts to establish a settlement in Botany Bay, about 13 km south of the centre of present day Sydney and now the site of the Sydney Airport runways. In 1770, James Cook's first landing on the continent of Australia in HMS Endeavour was in Botany Bay. He described the place as 'capacious, safe and commodious'. In August 1786, Lord Sydney asked the British Treasury to arrange for shipping to take 750 convicts to Botany Bay. Captain Arthur Phillip (see Fig 1) was appointed to lead the expedition and become the Governor of the new colony. The First Fleet was beginning to take shape.

Fig 1: Captain Arthur Phillip – who led the First Fleet
(*Courtesy: National Portrait Gallery, London*)

The composition of the First Fleet

The eleven ships of the First Fleet are listed below. The number of crew members is estimated because the names of about 100 crew members are not available.

Two Naval Escorts:
HMS Sirius: The flagship of the fleet with Captain Arthur Phillip on board. 511 tons. 71 marines on board. (See Fig 2)
HMS Supply: Naval escort. 175 tons. 42 marines on board.

Three Storeships carrying supplies required for establishing the new colony:
Borrowdale: 272 tons, 20 crew.
Fishburn: 378 tons, 30 crew.
Golden Grove: 331 tons, 20 crew.

Six Transporters carrying convicts:
Alexander: 452 tons. 40 crew.
Charlotte: 345 tons. 30 crew.
Friendship: 278 tons. 20 crew.
Lady Penrhyn: 338 tons. 32 crew.
Prince of Wales: 333 tons. 25 crew. Transported female convicts.
Scarborough: 418 tons. 35 crew.

Fig 2: HMS Sirius, 511 ton Flagship of the First Fleet, later wrecked on a Norfolk Island reef.
(Courtesy: Australian National Maritime Museum)

The Voyage of the First Fleet

The fleet set sail from Portsmouth Harbour on the first leg of its historic journey on 13 May 1787. The first port of call was Tenerife, in the Canary Islands, which they reached on 03 June 1787 after 21 days sailing. A convoy can only travel as fast as the slowest ship, which was the Lady Penrhyn, and Captain Phillip made sure that the ships kept together. In Tenerife they took on supplies of fresh water, vegetables, fruits and other supplies. Scurvy was a limiting factor in long distance sea journeys and was caused by lack of Vitamin C.

The fleet left Tenerife on 10 June 1787 and instead of hugging the west coast of Africa, they crossed the Atlantic Ocean and headed for Rio de Janeiro. Although this was a longer route, it was a faster route due to more favourable winds. They reached Rio on 06 August 1787 after 57 days sailing. After 29 days in Rio where essential repairs to masts and sails were carried out and fresh water and supplies obtained, including 115 bottles of rum, the fleet set sail for the Cape of Good Hope on 04 September, 3000 nautical miles away.

Table Bay in Cape Town was reached on 14 October, after 40 days sailing. In Table Bay fresh water and supplies were obtained. Also livestock was purchased for the new colony. This included horses, cattle, poultry, goats, pigs and geese. Plenty of live fruit plants and seeds were also purchased. The fleet set sail on 12 November on the last, but longest, lap of 6000 nautical miles non-stop to Botany Bay.

On 03 January 1788, the coast of Van Dieman's Land (Tasmania) was sighted but the Fleet sailed round it without stopping. The Fleet was now racing northwards parallel to the New South Wales coast (though in the opposite direction to the present day Sydney to Hobart yacht race) and there was considerable excitement among all on board that they were finally nearing their destination after nearly eight months afloat. The naval escort *HMS Supply* was leading the fleet and it anchored in Botany Bay on 18 January 1788, with the rest of the First Fleet following in the next day or two. The First Fleet had arrived safely. The route of the First Fleet is shown in Fig 3. Tremendous credit goes to Captain Arthur Phillip for shepherding the eleven ships for eight months over a distance of about 16,000 nautical miles and bringing them safely to Botany Bay, although there were many storms and gales along the way. At that time the only way of communicating between ships was by hoisting different flags and pennants and the amount of information that could be conveyed was necessarily limited.

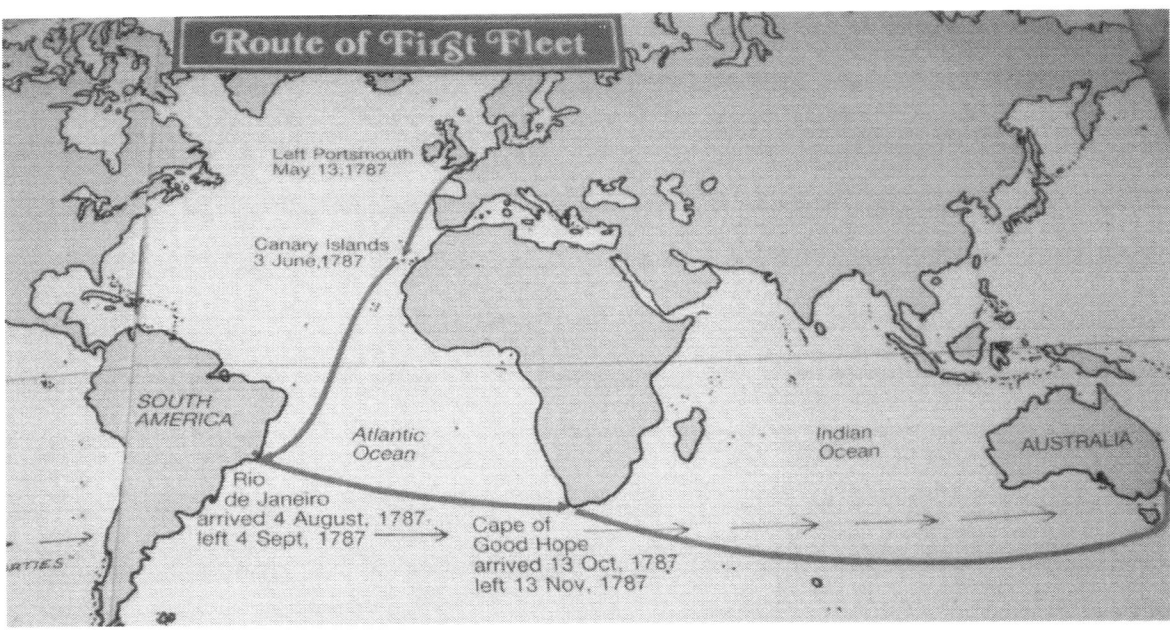

Fig 3: The Route of the First Fleet *(Courtesy: First Fleet Fellowship)*

However, Botany Bay was not found to be a promising site for a settlement. The bay was not well sheltered and was shallow, fresh water was limited and the soil did not seem particularly fertile. A few days later the First Fleet sailed 13 km north and found Port Jackson to be a large sheltered bay with ample fresh water and decided to found the first settlement here. Sydney and modern day Australia were born. See Fig 4.

Fig 4: The Founding of Australia, a painting by Talmadge
(Courtesy: State Library of New South Wales)

Rob Mundle in his book *The First Fleet* (Sydney, 2014) records the significance of the arrival of the First Fleet as follows in page 156 (Watkin Tench was a Captain in the Marines aboard the *Charlotte* and wrote a book about the first settlement):

The face of the modern world was about to change – the first pioneering steps towards European settlement of this unknown land were about to be taken. The enormity of the moment, and the hopes embedded in the hearts of those who had worked so hard to be there, were reflected in a note written by Watkin Tench, reading: 'To us it was a great, an important day, though I hope the foundation, not the fall, of an empire will be dated from it.'

Searching for the Ceylonese

There are many books on the subject of the First Fleet, but perhaps the most comprehensive book on the subject as regards the personnel is Mollie Gillen's *The Founders of Australia: A Biographical Dictionary of the First Fleet*. This 656 page book which was published by the Library of Australian History, Sydney in 1989 contains 1442 biographical entries of First Fleeters. All 1442 biographies were studied in the search for any Ceylonese. Gillen says that according to available records a total of 1420 persons embarked at Portsmouth, but details of about 110 more crew members are not available. During the voyage 22 babies were born, 69 persons died, were discharged or escaped at Rio and Cape Town. Her final total of arrivals at Botany Bay is 1373 persons, made up as follows: Male convicts 543, Female convicts 189, Convict's children 22, Ship's crews 306, Marines, their wives and children 299, and Officials and passengers 14.

Appendix 10, pages 453 to 529 of her book contain an Abstract of Biographical data of the 1373 persons who reached Botany Bay. A perusal of this Appendix does not show any names which are obviously Sinhalese, Tamil, Muslim or Malay. It is unlikely that a Ceylonese of that era would have an anglicized name because serious British presence in Ceylon commenced a decade later in 1796. That only leaves the possibility of a Portuguese or Dutch Burgher of Ceylonese origin.

The only name listed as being possibly of Portuguese origin is Paul Joseph (page 406). This is not a typical Portuguese name, so he could have been originally from Ceylon. The entry against his name says *"Paul Joseph a seaman aged 29, said to have come from Portugal, joined Sirius as able seaman on 28 March 1787, having previously served on HMS Elizabeth. He deserted Sirius on 14 September 1787 at Rio."* Since he deserted his ship in Rio he did not reach Botany Bay, so that leaves him out.

There is only one name listed as being possibly of Dutch origin. His first name is given as Cornelius and his last name as either Duhig or de Hague or Duhagen (page 110). The entry against his name reads " *Cornelius Duhig (de Hague or Duhagen), a seamen on the Friendship (who may have been Dutch)....*". The name is typically Dutch, so if he was not Dutch he may have been a Dutch Burgher, but as a seaman he did not settle in the colony. When his ship *Friendship* set sail for the return trip to England from Port Jackson seven months later on 14 July 1788, he is listed as being on board.

First Fleeters who may have settled in Ceylon

A careful search of the biographies of the First Fleeters does not reveal anybody of definitely Ceylonese origin. On the other hand, there is a possibility that the reverse may have happened and that some First Fleeters may have subsequently settled in Ceylon. The circumstances under which this arose is described below.

When the first settlement started in 1788, the Marines who arrived with the First Fleet were responsible for security. In 1791-92 these Marines were recalled to England and the New South Wales Corps was established to replace the Marines. The Officers in the Corps became very powerful obtaining large land grants and getting involved in the rum trade ending with the 'Rum Rebellion'. To control the Corps, England sent Lachlan Macquarie and the 73rd Regiment of Foot to Australia in 1810 and Macquarie took over as Governor of NSW.

Lieutenant Colonel Macquarie was with the 77th Regiment of Foot in Calicut, India when he was ordered to invade Ceylon. He and his troops landed in Negombo on 04 February 1796 and marched to Colombo. He started a siege of the Dutch Fort in Colombo and called upon the Dutch Governor to surrender, which he did two days later. On 19 February he set out for Galle and the Dutch there surrendered with hardly a shot being fired. The British had now taken over from the Dutch. A few days later on 30 March, Macquarie received a message that his wife was seriously ill and he returned to India. She died not long afterwards of tuberculosis.

In Sydney, Governor Macquarie did not get on very well with Lt. Col. O'Connell who was in charge of the 73rd Regiment of Foot. Macquarie persuaded England to re-deploy the Regiment elsewhere and they gave orders to O'Connell to proceed to Ceylon with his Regiment. O'Connell left for Ceylon with the main body of his Regiment by the sailing ship *General Hewitt,* leaving Port Jackson on 06 April 1814 and reaching Ceylon on 18 August 1814. The remainder of the Regiment followed in other ships and finally the wives and children of the Regimental soldiers sailed in the *Kangaroo* on 19 April 1815. On its return trip from Colombo, the *Kangaroo* brought the O'Dean family, the first Ceylonese family to settle in Australia (see *The Ceylankan*, November 2015).

In Ceylon, the 73rd Regiment of Foot fought against the King of Kandy in 1815. It was also involved in suppressing the Uva Rebellion of 1817-18, but at a heavy cost to the Regiment. Of the over 1000 regimental soldiers who took part, 412 were killed.

About a dozen or so soldiers who were First Fleeters had signed up and joined the 73rd Regiment of Foot and were posted to Ceylon. Apart from four of them, there are records to show that the others returned, either to Australia or to England, when the Regiment was disbanded a few years after the Uva Rebellion. There is a distinct possibility that any of these four plus the wife of one of them may have decided to settle in Ceylon, or perished in the Uva Rebellion and are buried somewhere in Ceylon. The details of these First Fleeters, as given by Mollie Gillen are as follows:

Laurence Richards (c1759-)

He was a Marine from Devon who embarked on the *Prince of Wales* in the First Fleet, with his wife Mary. He decided to become a settler and was given a government grant of 60 acres of land in the Sydney suburb of Bankstown. Imagine what that would be worth today! He and his two sons joined the 73rd Regiment in 1810. Laurence sailed to Ceylon by the *Windham* in April 1814. There is no record of his return to Australia or England.

Mary Richards (c1765-)

Mary was the wife of Laurence Richards, and had come with him on the *Prince of Wales*. They had eight children, seven of them were born in Australia. There is no record of her death in Australia, so she must have accompanied her husband to Ceylon.

Samuel Richards (1787-)

Samuel was the son of Laurence and Mary Richards above, and he was born in the *Prince of Wales* while on its First Fleet voyage to Australia. He joined the 73rd Regiment and sailed for Ceylon in the *General Hewitt* in April 1814. He was stationed in Kandy in December 1815 but there are no subsequent records of his return to Australia or England.

James Walbourne/Walburn (c1765-)

James was born in North America. 18 year old James was convicted at the Old Bailey, London in 1783 and sentenced to transportation for seven years for the theft of a linen handkerchief valued at 12 pence. He was caught pickpocketing it from a gentleman at Temple Bar. (Shades of Charles Dickens' *Oliver Twist*! published a few decades earlier). He was transported in the *Scarborough* in the First Fleet. He later joined the 73rd Regiment and was sent to Ceylon. He was separated from his wife and she did not accompany him. He is recorded as being in Ceylon in December 1815. There is no record of his death or return to Australia.

Peter Wilson (c1766-)

Eighteen year old Peter was convicted of theft of a purse in Manchester and sentenced to transportation for seven years. He was transported by the *Alexander* in the First Fleet. Having served his term he joined the NSW Corps. He was transferred to the 73rd Regiment in 1810 and in April 1814 he sailed for Ceylon in the *Windham*. He is recorded as being in Ceylon in December 1815 but there are no further records.

Conclusion

Al Grassby in his book *The Tyranny of Prejudice* written in 1984 claims that there were Ceylonese in the First Fleet but does not state his source. A study of Biographies of First Fleeters in a subsequent book by Mollie Gillen published in 1989 does not show conclusive evidence of a First Fleeter from Ceylon. Al Grassby wrote about 25 books, in addition to a busy Parliamentary Ministerial career, so perhaps he was pressed for time to check his facts.

On the other hand, there is a distinct possibility that up to five First Fleeters may have subsequently settled in Ceylon and/or are buried there. Further research is required to verify this possibility.

To be submitted shortly for consideration for publication, to the Editor of The Ceylankan.

Made in the USA
Middletown, DE
08 May 2016